THE MYCENAEAN WORLD

JOHN CHADWICK

THE MYCENAEAN WORLD

CAMBRIDGE UNIVERSITY PRESS
CAMBRIDGE
LONDON · NEW YORK · MELBOURNE

Published by the Syndics of the Cambridge University Press
The Pitt Building, Trumpington Street, Cambridge CB2 1RP
Bentley House, 200 Euston Road, London NW1 2DB
32 East 57th Street, New York, NY 10022, USA
296 Beaconsfield Parade, Middle Park, Melbourne 3206, Australia

Library of Congress Cataloguing in Publication Data
Chadwick, John, 1920–
The Mycenaean world.
Bibliography: p.
Includes index.
1. Civilization, Mycenean. I. Title.
DF220.C43 938'.01 75-36021
ISBN 0 521 21077 1 hard covers
ISBN 0 521 29037 6 paperback

First published 1976
Reprinted 1976

Printed in the United States of America

CONTENTS

ILLUSTRATIONS

ACKNOWLEDGEMENT is due to the following for their permission to reproduce the illustrations indicated: the Ashmolean Museum: 35; the Athens Archaeological Society: 2, 62 (from S. Marinatos, *Thera* VI, pls. 6 and 9); the British School at Athens: 43, 64 (from *BSA* 7, fig. 12 and 47, pl. 50); J. Allan Cash: 30, 32, 33, 47, 49; H. W. Catling: 57; Department of Archaeology, University of Cincinnati: 8, 10, 20, 36, 38; the Clarendon Press, Oxford: 13 (from A. J. Evans, *Scripta Minoa* II, pl. 38); the Deutsches Archäologisches Institut, Athens: 64, 75; Henry Hankey: 9; Hirmer Fotoarchiv München: 23, 55, 56, 60; Macmillan London and Basingstoke: 3 (from A. J. Evans, *The Palace of Minos* III (1930), p. 224, fig. 157); the National Museum, Athens: Princeton University Press: 34, 69, 74 ('Battle Scene III-Starfish', 'Battle Scene V-Chariot', and 'Lyre Player and Bird' in Vol. II, *The Frescoes* of Mabel L. Lang, *The Palace of Nestor at Pylos in Western Messenia* (copyright © 1969 by Princeton University Press), published for the University of Cincinnati: Plate 124 24H64, Plate 123 26H64, and Plate 126 43H6. Reprinted by permission of Princeton University Press); Miss C. W. Shelmerdine: 27; Edwin Smith: 5, 54; Lord William Taylour: 40; Mrs A. J. B. Wace: 61.

PREFACE

There is no shortage of books describing the civilization which developed in Greece in the Late Bronze Age, the period of the sixteenth to thirteenth centuries which we call by the name Mycenaean. But this remote epoch has been until recently the jealously guarded preserve of the archaeologist, since it was directly known only from the mute testimony of palaces, tombs, pottery, seal-stones, frescoes, and such other durable objects as have withstood more than thirty centuries of burial. Nearly all the books up to the present which have sought to describe this civilization have been written by archaeologists, and their interest has been centred on the material remains, even when they have shown awareness of another dimension.

Since 1939 we have known that Mycenaean palaces made use of writing, and since 1952 that their script, identical with that used in fourteenth-century Knossos, concealed an archaic form of the Greek language. I described the decipherment of that script by Michael Ventris in my small book, *The Decipherment of Linear B* (Cambridge 1958, 2nd edition 1967). A chapter of that book was devoted to a brief description of life in Mycenaean Greece, as it emerged from the new documentary evidence. But research into these written sources has now progressed so far that no revision can do justice to the subject. It is necessary to write a whole new book to describe Mycenaean Greece as it now begins to emerge from the tablets.

At first sight their contents are deplorably dull: long lists of names, records of livestock, grain and other produce, the account books of anonymous clerks. Here and there a vivid description of an ornate table or a richly decorated chariot breaks the monotony. But for the most part the tablets are drab and lifeless documents. Their one virtue is their utter authenticity, for they contain the actual words and figures noted down by the men and women who created the same civilization that has yielded such splendid treasures to the archaeologist's spade. The facts written down by the clerks and officials of four different royal establishments are now accessible to us; and they are historical evidence as solid, and may serve as foundations for historical deductions just as reliable, as the material remains.

Progress in interpreting the documents has been possible for a number of reasons. The script and the rules governing its use are now better understood; the nature of the dialect has become much clearer, and the meaning of words which at first seemed obscure has often been elucidated. The study of the original texts has enabled us to propose many improved readings; and in particular the location of the different fragments that make up a single tablet has allowed us to reconstitute, wholly or in part, many new texts from unintelligible pieces. But perhaps the greatest step forward has been due to the identification of the contents of the individual baskets, files as we might say, in which the tablets were stored, before a conflagration precipitated them to the floor in a confused heap. This has been possible in many cases through the recognition of the handwriting of different clerks. Where a single tablet is often like a single card removed from an index-file, a whole basketful can reveal a great deal of the facts underlying the records.

There seemed therefore to be a need for a book which would present a picture of Mycenaean Greece as it can now be reconstructed from the documentary evidence. This is of course complementary to the archaeological sources, on which I have also drawn heavily; but the main emphasis is on the new evidence which we now possess for economic life in this period. However, a detailed discussion of every group of documents so far known would quickly become tedious; all the main groups are discussed in *Documents in Mycenaean Greek* (Ventris and Chadwick, 1956; 2nd edition, Chadwick, 1973). There are still some groups which are too little understood to contribute much to a synthesis of the type attempted here; but when I look back on the progress we have made over the last twenty years, I feel sure that as time goes on, and especially if new texts are found, it will become possible to extract from these too fresh items of information which can contribute to the general picture.

Some of my colleagues will doubtless think I have in places gone too far in reconstructing a pattern which will explain the documents. Here I can only say that some pattern must exist, for these are authentic, contemporary sources; and if the pattern I have proposed is the wrong one, I will cheerfully adopt a better one when it is offered. But what I do reject is the defeatist attitude which refuses even to devise a pattern, because all its details cannot be proved. The documents exist; therefore the circumstances existed which caused them to be written, and my experience has shown me that these are not altogether impossible to conjecture.

In seeking to bring together all the evidence on each topic considered, it is often necessary to treat the same document under different headings. So far as possible repetition has been avoided by means of cross-references; but the reader must accept that these refer forwards as well as backwards, and he may have to wait until later for the evidence on which some conclusions are based. I have of course not had room to discuss all the rival theories that have been advanced; but I have tried to present what I now judge to be the most likely interpretation of the documents, following for the most part the consensus of opinion; though in places I have adopted solutions of my own against widely held views, and I have from time to time found myself obliged to advance new solutions. In some cases fuller justification of my views is being presented elsewhere; as for instance my detailed refutation of some current views on Pylian geography. I have given references to new work so far as I can without overloading the text with notes; these are in the form of author's name, date of publication and page number if appropriate, and the full reference will be found in the bibliography, which in a book of this kind must inevitably be selective.

It is as irritating for the expert to read 'a tablet from Knossos' as it is for the more general reader to be confronted with strings of unintelligible numbers. I have tried to compromise by inserting, usually in parentheses, the exact reference to tablets in such a way as not to interrupt the discussion. For those who wish to look up these references I must explain the conventions now in general use. The site from which the document comes is abbreviated to the first two letters of its name: KN = Knossos, MY = Mycenae, PY = Pylos, TH = Thebes. The tablets are further classified by series of two-letter prefixes, which give the expert further information about the subject to which they refer; e.g. prefixes beginning A- indicate lists of men and women, C- livestock, L- textiles, R- weapons and so forth. Finally each tablet has a serial number, which, after an early experiment at Pylos, is now regarded as fixed; though apparent changes may occur if two numbered fragments are shown to belong to a single tablet. The texts are normally quoted after the latest edition: KN = J. Chadwick, J. T. Killen and J.-P. Olivier, *The Knossos Tablets IV* (Cambridge 1971); MY = J.-P. Olivier, *The Mycenae Tablets IV* (Leiden 1969); PY = E. L. Bennett and J.-P. Olivier, *The Pylos Tablets Transcribed* (Rome 1973); TH = J. Chadwick, *Minos* (Salamanca) 10 (1969), 115–37 and 'Thebes Tablets II', Supplement to *Minos*, No. 4 (1975).

This is perhaps the point at which to say something about the Linear A script, for although it lies strictly outside the scope of this book, some references have to be made to it. Between the eighteenth and fifteenth centuries B.C. the Cretans employed an indigenous script, which they used both for keeping accounts and for dedicatory inscriptions. This was patently the source from which Linear B was borrowed; indeed it is likely that the Greeks began by borrowing Minoan scribes, who then adapted their script to represent the Greek language. Thus we can understand much of the content of the Linear A tablets; we know how the writing system works and we can assign approximate values to most of the syllabic signs. But although we know the meaning of a few words, it has so far proved impossible to demonstrate convincingly what the underlying language is. Further progress will depend largely on the discovery and publication of more texts.

It may be useful to insert here a brief note on chronology. There is no exact means of dating events in the whole of the Greek Bronze Age; we rely on a sequence which is primarily that of pottery styles, and in a few places we can synchronize these with the more exactly dated history of Egypt. The archaeologists therefore use a classification into Early, Middle and Late Bronze, employing the terms Early, Middle and Late Helladic for the mainland, Minoan for Crete. These periods are further subdivided into three, and each sub-period may be further divided into phases. As far as possible this book makes use of dating by centuries, but it must be remembered that even these are merely approximations. The following table will give some rough indication of the principal events.

Century	20th (or earlier)	Ancestors of the Greeks enter Greece; beginning of Middle Helladic period.
	16th	Beginning of Late Helladic or Mycenaean period.
	15th	At beginning, major eruption of Thera; around the middle of the century, Greek invasion of Crete.
	14th	(Early) Destruction of Knossos (Late Minoan III A period). (End) Beginning of Late Helladic III B period.
	13th	*Floruit* of Mycenaean civilization. Towards end, destruction at Thebes, Mycenae, Pylos and elsewhere.
	12th	Late Helladic III C period.
	8th ?	Date of Homer.

In the course of this book a number of Mycenaean words are quoted, so it is necessary to explain the system of transcription employed. The Linear

B signs can be transcribed alphabetically according to a system devised in the earliest days of the decipherment. In this, each syllabic sign is replaced by a conventional alphabetic form, which gives an approximation to the sound of the word as we can reconstruct it. But since a number of sounds are omitted by the script and left to the reader's imagination, we must often give two transcriptions: a straight representation of the Linear B signs, which is indicated by the use of hyphens to space out the syllables (e.g. *a-to-ro-qo*); and a reconstructed form representing the pronunciation we believe the word would have had (for this word *anthrōquōi*). Classical Greek words too are here transliterated into the roman alphabet.

The system used for Linear B requires some explanation. The syllabic spellings are only approximate, because the script does not make distinctions which are important for Greek. Thus the aspirated form of stops, which in ancient Greek were pronounced like the plain stops but with a puff of breath, are not separately noted; *k* may stand for *kh*, *t* for *th*, *p* for *ph*. Nor are the voiced equivalents noted, except in the case of *d*; thus *k* stands equally for *g*, and *z* probably has the values *ts* and *dz*. The letter *r* is used in transcription, but may be read as either *r* or *l*. The letter *q* is used with the value of *qu* (or *kw*), and may be aspirated (*quh*) or voiced (*gu*). There is ordinarily no sign for *h*. The letter *j* is to be pronounced like English consonantal *y*; *w* as in English. In the course of the decipherment it was observed that certain signs appeared to duplicate the values of others, and these were labelled by adding a numeral: thus ra_2 and ra_3. But it is now known that all signs of this type have special values: ra_2 stands for *rya* or *lya* as a single syllable, ra_3 for *rai* or *lai*. Similarly a_2 stands for *ha*, a_3 for *ai*, but both of these are optional, and *a* may be used with these values. There are also syllabic signs containing the semi-vowel *w*: e.g. *dwe, dwo, nwa;* they also occur rarely since Greek words which contain them are rare, and the *w* had been eliminated in classical Greek.

The transcription of numerals is simple, but it needs to be remembered that the Mycenaean are like the Roman numerals and do not rely on position. But ideograms are more difficult, since these are not ways of writing Greek words, so much as counting symbols added to numerals in order to specify what is being counted. There seems to have been a certain freedom to devise an ideogram; for instance, the signs for different kinds of vessels are in effect small schematic pictures. But the majority had already in the parent script, Linear A, become formalized, and these were simply conventional patterns. We have been able to work out the meaning of most of these, though there are still a few which are obscure. The method of transcription now internationally adopted is to represent ideograms by appropriate Latin words, which are then, if necessary, abbreviated. Hence if you look up recent editions, you will find such curiosities as VIR, MUL, GRA, OLIV, CUR, EQU: but in this book these are always interpreted, and will be described in English as *man, woman, wheat, olives, chariot, horse,* and so forth.

The metric signs for weights and measures of capacity are a special problem. After some experiment, we fixed upon a conventional system using capital letters of the alphabet to represent them, ranging from L to Z. Their use will be apparent from the discussion in Chapter 7, pp. 102–8; see also figs. 42, 44 and 45.

Another problem confronts us in dealing with Greek place names. In some cases there are specifically English forms and pronunciations in regular use, and it would be pedantic to alter familiar names like *Athens, Corinth* or *Mycenae.* But even when a place has retained the same name from the Bronze Age to the present day, its pronunciation has of course changed. Thus what in the Mycenaean period was (presumably) *Mukānai* became in classical times *Mykēnai* (where *y* has the value ü) and is known to the Greeks of today as *Mikíne.* Thus reconstructed Mycenaean words are written with *u* rather than *y, ā* for later *ē, qu* and *gu* for later *p* and *b* or *t* and *d* according to context, and with *w* where nothing survives later; hence *guasileus* for classical *basileus, wanax* for classical *anax,* and so on.

The spelling of modern Greek place and personal names raises a further difficulty. After much hesitation I have decided to adopt a compromise, with the intention of enabling the user to arrive at something like the correct pronunciation, while keeping reasonably close to the official spelling. But I must explain how the system works.

Vowels and diphthongs are pronounced long or short depending upon whether or not they carry an accent, which is therefore always marked. The foreign visitor is often left helpless by guide-books which omit this indispensable feature. But although the foreigner who asks for *Knósos* instead of *Knosós* will be instantly corrected, it needs to be said that sometimes more than one accent may be heard: *Monemvásia, Monemvasía* and *Monemvasiá* are all in use. It should also be noted that in speaking Greek the accent may change in the inflexion: Athens is (in the literary form) *Athíne,* but 'of Athens' is *Athinón.* The vowels *a, e, i* and *o* are pronounced more or less as in Italian, when short something like the vowels of English *pat, pet, pit, pot; ou* is pronounced as Italian *u* (English *ou* in *you*).

The consonants as transcribed are more or less as in English, except in the following combinations: *dh* like *th* in English *then; ph* like English *f, th* like English *th* in *think, kh* like a rough *h* or Scottish *ch* in *loch, gh* a similar voiced sound, but almost like *y* before *e* or *i.* Initial *h* is not pronounced;

thus the common element in place names meaning 'Saint', *Hághios*, is pronounced something like *Áyos*. There are of course many subtleties not mentioned here, for which the reader must refer to books on modern Greek.

It hardly needs saying that this book could never have been written without the help and advice of many friends. But it is a pleasure to record the names of those who have read and criticized drafts of the whole or parts of the book: Dr J. T. Killen, Dr C. G. Thomas, Miss C. W. Shelmerdine and Mrs C. Murray. Mrs B. Black has done most of the typing. I am much indebted to a number of people and institutions for permission to reproduce photographs; a full list of these appears separately. But I must mention specially Mr Henry Hankey, who painted the picture of the Mycenaean scribe at work. To all of these I offer my thanks.

It is my hope that the book will be of interest not only to students of the early phase of Greek civilization, but also to the more general reader. I should like here to remember particularly my many Greek friends, and to offer them this small contribution to their history in return for many enjoyable visits I have made to Greece, and for several honours received at their hands. The Greek language has a continuous line of development from the fourteenth century B.C. down to the present day, and the echoes of Bronze Age Greek have been well described by a contemporary poet, Mr P. A. Sinopoulos:

xekhíthike kambanolálima triandatrión eónon.

'There rang out a peal of bells thirty-three centuries old.'

Cambridge J.C.
June 1975

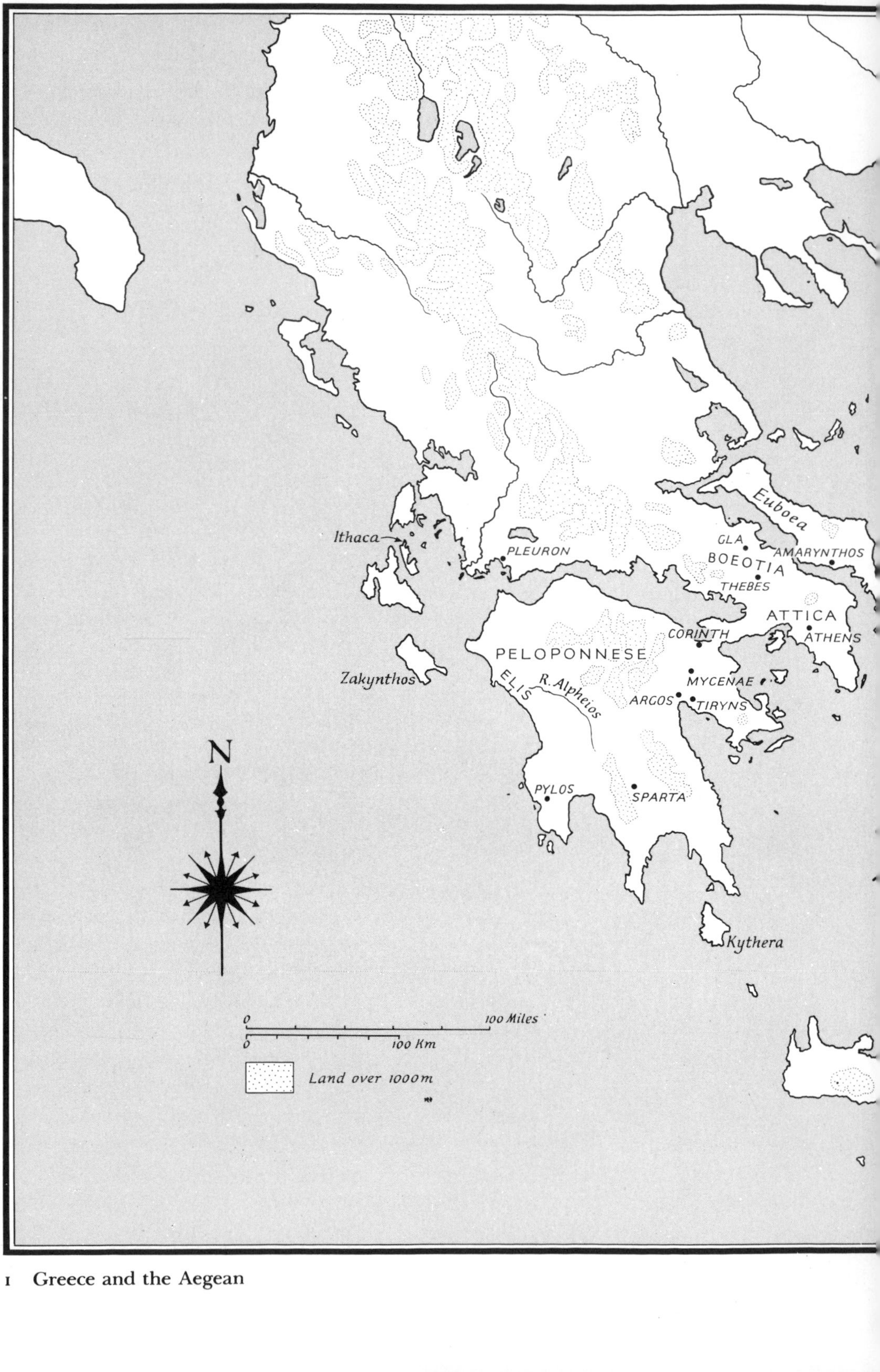

1 Greece and the Aegean

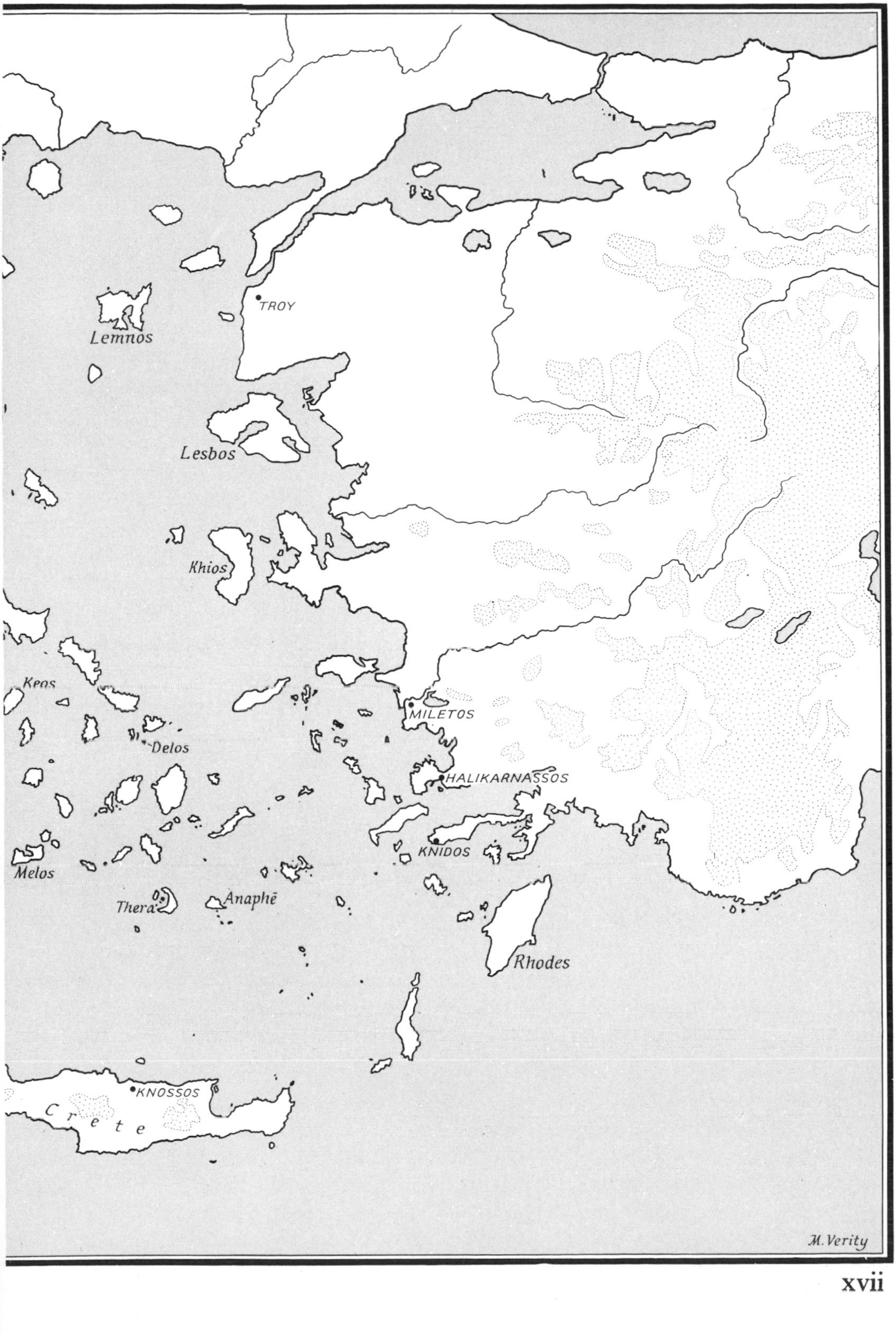
TROY
Lemnos
Lesbos
Khios
Keos
MILETOS
Delos
HALIKARNASSOS
KNIDOS
Melos
Thera
Anaphē
Rhodes
KNOSSOS
Crete
M. Verity

1 THE HELLENIZATION OF GREECE

There is nothing easier in talking about the past than to ask meaningless questions, which nevertheless still appear sensible. If we ask: 'Where were the English when Julius Caesar invaded Britain?' there is no answer; at that date there were no inhabitants of Britain who could be identified as 'English'. Similarly we must beware of asking questions like: 'When did the Greeks reach Greece?' for this presupposes that there were any Greeks outside Greece. Yet this is a question which has often been asked and usually answered.

In both these examples the vital point is the meaning of 'the Greeks' or 'the English'. I intend by these terms speakers of the Greek or English languages respectively, for if they meant simply the inhabitants of Greece or England, the questions would be superfluous. Thus my question about the Greeks supposes the pre-existence of the Greek language outside Greece, a hypothesis for which there is no evidence. The Greek language is known from documents written in Greece from the fourteenth century B.C. onwards, and at various later periods in other countries too as the result of colonizing movements; but its motherland has always been, roughly speaking, the area occupied by the present state of Greece, though perhaps not originally extending as far north as the present frontier.

However, the present domain of a language is not necessarily its original home; the Hungarian language or the Turkish, for instance, must have reached their present areas from much further east. All we can say about Greek is that it seems to have left no traces outside Greece, except where it has spread in historical times. But the existence on the map of ancient Greece of dozens of place names without a meaning in Greek strongly suggests that at one time another language was spoken there, though what this language was we have no means of knowing. Names such as *Korinthos*, *Zakunthos*, *Athānai* (Athens), *Mukānai* (Mycenae), *Knōsos* (the traditional spelling Knossos is strictly incorrect), *Amnisos*, *Tulisos* are certainly derived from one or more unknown languages previously spoken in Greece.

It is this fact, the evidence for a non-Greek-speaking population in prehistoric Greece, which has led serious scholars to ask: 'When did the

Greeks enter Greece?' However, the analogies of well-known historical cases like 'When did the English enter New Zealand?' must not blind us to the possibility that the Greek language did not exist before this presumed event, but was formed on Greek soil, just as Modern English was formed in England out of Anglo-Saxon heavily contaminated with Norman French and a few other foreign bodies. Is there any reason why this theory should not be preferred?

The traditional view of waves of Greek-speaking warriors marching down through the Balkans to subjugate Greece is an old one, best supported by the work of an eminent Austrian linguist, Paul Kretschmer, as long ago as the end of the nineteenth century. The form in which this theory has been most often held is that there were three such waves of invaders, usually called Ionians, Achaeans and Dorians, after the classical divisions of the Greek dialects. It was even possible to date these invasions archaeologically: the Ionians would be the people who entered Greece around the twentieth century B.C., the Achaeans about the sixteenth, the Dorians about the twelfth. But this serves to expose one weakness in the theory, for it implies that the Dorians of the twelfth century were still speaking what was recognizably the same language, despite minor differences, eight hundred years after losing contact with their Ionian cousins. Parallels suggest that the differences arising over such a long period would have been far greater than those which can be observed. Although the science of glottochronology, which aims to establish the dates of prehistoric linguistic events from the comparison of dialects or related languages, is not sufficiently exact to enable us to reject the traditional view on these grounds alone, it offers a strong counter-argument. Let us therefore explore the alternative view.

This hypothesis is that the Greek language did not exist before the twentieth century B.C., but was formed in Greece by the mixture of an indigenous population with invaders who spoke another language (Chadwick, 1963). What this other language was is a difficult question. We know that Greek belongs to the great family of Indo-European languages stretching from Iceland and Ireland to the north of India, without counting their extension in comparatively recent times to the Americas, Africa and Australasia. By a comparison of the earliest recorded languages of this family it is possible to reconstruct a great deal of a prehistoric language we call proto-Indo-European, in much the same way as it would be possible to reconstruct Latin, if we did not know it, from Italian, French, Spanish, Portuguese and Romanian. Whether the invaders of Greece spoke pure proto-Indo-European is doubtful; but at least we can be sure of many features of their language, even if the exact stage reached in development at the time of their arrival is hard to predict.

When these proto-Greeks, as I shall call them, reached Greece, they mixed with the previous inhabitants, whom they succeeded in subjugating, and borrowed from them many words for unfamiliar objects; and the mispronunciation of Greek by these aboriginals led to permanent changes in the phonetics of the language. The borrowed words are particularly interesting, for they include the names of many plants and animals, as well as terms indicating a high degree of civilization, such as the word for 'bath' or the many terms to distinguish different kinds of pot. Now among the plants are the words for two trees, the cypress and the turpentine-tree. Neither of these grows freely in areas liable to hard frost, hence they are found in the Balkans north of the Aegean basin only in specially sheltered locations. It is therefore unlikely that the proto-Greeks encountered these words outside that area; but since the word for 'cypress' shows a characteristic divergence in the later Greek dialects, it is probable that the splitting of Greek into dialects, in this respect at least, took place inside Greece. Nor does this theory encounter any problems on the archaeological level. The entry of the proto-Greeks can be placed not later than the nineteenth century B.C.; there is now some evidence that the major change occurred in some places even earlier, as long ago as the twenty-second century, when many towns were destroyed and rebuilt on new lines. The changes apparent archaeologically in the sixteenth century are not necessarily to be connected with the arrival of new peoples: the chief effect seems to be an increase in the influence of Crete on Greece.

The events at the end of the Mycenaean period are a problem. Greek traditions suggest that around this time a new branch of the Greek race, the Dorians, moved into the Peloponnese. Certainly the people who occupied all except the centre of the Peloponnese in classical times called themselves Dorians, and spoke closely related dialects. But it has proved impossible to find any unambiguous trace of this movement in the archaeological record; and if they did come from northern Greece, it cannot have been from Thessaly, which seems to have shared in the Mycenaean civilization. The only area they could have started from is the north-west, and this is in keeping with the scraps of information the classical Greeks remembered about the event. But it hardly seems likely that the rugged mountains of Aetolia and Epirus could generate a large enough population to colonize southern Greece on the scale required, however weak the Mycenaean resistance. I now think that we may have to seek a much more fundamental solution to this problem, but since it lies outside the scope of this book, I propose to reserve this for further discussion.

Reconstruction of prehistory

We can now attempt a summary reconstruction of the history of Greece from the twenty-second to the twelfth centuries B.C. The period begins with the incursion, from where we still do not know, of a warlike people possessing the horse, but of a smaller type than those we use now, and with a distinctive kind of pottery. These people establish themselves, perhaps first in central Greece and the north of the Peloponnese, and by mixing with the indigenous peoples create the Greek language, which is extended to the remainder of the mainland, except probably Macedonia. At what date Greek reached the islands is unclear; Thucydides (1.4) talks of Cretan supremacy in this area, and deduces archaeologically the presence of Carians (i.e., the people whom he knew as the inhabitants of south-western Anatolia) in the islands (1.8). Crete was occupied down to the fifteenth century by people who did not speak Greek, for we have their language in written form, and although we cannot securely identify it, there is no doubt that it was not Greek (Chadwick, 1967*b*, 12–15, 154–6). This is the language of the clay tablets and other inscriptions in the Linear A script, which has been found in many parts of Crete, and in traces in the Aegean islands. The Cretans certainly established themselves outside Crete: the islands of Keos (Kéa, off Attica), Kythera (Kíthira, off Lakonia), Melos (Mílos), Rhodes and above all Thera (Santoríni).

It is from Thera that we know most of the Minoan period in the islands, thanks to the immense archaeological excavations at Akrotíri undertaken recently by the Greeks under the late Professor S. Marinátos. At the moment of writing only the southern tip of what may be a large town has been exposed; yet this has revealed large complexes of buildings, streets and squares with walls standing as much as seven or eight metres high. Although none of the buildings so far explored has the typical plan of a Minoan palace, now well known from Crete, the excellent masonry and Fig. 2 magnificent wall-paintings prove that we are dealing with more than private houses. At the least this area must have been inhabited by important officials, and it gives the impression of a Kremlin complex rather than a Buckingham Palace.

Around the sixteenth century the Minoan influence on the mainland becomes very marked. Military conquest seems unlikely; the mainlanders, who by this time might deserve the title of Greeks, were always warlike, interested in weapons and hunting, while the Minoans lived in open palaces on sites offering no natural protection. All the refinements of civilization on the mainland in arts and crafts seem to have been borrowed from Crete. The most famous Minoan sport, recorded on frescoes and

2 Fresco of a fisherman from Thera

Fig. 3 many other works of art, was clearly connected with bulls. But there is nothing to suggest any resemblance to the Spanish *corrida de toros*, for all the human participants are unarmed. As Professor Sir Denys Page has pointed out, the traditional view of this sport must be wrong. It is physically impossible for even the most highly trained athlete to perform a somersault over the back of a charging bull, even less to be caught by another performer stationed behind the bull. The apparent positions are due to the artist's failure to show perspective. The sport must have been for the performer to excite the bull to charge him, and then at the crucial moment to leap high in the air, allowing the bull to pass harmlessly underneath, and tucking his legs up so that no contact took place, for contact with an object moving at 50 km.p.h. is likely to be disastrous. Something similar still takes place in the south of France. It must have been a thrilling sport with serious risk to the competitors, but it confirms the impression of the Minoans as a civilized, controlled people, while not lacking in courage. Small wonder that later Greek tradition looked upon the game as a sort of gory sacrifice; the people who made the word for 'foreign-speaking' mean 'barbarous' would not have allowed the Cretans an honourable sport.

Cretan art and craftsmanship, and hence no doubt artists and craftsmen, are now found freely on the mainland. I believe it is to this period that we must assign the adoption, again from the Minoans, of a script as a means of keeping accounts. So long as you manage a small estate, you may be able to exercise adequate control without written records; but as the area under your control grows, the need for an accounting system becomes imperative. This is very likely what happened in the mainland at this time (see Chapter 5); small units ruled by a local baron became amalgamated, whether by peaceful means or imposed unions, until the kingdoms resulting from them needed an army of officials to govern them and direct their production, and hence arose the need for accounts. The Minoans had long since devised a system of keeping accounts, and had gone on to use their script also for recording dedications in shrines. The Greeks borrowed from them the system of writing, both adapting it to their own language and improving the book-keeping. A very simple reform which they introduced was the practice of starting each entry on a new line, and consequently having the tablets 'tailor-made', the dimensions suiting as a rule the text that they were to carry. At this time too there is an obvious access of wealth, and the Mycenaean economy 'took off', as modern economists say. Later on we shall be examining the economic basis for this leap forward.

But all was not well in the Minoan world. During the sixteenth century

3 Bull sports from a vase found at Hághia Triádha

a serious earthquake caused heavy damage in Thera, and apparently simultaneously in Crete, for the same event seems to be recorded in the archaeological strata at Knossos, Phaistos and other Cretan sites. The southern edge of the Aegean is especially liable to earthquakes, for a reason which is easier to grasp now that new views of the movement of the earth's surface have been confirmed. It appears that Greece and the Aegean is carried on a very small 'plate', which is being overridden on its southern edge by the huge African plate as it moves northwards. The result is a deep trench in the sea-floor south of Crete, and frequent earthquakes around the borders of the Aegean plate. The event of the sixteenth century, following upon another a century or so earlier, seems to have been particularly severe. Yet as soon as it was over, the Minoans immediately rebuilt their towns and life continued as before; indeed there are signs of growing development and prosperity in the succeeding period.

A short time later, around 1500 according to Professor Marinátos, a further earthquake, which was not so violent as the previous one, shook Thera. But it must have been accompanied by a more alarming event, a volcanic eruption; for Thera was then a fair-sized island, about 16 km in diameter, roughly circular and rising to a huge conical mountain in the centre. The hitherto dormant volcano must have shown signs of coming to life, for the elegant buildings were abandoned, and we may conjecture that their inhabitants retreated to the greater safety of Crete. Of course, only the upper class could make their getaway; the humble people stayed on, and began to clear the ruins of the earthquake, so that they could occupy the undamaged part of the old buildings.

A short time later, to be measured in months rather than years, the anticipated disaster took place. The volcano began to erupt in earnest, and the town was covered in a deep layer of ash, from which it is now being resurrected by the archaeologists. As the eruption continued, its ferocity increased until the solid mountain was nothing but a hollow shell out of which all the molten rock had been ejected; until in a final paroxysm the whole mountain exploded and the sea rushed in. So all that survives today is a crescent-shaped sector in the east and a much smaller island which was once part of the west coast. An exploding volcano is a rare event, but the eruption of Thera seems to have been closely parallel to the eruption of Krakatoa in the strait between Java and Sumatra in A.D. 1883. There was, however, one important difference; the volume of matter lost from the island, and hence the violence of the eruption, was greater in the case of Thera by a factor of at least four, possibly as much as ten, times. For other parallels we must go back to geological times, when, for instance, the island

Fig. 4

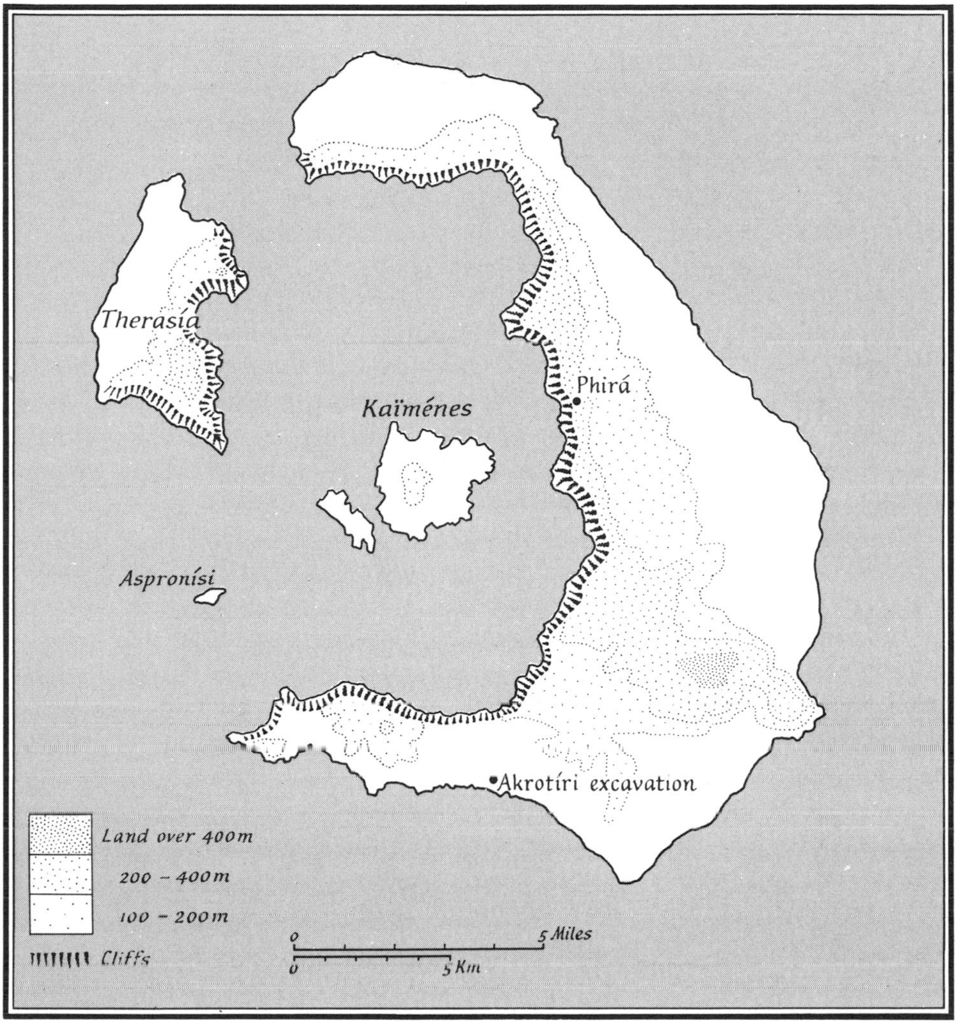
Therasía
Kaïménes
Phirá
Aspronísi
Akrotíri excavation
Land over 400m
200 – 400m
100 – 200m
Cliffs
0
5 Miles
0
5 Km

4 Thera

of Ischia erupted in a similar way.

This scientifically attested event has given rise to much controversy. The alleged connexion with Plato's strange tale of a sunken land called Atlantis can be easily dismissed, for the Platonic account contains three major errors (size, date and position), not to mention less serious ones, if it refers to Thera; and if it is really a distant reflexion of this event, it is too distorted to be of any assistance to us in our search for the truth, though it may entertain those who enjoy guessing games.

The more important argument concerns the effects that the explosion would have had elsewhere. We can be sure that the noise was incredibly loud and alarming; Krakatoa was heard in Australia, and the whole Aegean must have been made aware of the fate of Thera by a terrifying roar. The cloud of ash ejected from the volcano will have darkened the sky for hundreds of kilometres around. But the most unpredictable effect will have been on the sea. When the outer wall of the mountain was shattered in two places and the sea rushed in, immense tidal forces were generated, and a wave, known by the Japanese term *tsunami* 'shock-wave', would have been propagated throughout the Aegean. Clear evidence of the wave exists on the island of Anáphi, 27 km to the east, in the shape of layers of pumice at heights up to 250 metres. Pumice has been reported elsewhere, for instance on the site of Nikhória in the southern Peloponnese, but although it can be identified as belonging to a stratum of this date, it clearly reached the site by deliberate cartage, for it is much too high and far from the sea to have been carried by a wave. In fact, the search for wave-damage has been disappointing. The *tsunami* caused by Krakatoa did damage and caused loss of life as far away as Hawaii; how could Thera have failed to cause far worse in the confined waters of the Aegean?

No doubt many coastal settlements were swamped, but archaeological traces are very difficult to find. Moreover, the behaviour of waves in the sea is very complex. The immediate result in the neighbourhood of the volcano would be a slight lowering of the sea level over a large area, so slight that vessels sailing near Krakatoa reported no abnormal waves. Had the Minoan fleet been at sea, it would probably have survived unscathed. But where the wave encountered shallow water, it would build up to a great height; the wave generated by Krakatoa at places reached a height of more than 30 metres. But this would not be true on all coasts, for where the water is deep close inshore, the wave is reflected back and its energy is thus gradually dissipated. Hence we must not suppose that a settlement such as Gourniá, on a low hill a few hundred metres from the sea on the north coast of Crete, would inevitably be swamped. Probably more evidence will come to light as archaeologists begin to look for it.

But even without direct archaeological evidence there is here an effect which can be securely predicted. Ships at sea in deep water might survive unscathed; but any ship near the shore or inside a harbour, even if pulled up on the beach, would undoubtedly have been lifted by the force of the wave, probably carried some distance inland, and certainly smashed to pieces. If the Minoan fleet had been in any harbour on the north coast of Crete, it must have been destroyed at a single stroke; and the same blow probably fell on shipping throughout the harbours of the Aegean. Only on the south coast of Crete is the effect likely to have been less devastating. It is reasonable to suppose that most of the Minoan fleet was put out of action, and this has always been presumed to be the force which kept Crete so long inviolate and enabled its inhabitants to dominate the Aegean. The rulers of Greek states facing the Aegean may have suffered similar disasters, but their naval forces were probably much smaller, and shipping on the west coast of Greece or in the Corinthian Gulf would surely have escaped. Hence the Greeks would, once they had recovered from the initial loss, have been able to re-equip with new vessels, and they may well have felt the need to do so to defend themselves, once the Minoan control of the sea had been broken. It is around this date that the epoch of fortification seems to begin in Greece, though most settlements remained unfortified. If the Minoans were less well placed to rebuild their fleet, this would explain why the Greek invasion of Crete was possible, but only after the Greeks had had the time to build new fleets and organize the immense joint enterprise that would have been necessary to mount a successful invasion.

The third effect is the hardest to predict, but potentially the most damaging. The volcanic ash ejected would have risen high into the atmosphere, to descend like rain on the areas downwind. The work of two American geologists, D. Ninkovich and B. C. Heezen (1965), has shown the existence of such a deposit of ash on the sea-bed around Thera, and its relative thickness in different directions indicates that the wind was in the north-west. The ash was therefore carried towards central and eastern Crete and the Dodecanese. How thick was the layer deposited on Crete it is hard to tell; its existence, in microscopic quantities, has been reported at the site of Mírtos, more than 80 nautical miles (146 km) away on the south coast of Crete and in the lee of Mount Dikte (Dhíkti). If the ash were as much as 10 cm thick, as has been suggested, its effect upon plant life would have been devastating, for although in small quantities it can act as a fertilizer, larger amounts will kill all vegetation. The effects of wind and rain will in due course disperse the layer of ash and the land will regain its fertility; this happened with great rapidity on Krakatoa, but this is doubtless because it lies in a tropical rain-belt. Thus there may have been a period when eastern Crete became barren, but nothing in the archaeological record shows this; the palaces continued to flourish, apparently without interruption.

The next major event is still a mystery. The eruption of Thera seems to be securely dated to the end of the Late Minoan I A period, around 1500 B.C. At the end of the I B period, perhaps around 1450, a major catastrophe struck the Cretan palaces. All over Crete, but perhaps with the exception of Knossos, Minoan buildings went up in flames. Now the temptation to squeeze the chronology, so that the destruction of Minoan Crete can be attributed directly to the effects of the Thera eruption, is very strong. But although it is hard to calculate the time interval, there does appear to be too long a gap for us to bring the events together. Moreover, how does a volcano cause fires at a range of 160 km? Even the shock-wave generated in the air is hardly likely to have overturned lamps so consistently at such a distance. It begins to look as if the effects of Thera were to weaken the Minoan power to such an extent that the Greeks from the mainland judged it safe, as much as a generation later, to attack in strength and destroy all the centres of Minoan power save one, Knossos, where they installed themselves in luxurious surroundings, having some parts of the palace remodelled to suit their own taste.

One result of the Greek take-over in Crete was doubtless to reinforce the movement of Cretan craftsmen to the mainland, and we shall see evidence later which suggests their presence there in the subsequent period. Crete enjoyed a period of strongly centralized rule, but this too lasted only a short while, for the destruction of Knossos had only been delayed, not averted. Again for unexplained reasons, and at a much disputed date, but probably in the first half of the fourteenth century, the huge palace of Knossos was burnt, and was never again the seat of a major power. This does not of course mean that there was never again a king at Knossos; but if so, he built a new palace on another, as yet undiscovered, site; and he may well have been only a petty prince, unable to impose his will on the other rulers of Crete.

At this period our attention must shift to the mainland. The whole of southern Greece, at least as far north as Boeotia, and possibly including Thessaly, was the home of an advanced Greek society, which we qualify by
Fig. 5 the name Mycenaean after Mycenae, the first and most important site to be thoroughly excavated. It would appear that the country was divided into small states, but in some cases bigger than the city-states of classical times. We know of palaces at Thebes, Athens, Mycenae, Tiryns and Pylos; but there were undoubtedly others, for instance at Sparta, in Elis or the Corinth area. Only where the archives of clay tablets have survived can we

5 Mycenae: the citadel

hope to delimit the areas controlled by these palaces, and that means at present Pylos, for the tablets from Mycenae and Thebes are too few to enable work on this to proceed. But the size of the Pylian kingdom can be determined with reasonable certainty, and we may presume that other kingdoms occupied similar, geographically determined, areas. It would be surprising if the whole of Lakonia were not administered from a palace in the neighbourhood of Sparta. There may have been two palaces as close as Mycenae and Tiryns (15 km apart), but for strategic reasons it is impossible that the Argive plain was divided between them; Tiryns must have been a dependency of Mycenae.

Mycenaean Greece seems to have reached its zenith in the early thirteenth century. It was in this century that the settlement at Troy known to archaeologists as Troy VII A was destroyed, apparently by enemy action, though there is no archaeological evidence that the destroyers were Mycenaean Greeks. But by the middle of the century the tide was on the turn, and we encounter once again the familiar tale of settlements burnt and sites abandoned. Clearly the whole of Greece was in a ferment, and one after another the magnificent palaces went up in flames, and although life continued it was henceforth at a much lower level of civilization. The higher arts, like building in stone and writing, wither away, and life returns to its agricultural base.

If we could plot accurately the dates of these destructions, the pattern would doubtless be instructive. But archaeological dating cannot be precise enough, nor can modern scientific methods like radio-carbon give the required degree of accuracy. At some sites there seem to have been two or even three destructions; at Mycenae the houses outside the walls were burnt long before the buildings within them, and then there seems to have been another interval before the final destruction. At Thebes too, two destructions are apparently recorded within a short time; but the overall picture does not allow any precise deductions. All we can say for sure is that the Mycenaean kingdoms with their large thriving population came to an end, and the next century sees Greece sparsely inhabited and the survivors seeking sites less exposed to piratical raids from the sea.

2 THE DOCUMENTARY EVIDENCE

The outlines of the historical summary given in the last chapter come from archaeology, the collective efforts of scholars of many nationalities over a period of a hundred years. But ever since the achievement of Michael Ventris in 1952 in deciphering the Linear B script, we have had another means by which to investigate Mycenaean Greece. The main purpose of this book is to show what the tablets, taken in conjunction with other sources, can tell us and how those results have been obtained.

The written documents of Mycenaean Greece are relatively few. Tablets have been found in large numbers only at Knossos and Pylos; small numbers so far come from Mycenae and Thebes; and Tiryns has produced only enough to show that here too they existed. Our information is therefore extremely patchy, and in some cases it may not be safe to generalize from it; but the homogeneity of Mycenaean culture is so marked, that it would be strange if other parts of Greece behaved very differently.

It is hard to be precise about numbers of tablets, because the great majority are made up of at least two fragments, and often many more. To count a small fragment as a tablet is misleading, yet it may belong to an otherwise unknown document. It is safer to talk in round figures of some 3,000 tablets at Knossos and perhaps 1,200 at Pylos; but since the average size is greater at Pylos, it is in fact our major source of information.

What makes these unpromising lumps of clay so precious is the fact that they constitute a totally new source of unimpeachable information about the earliest Greek civilization, which is otherwise known only from archaeology and the vague traditions of the classical period. That they do not tell us anything about the history or thought of the people who wrote them is regrettable; but it may come as a surprise to some to discover how much can be deduced from them. If the Mycenaeans did not consider it necessary to preserve their history or their diplomatic correspondence, at least they did leave a record of the administration of their kingdoms and the operation of some parts of their economy. Fig. 6

In addition to the tablets we have Linear B inscriptions painted on vases

(a)
(b)
(c)
(d)
(e)
(f)

6 Tablets from Knossos: (*a*) Ra 1548: three swords: (*b*) Sc 230: a chariot, a pair of horses and a tunic for Opilimnios; (*c*) K 875: a list of handleless vessels; (*d*) Gg 701: jars of honey; (*e*) L 693: linen and bronze; (*f*) Od 690: wool

from a number of sites, and more are still being found. Single signs, usually incised on a finished pot, occur frequently, and may generally be taken as marks indicating ownership or perhaps in some cases maker. Many of these signs are taken from the repertory of Linear B; but they are almost invariably simple signs requiring only a few strokes, and could therefore be duplicated accidentally by men who did not know how to read and write. It is never safe to talk of a true inscription until we have a sequence of at least three consecutive signs.

In this sense inscriptions do occur on Mycenaean vases, as a rule storage vessels; these are painted on before firing and could not have been added after manufacture. By far the greater number of such inscriptions, when complete, consist of one word; and when this word can be identified, it seems always to be a personal name. But there exists also a relatively small group of vases with longer inscriptions; most of these are from the small areas so far dug of the Mycenaean palace of Thebes. These typically have a three-word formula, and owing to the spacing of the words round the jar, it is not always easy to tell where the inscription begins. But the pattern seems consistently to be: man's name, place name, and another man's name in the genitive case. The place name may appear directly as such or as the derived adjective; in one case it appears to be replaced by the adjective 'royal'. The curious fact, however, emerges that no less than four of the place names found on jars from the mainland are known on the Knossos tablets as belonging to towns in Crete. No jar has yet been found Fig. 7

7 Inscribed 'stirrup-jars' from Thebes

8 The palace at Áno Englianós, showing the Archive Room in the left foreground

in Crete with the extended formula. But some of these jars from Thebes appear to have been probably made in Crete (see p. 59); thus it would seem that the practice of recording place of origin on jars for export was a Cretan habit. Presumably the purpose of these inscriptions was to act as a kind of label or trade-mark guaranteeing the origin of the liquid they contained. No doubt future archaeologists, when they come to study the glass containers of twentieth-century Britain, will compile long catalogues of our trade-marks.

The tablets were made of ordinary clay, sometimes being formed around an armature of straw; this of course perished, but the hole which it left is clearly visible when the tablet is broken. Writing was done with a needle-sharp stylus – perhaps a thorn mounted on some kind of holder – and then left to dry. After a few hours, perhaps a day at most, the clay became too dry for additions or deletions to be possible. Hence mistakes discovered after this time could not be corrected. It is sometimes possible to see that a sign has been added after the clay had begun to dry. Unlike the clay tablets of Assyria, in Greece they were never deliberately baked, and they would have long since crumbled away, but for the accident that the buildings in which they were kept were destroyed by fire. The fire, ironically enough, preserved the tablets by baking them, in a rather patchy manner, so that the colour varies from one part of the tablet to another.

The tablets, once written, were stored away in baskets, perhaps also wooden boxes, since some hinges were found associated with them, and, it seems probable, ranged on shelves round the walls of the offices. The baskets could be identified by labels, small blobs of wet clay pressed onto

9 A reconstruction of the Archive Room at Pylos, showing a scribe at work

the outside of the basket; some of these have survived and are recognizable by the impression of basketry on the back. The inscriptions on the labels were usually terse; that for the basket containing a series of tablets at Pylos recording body-armour (Sh) had only the single word 'corslets' (Wa 1148). Fig. 10

Figure 9 is an attempt to reconstruct the scene in the Archive Room at Pylos while it was in use. I am much indebted for it to the Hon. Henry Hankey, who very kindly painted the picture following a brief I drew up. The scribe sits on a stool (*thrānus* on the tablets) in the Main Archive Room; through the door at the back we can see through into the Annex, where

10 Clay label from Pylos, showing marks of basketry on the reverse

most of the tablets were found. The written tablets are tidily filed in their labelled baskets; a few lie exposed drying before being put away.

The scribe holds the tablet he is working on in his left hand; it is quite often possible to see the fingerprints on the reverse where a tablet was held, and large tablets have sometimes here depressions corresponding to the positions of the thumb and fingers. Next to him stands an official who has returned from a tour of inspection and is dictating the details he wishes to record; he has brought with him a tally-stick to remind him of the correct figures – a gratuitous invention, but it is certain that some form of temporary mnemonic would have been needed to ensure that the official got his figures right. In the foreground a small boy is kneading clay ready to make the next tablet for the scribe.

The result of a fire in such a room can easily be guessed. There was inflammable material in the baskets or boxes containing the tablets, and if we are right in restoring wooden shelves these would have made a good blaze; in any case the walls contained wooden beams. Thus the destruction of the shelves would have scattered the tablets in fragments all over the
Fig. 11 floor. Sometimes fragments were found close together and were duly glued by the excavation's pot-menders; at other times it has taken much patient research and inspired guesses to see which fragments fit together. For unfortunately during Evans' pioneering dig at Knossos it was not thought necessary to keep accurate records of the position of each piece,

11 Knossos Tablet (De 5032) reconstructed from fragments

and only the general area was indicated in the day-books of the excavation; and for many of the smaller pieces even this information is lacking.

It would have much simplified the task of the editors of these documents, if more detailed and accurate records had been kept. Instead I and my colleagues who have worked on the Knossos tablets have had to face the prospect of a gigantic jig-saw puzzle; or rather, it is like doing some two thousand or more small jig-saw puzzles simultaneously, knowing that many of the pieces are missing. This is a good opportunity to pay tribute to the members of the team who have done most of the work. I was joined first by John T. Killen, who came to Cambridge from Dublin and stayed to make a career as University Lecturer; then by a Belgian, Jean-Pierre Olivier, who displayed not only a rare talent for Mycenaean epigraphy, but such zeal that it was impossible to prevent him from working fourteen hours a day; and through him we were finally joined by another Belgian, Louis Godart, who has now a teaching post in Italy. All of these, and others too, have rendered notable service in this sport of 'join-hunting', and it has been a pleasure to lead such a brilliant international team. The result of their years of toil in Iráklion Museum is that the Knossos tablets are now much more complete than when Evans left them. Even so, the task is not finished, and perhaps never will be; but we have reached the point where the law of diminishing returns is operating so strongly that it is doubtful whether much more work would be worth the effort. Sometimes even when a true join between fragments cannot be found, it is possible to demonstrate that two fragments belong to the same tablet, and even to conjecture what was on the missing piece.

The Pylos tablets were much better treated, and their original editor, Professor Emmett L. Bennett, Jr, of the Institute for Research in the Humanities at Madison, Wisconsin, U.S.A., worked closely with their excavator, Carl Blegen, and his team. The first edition in 1951 was a fundamental step towards the decipherment of the script, for it established with hardly any errors the Pylos repertory of signs. Bennett's subsequent editions have added new texts and improved the reading of the older ones; but the original work was so good that relatively little improvement was needed here. Bennett was also a major contributor to the work on the Knossos tablets, and his pioneering season in 1950 produced the first satisfactory classification of these texts.

This is the other fundamental task of the epigraphist: to reconstruct not only the individual tablets, but the files to which they belonged. A group of tablets precipitated from a high shelf would have been scattered over a wide area of floor, even if never disturbed before the archaeologists penetrated to them. In practice of course such a desirable situation is rare, and human interference – hunters for re-usable stone rather than buried treasure – or even burrowing animals, not to mention natural forces, have all contributed to blur the record. This is partly why so much controversy still surrounds the dating of the Knossos tablets.

The grouping of the tablets into series was accomplished by Bennett in
Fig. 12 advance of the decipherment by studying the ideograms. Tablets listing, say, men and women could be easily distinguished from those listing sheep, cloth or chariots. Further refinement of this classification became desirable after the decipherment, since we need to know, if possible, the actual files in which the tablets were stored, because the complete contents of a file may be regarded as a single document. I proposed therefore the term 'set' as a sub-division of a series, meaning a group of tablets intended by their authors to be kept together and read as a single document. Since this implies penetrating the minds of men who have been dead for thirty-two centuries, it is an ideal rather than a practical aim. But we have made remarkable progress in working towards it, and these sets offer useful insights into the way Mycenaean officials worked.

In a few cases the archaeological record has actually preserved for us not merely the set but the order in which the tablets were filed. The best

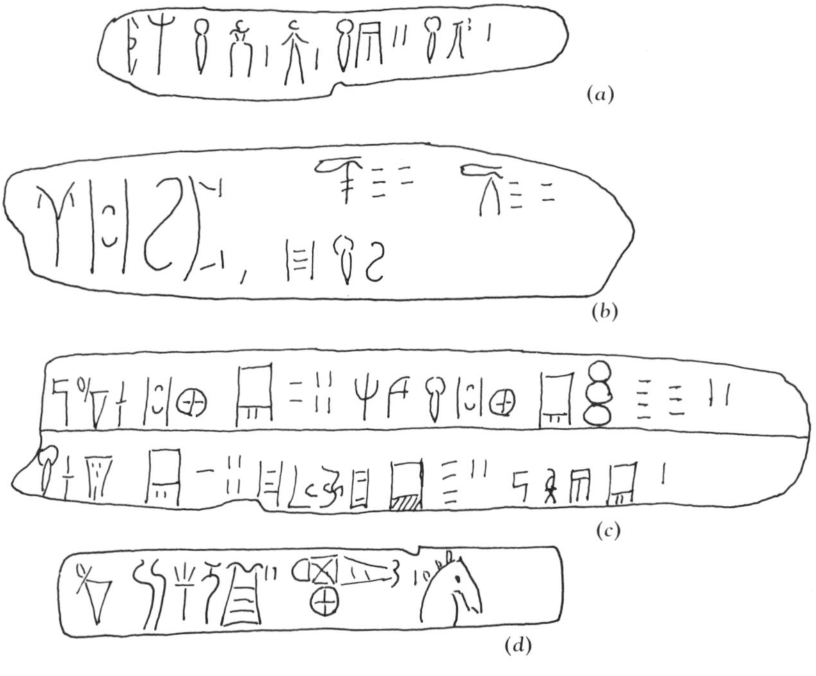

12 Knossos tablets: (*a*) Ag 88: a man, a woman, two girls and one boy; (*b*) Db 1227: fifty rams and fifty ewes; (*c*) Ld 587: different kinds of cloth; (*d*) Sc 103: horse, chariot and tunic

13 The Knossos Pp series of tablets as found

example is shown by the photograph reproduced in fig. 13. This was taken by Evans in the course of his dig at Knossos, and shows the Pp series of tablets as actually uncovered. The tablet at the bottom of the picture is the totalling document frequently included in a set such as this, and simply records the total of all the others. Whether it was the first or the last in the file we cannot infer from its position; but it is more likely to have been on top of the pile, so that the original order will have been reading from bottom to top of the picture. Such details are not merely pedantic, for when we find place names listed in such a set, as they are in the Pp series, the order may be a clue to their geographical location.

The task of distributing the tablets into their correct files has been enormously helped by the study of handwriting. Just as modern handwriting differs, so too Mycenaean scribes had characteristic hands; the way in which they make some of the common elements of signs allows us to classify them. For instance, an inverted V forms the basis of several signs, and scribes can be grouped according to whether the sides of the V are straight or convex. By careful examination of the ridges formed by pressing the stylus in the clay, we can tell the order in which intersecting strokes were written. The cross element, which recurs in a number of signs (e.g. *ka*, see fig. 14), may be made with the vertical stroke crossing the horizontal, or vice versa, or the strokes may even be curved. Equally

14 Variant forms of signs used by different scribes

significant at this level are the way adjacent strokes are spaced, joined or left unjoined, the position and shape of minor elements, the doubling of lines. By this means Bennett (1958) and Olivier (1967) have been able to identify securely a large number of the more prolific scribes at Knossos and Pylos.

As a rule, all the tablets in a single file were written by the same scribe, though exceptions occur; and there are cases where two scribes have written on the same tablet, as if the appropriate clerks have each been ordered to add their own quota of information (e.g. PY Ed 411). The number of different hands at each site is large, probably as many as seventy at Knossos, at least forty at Pylos. This means that the scribes are not professional writers, as in the Near East, but are literate officials who can write a tablet as and when required, but have other duties as well. Some senior officials seem rarely to have written a tablet themselves, no doubt leaving their subordinates to do most of the work, but occasionally they take the stylus in their own hands.

The total number of documents at each site gives a very small average production per scribe; but in fact some scribes are prolific, others do very little. We must not, however, infer that Mycenaean scribes were any more idle than modern typists; it is likely that most of them had other duties than writing, since one scribe could easily have written all the surviving documents from either Pylos or Knossos in a few weeks. No doubt work in the offices had its moments of tedium, when a clerk would turn his tablet over and draw a sketch or a pattern. We are lucky to have three good examples of this kind of doodling; most must of course have ended in the Fig. 15

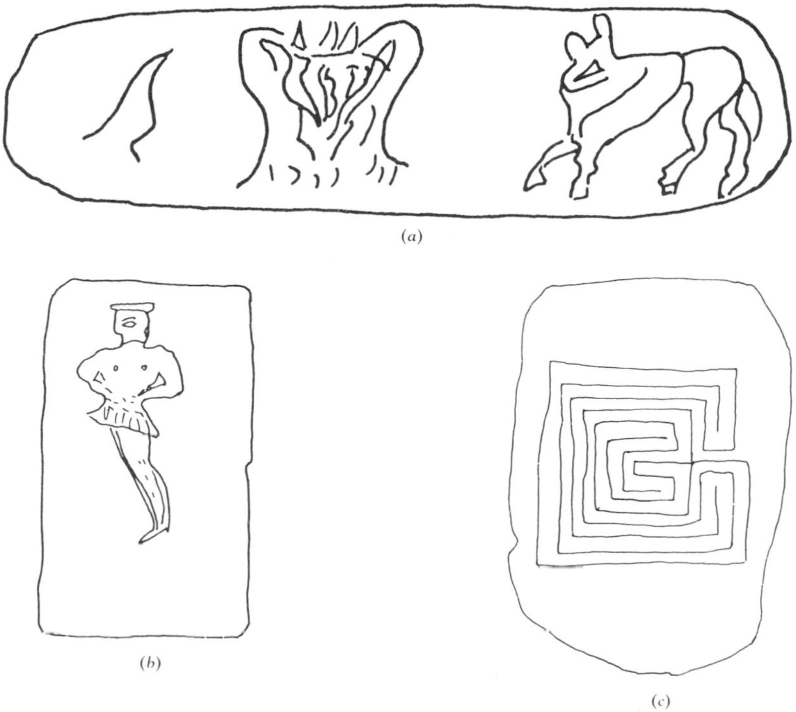

15 Examples of 'doodling' from (*a*) Knossos, (*b*) Mycenae, (*c*) Pylos

scrap basket. Evans thought the Knossos example was a gem-engraver's preliminary sketch, but it is hardly necessary to take it so seriously. The one from Pylos is the crudest drawing, but it is very interesting to see this early example of the famous 'labyrinth' pattern, varying forms of which have been found on stone as far distant as Ireland.

If each official was in charge of a particular department, then bringing together all the tablets he wrote may allow us to see what his particular responsibility was. At Pylos, for instance, there was an official who seems to have written nothing but the tablets dealing with chariot wheels (Sa) and a label (Wa 1148). The label might otherwise not have been associated with this group, but the handwriting shows that it belongs here. At Knossos we find the same official dealing with wool, cloth and women workers; he was obviously concerned with the organization of the textile industry.

Once written a tablet dries rapidly and further entries cannot then be made. It follows that a large tablet with many entries could not have been used unless all the information on it was available at the same time; if the information came in one item at a time, it would have been necessary to use small individual tablets for each piece of information, which could then be filed in any order, like a card index. Once the file was complete, the information could, if required, be recopied onto large tablets. We have excellent examples of this in the 'land-tenure' tablets from Pylos, where a large set of small, individual tablets (as the Eb series) has been recopied in groups on large tablets (Ep) to form a long continuous document. There are slight discrepancies between the two versions, and efforts have been made to assign them to different dates. But it seems much more likely that the differences are merely verbal, and the essential details, the figures, are, so far as the completeness of the documents allows us to judge, apparently repeated unchanged (see pp. 111–14).

There are also problems caused by scribal errors. Mycenaean writers were no more reliable than we are, and were quite capable of leaving out a sign by accident, writing the wrong sign, or spelling the same name two different ways. These errors can hardly have caused much trouble to the people who were intended to read these documents; but for us they constitute a severe obstacle. Sometimes a repeating formula is slightly varied; how can we be sure if this was without significance or was intended to convey a different meaning? We were puzzled for a long time by a form *wo-zo-e*, until another tablet was found bearing the same formula, which showed that the mysterious word was an error for *wo-ze-e* 'to work'. If the parallel text had not turned up, we might still be racking our brains to explain that erroneous form; so some at least of the words that still defeat us may be due to errors. When what is indubitably the same word is repeated, but with an extra syllable inserted, are we to assume that one is wrong, and if so, which?

It often happened that the scribe discovered his error and corrected it while the clay was still wet. We can sometimes make out what underlies a deletion, or observe that a sign or two were added as an afterthought, after the surrounding words were already complete. When a scribe runs out of space, he may squeeze a word in above the line, continue over the right edge, and even go right round to the back (PY Va 1324). As a rule, the back is not inscribed, but can be used if the space on the front proves inadequate. But sometimes it looks as if the back was inscribed with a text unrelated to the front; it is hard to see any connexion between the miscellaneous catalogue of jars, bowls and other vessels on MY Ue 611 and the note of olives, figs and wine on the back – they could not be merely the containers. There are occasionally entries on the lower edge of a tablet.

It cannot be too strongly emphasized that what mattered most to the users of these documents was the numerals. The numbers and quantities are the important details which cannot be confided to the memory; the remainder of the text is simply a brief note of what the numerals refer to, headings to enable the reader to identify the person or place associated with the quantity recorded. Thus the interpretation of these documents must start from these figures, and any explanation which ignores them does so at its peril. Some promising theories have foundered upon this rock, but where theories are built upon it, they are likely to stand firm. Many of the deductions which supply the material for this book began from observations of the numbers on the tablets.

The incomplete condition of the archive that has come down to us presents us with many problems; but we have found means in some cases to overcome this deficiency. Where we have two sets of tablets containing the same information, it is of course easy to use one to supplement the gaps in the other. But another method which has proved useful is the existence of tablets giving totals: if the figures preserved on the relevant series of tablets add up to seventy per cent of the total given, we can infer that thirty per cent of the entries are probably missing. In other cases it seems that a series is preserved intact; the *o-ka* tablets from Pylos, which will be discussed at length in Chapter 9 (pp. 173–9), seems to be complete, for not a single scrap can be identified as belonging to a missing member of this set, and there are other reasons for thinking it is complete.

But the major gap in our knowledge is due to another fact that we can only infer: the existence of records on some perishable material, that was consumed by the fire which rendered the tablets durable. It is hard to believe that such careful accountants did not keep at least a summary of their operations from year to year. Yet it is clear that the tablets we possess are all from the last year of the palace's existence, for their references to 'this year' and 'last year' would be meaningless if the records of several years were kept together in the Archive Room, and the presence of month dates combined with the absence of year dates also confirms this. Even the very forms of the signs with their elegant curved strokes and complex patterns suggest that this script was not designed for writing on clay. Pen and ink must have come as naturally to the Mycenaean scribe's hand as the stylus, and clay was obviously the second-class writing material which could be thrown away, or soaked, pounded up and re-used. Thus inferences from what is not in the tablets must be treated with caution; only in respect of the current year are the gaps in our knowledge sometimes important.

The superior writing material was clearly expensive, while clay was cheap. This suggests that although papyrus might have been imported from Egypt, skins of some sort are more likely. It may be not just a coincidence that in Cyprus, where so many Mycenaean traditions lingered on into the classical age, a school-master was called *diphtheraloiphos*, literally 'one who paints on skins'. There are references in the tablets to skins (*diphtherai*), but none apparently in connexion with writing; and there are men described as *a-ro-po*, which could represent *aloiphoi*, the second half of the Cypriot compound, but they are too rare to be the ordinary scribes. The absence of a word for scribe on the tablets goes to support the inference that literacy was expected of clerks and officials, and the man who knew how to write had therefore no special name.

Some gaps in our information may be due to the accident of preservation. At Pylos we have records of large numbers of chariot wheels, but none of chariot frames, though at Knossos both are found. It seems clear that the relevant tablets at Pylos were simply not recovered, possibly because they were kept with the chariots on a part of the site not excavated. As we shall see later, the excavated areas of Knossos and Pylos were only a fraction, though the most important fraction, of the towns to which they belonged. One reason for the absence of certain records is undoubtedly the time of year when the palaces were destroyed (see pp. 188–92); it would appear that there was an annual clearance of the clay tablets of the past year and they started the new year with a clean slate.

The ordinary small tablet of elongated shape has been compared with a reference in an ancient author to writing on leaves, and the name of 'palm-leaf' has been applied to these tablets. It is possible that leaves were used for rough jottings, but the characteristic shape of a 'leaf' tablet is explained more simply by the way in which clay handles. If you roll a lump of clay between the hands, the result is a cigar-shaped object, and if this is then squashed flat, we get exactly the shape of this type of tablet. Tablets are usually 'tailor-made', adapted in size to the length of the text to be written on them; sometimes a group of small tablets (e.g. Pylos Ed series) is used in preference to one large tablet, if a summary had to be filed together with the documents on which it was based. The largest known

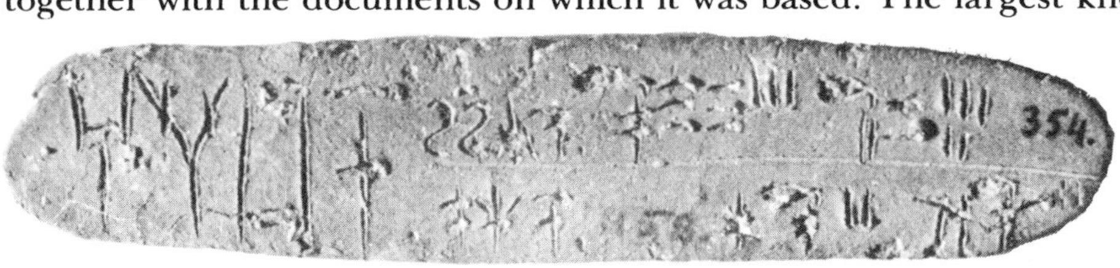

16 A sheep tablet from Knossos: Dg 1158 (see text)

tablet measures 16×27 cm and is about 3 cm thick; most are much smaller.

A typical small tablet must be read, like a card in a filing system, in connexion with the other members of the series. A typical example is shown in fig. 16. The entries are: (1) the name of a shepherd, *Aniatos*, in large characters; this is the key-word by which the flock is identified; (2) in smaller characters in the lower line *Phaistos*, the name of the district where the flock is kept; (3) above this a man's name, *Werwesios*, apparently an official to whom this flock is allocated; (4) the numbers of sheep: male 63, female 25, 'old' 2 (making an unrecorded total of 90); (5) the number of sheep required to bring the flock up to nominal strength: 10 (i.e. the nominal total is 100). It can be seen that the last figure was corrected from 12; at some stage the writer had forgotten the two 'old' sheep. It is only by comparing this with all the other similar tablets that we can interpret the entries as given above. The indication of the sex of the animals is shown by means of marks added to the sheep ideogram; the words for 'old' and 'to be supplied' are reduced to abbreviations; and the rest of the text, apart from the numerals, consists of the three names. It is obvious from this that when we have to interpret an isolated document there is often little we can do; only when put into its correct context in the archives can we grasp its significance.

The other elements in the writing system are the numerals and ideograms. The numerals present no problem, except that they are often damaged and incomplete. Ideogram is the name given to signs which stand before numerals and indicate the commodity which is being counted. These are often pictorial, and it is easy to recognize men, women, horses, chariots, wheels, swords, cups and vessels of various sorts. Other

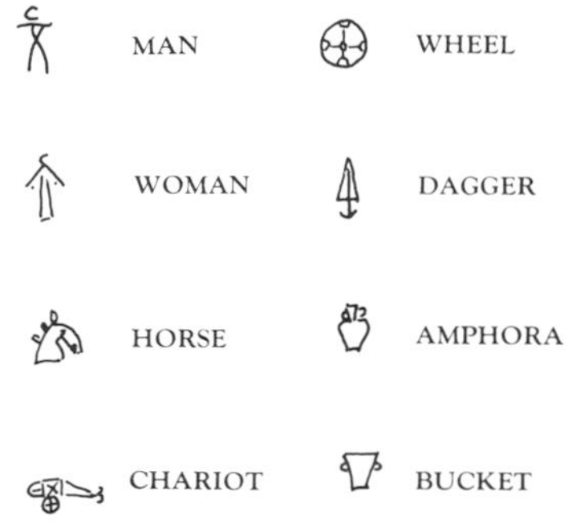

17 Recognizable ideograms

18 Conventional ideograms

signs are so stylized that it is difficult to guess them from their appearance, and we must rely on deducing their meaning from context; examples of this class are sheep, goats, oxen, olives, wheat, barley, bows, cloth. Sometimes there was no conventional sign, but a syllabic sign was used as a sort of abbreviation; but unfortunately the abbreviation is sometimes of a word unknown to us, thus flax is written *SA*, although the Greek word for 'flax' is *linon;* but since this is once used as a description of *SA*, we can infer that this is its effective meaning. The same abbreviation can be used for different meanings in different contexts. It is thus not surprising that there are still a number of these signs which we cannot interpret, or at least only speculatively.

The large 'page-shaped' tablets do not follow any very regular pattern. Fig. 19 A large tablet may be a complete document in itself (e.g. KN U 4478, PY Tn 316); or it may form part of a set. One of the best examples of such a set is the 'coastguard' tablets of Pylos, a set of five large tablets making up a single long document. Such a document often begins with a heading, often only a single line (e.g. PY An 654.1), but sometimes as much as three lines (e.g. PY Jn 829), specifying in general terms the subject, which is then recorded in detail in a series of entries. The document is sometimes split up into paragraphs by inserting one or two blank lines; a clear indication of a continuation of the subject in a new paragraph, whether on the same tablet or a subsequent one of the set, is the word *o-da-a*$_2$, which must mean approximately 'and also as follows'; it not only connects the new paragraph with what has gone before, but saves having to repeat the introductory formula each time.

All too often large tablets prove to contain nothing but a list of personal names, and the heading is only a terse formula which is obscure owing to our ignorance of the circumstances. All too often the upper edge of the tablet is damaged, and the introductory words, which might have made sense of the document for us, are lost or fragmentary. A list of women's names from Mycenae (V 658) has as its heading apparently the single word *demnia* 'bedding'; and a somewhat similar list at Pylos (Vn 851) has lost all its heading except for this same word. Are we to suppose that these persons were guests being accommodated, who had each been issued with blankets for the night? The Mycenae tablet incidentally couples the women in pairs; in two cases the second woman is not named, but is merely given as 'and daughter'. Dare we suppose that these pairs had to share the same bed?

The writing system is clumsy, but adequate for the kind of material the archives contain. The names and vocabulary words are written by means of syllabic signs, and these are transcribed conventionally by syllables linked with hyphens (e.g. *de-do-me-na*, *i-je-re-ja*, *a-re-ku-tu-ru-wo*). These transcriptions give only a clue to the possible interpretations, which have to be deduced according to a complicated set of rules; and from the possibilities we have again to reconstruct a form of the word which will

19 A page-shaped tablet: Knossos U 4478

answer to our knowledge of the Greek vocabulary. Thus *de-do-me-na* can be reconstructed without difficulty as *dedomena*, 'contributed', 'given'; *i-je-re-ja* stands for *hiereia* 'priestess'; *a-re-ku-tu-ru-wo* for the man's name *Alektruōn*. In some cases the reconstruction has to take account of dialect features absent from the classical language (e.g. *qa-si-re-u* reconstructs as *guasileus*, where the classical form is *basileus*), and the meaning may be slightly different, as in the same word which in Mycenaean means 'chief', 'head-man', but in later Greek has become the regular word for 'king'. In some cases, especially technical terms, the word disappeared from Greek between the Mycenaean period and the classical, so that it is impossible now to reconstruct the form; even so, it may sometimes be possible to deduce its approximate meaning from the way it is used. Where Mycenaean words are quoted in this book, the reconstructed form will be given where possible; where a straight transcription of the Linear B signs is given, these will be separated by hyphens, as shown above.

The very simple numeral system is adequate for recording numbers, and we have examples of up to five-figure numerals. But like all systems known to the ancient world, it lacked the positional notation which makes arithmetical calculation so easy for us, and there is no sign for zero. We may presume that some kind of abacus was employed in the arithmetical sums which we can see were performed. Large quantities of commodites such as grain or wine were measured in units of decreasing size, like the British *bushel, gallon, quart, pint* and *gill*, for unlike the metric counterparts the Mycenaean units are linked in a complicated system of relationships, which shows signs of being based upon the sexagesimal system used by the Assyrians. Thus the basic unit of dry measure is divided into tenths, which are further divided into sixths ($10 \times 6 = 60$), and these again into quarters. Similarly the major weight is divided into thirty double units, and these again into quarters (see further pp. 102–8). No difficulty seems to have been experienced in addition, when it was necessary to reduce a large number of minor units to the next higher unit of the system; though there is one clear case (PY Jn 658.11) of a mistake at this stage, and in other cases we may suspect the addition.

One method of adding was the use of tallying. We find tablets used for rough working, and one revealing tablet (PY Ea 59) has on its back a clear example of how addition sums were sometimes done: single strokes were written for each unit, and these were arranged in groups of ten, each ten being written as two fives one above the other. The text is unfortunately incomplete owing to the damaged state of the tablet, but what appears to be the total has been written in normal style underneath: 137.

Fig. 20

Yet despite all the complications and unsolved problems, we are now in a position to read a tablet almost completely, even if we cannot assign a value to every sign. The syllabic signs of uncertain value are only a few, and these the rarest; and for some of them we have tentative values which cannot yet be proved for lack of evidence. Most of the ideograms are identified, though a few remain obscure or disputed. The most troublesome items are the abbreviations; for instance, a squarish box with the syllabic sign for *ke* inserted in it is probably intended for a word of which *ke* would in the Mycenaean spelling be the initial syllable, but in default of further clues, it has so far been impossible to guess which of many possible words it was meant to represent.

The major difficulty now is not the 'reading' of the documents, but understanding what they were meant to convey; not the words, but the physical operations they record. Little by little progress is being made in understanding the world in which documents of the kind came to be written. This book is an attempt to reconstruct as much of that world as present knowledge allows.

20 Tallying on the reverse of a Pylos tablet: Ea 59

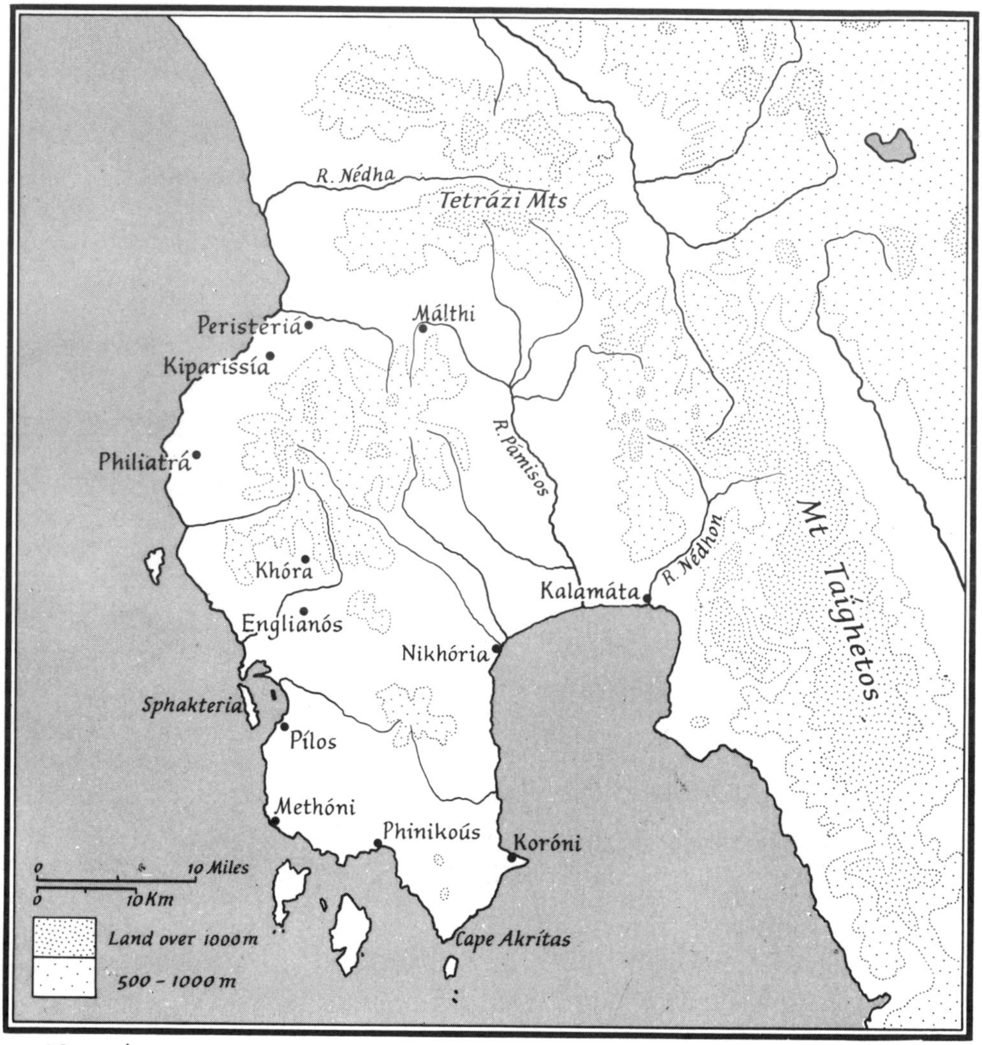
R. Nédha
Tetrázi Mts
Peristériá
Kiparissía
Málthi
Philiatrá
R. Pámisos
Mt Taïghetos
R. Nédhon
Khóra
Kalamáta
Englianós
Nikhória
Sphakteria
Pílos
Methóni
Phinikoús
Koróni
0 10 Miles
0 10 Km
Land over 1000 m
500 - 1000 m
Cape Akrítas

21 Messenia

3 MYCENAEAN GEOGRAPHY

22 The Haghiá ridge from Englianós

Messenia

If the king of Pylos climbed on to the roof of his palace, he must have had a fine view of a large stretch of country running down the southern part of the west coast of the Peloponnese. Away to the north-east his view was cut off by the jagged mountain ridge now called Haghiá, rising to 1,218 metres. This ridge runs approximately north and south, and reducing gradually in height leads eventually to the low saddle over which the modern highway runs to Kalamáta. To the south he could have seen the mountain, now called Likódhimos, which lies beyond and inland from the modern town of Pílos, at the south of the Bay of Navaríno; much of the bay too would have been visible. It forms a magnificent harbour, protected from the open sea by the rocky barrier of Sphakteria island, where a Spartan force was cut off by an Athenian fleet in 425 B.C. The main entrance to the bay is at the south-west, and though the shoreward side is Fig. 22

23 Voïdhokiliá bay, looking south with the Osmanagha lagoon and the bay of Navaríno in the background; modern Pílos is in the distance to the left of the conical hill

very shallow, it offers excellent anchorage for even large ships. Ancient ships, of course, when not in use, were drawn up upon the beach. At the north of the bay is a narrow passage between Sphakteria and the mainland, hidden from the king's viewpoint by a large cliff which overlooks the lagoon, now drained, at the north end of the bay. The coastline here may have changed since antiquity, but expert opinion inclines to the view that silting of the lagoon has probably kept pace with the slight rise in sea-level, so that the situation would not have been very different. Just to the north is a curious little bay, now called Voïdhokiliá or 'Ox-belly', formed by a sand-bar which runs in a crescent round more than three-quarters of a circle. If this was in existence, it would have provided an excellent harbour for ancient ships, with its sandy beach for hauling out, and the rocky entrance should not have been too difficult to negotiate. Traces of Mycenaean occupation have been found near by, and a *tholos* (beehive-shaped) tomb on the headland to the north points to the existence of a settlement in the vicinity. It is highly probable that the king of Pylos had his port here about 6 km from the palace. Fig. 23

To the west the sea is invisible, hidden behind the broken, low hills which form a series of obstacles in this direction. Was all this stretch of territory, about 20 by 10 km, under the king's control, and, if so, how much further

did his writ run? This is the first question we must try to answer.

We can begin with some general geographical considerations. The palace was clearly, as its archive implies, the administrative centre of an extensive area. Such centres are normally placed in a convenient place for communications, and not as a rule highly eccentric unless for obvious physical reasons. All communications in this coastal strip must run roughly north and south, because the mountain range can be penetrated easily by roads only at two points: beyond Kiparissía, 30 km to the north, where a broad river-valley gives access to the interior, and over the saddle to the south, opposite the Bay of Navaríno. This in itself suggests that the kingdom stretched at least as far as Kiparissía to the north, since there is no defensive line to provide a satisfactory frontier south of this strategic point, where the mountains come close to the sea. To the south again there is no barrier until we pass modern Pílos, and beyond that is only a short peninsula, much of it high and broken ground, leading eventually to the barren tip of Cape Akrítas. The kingdom surely extended throughout the coastal strip from Kiparissía to Methóni.

But although Kiparissía offers a defensive line, we know that the broad valley north of it was densely populated in Mycenaean times; both the main valley and the side valleys opening off it to north and south have

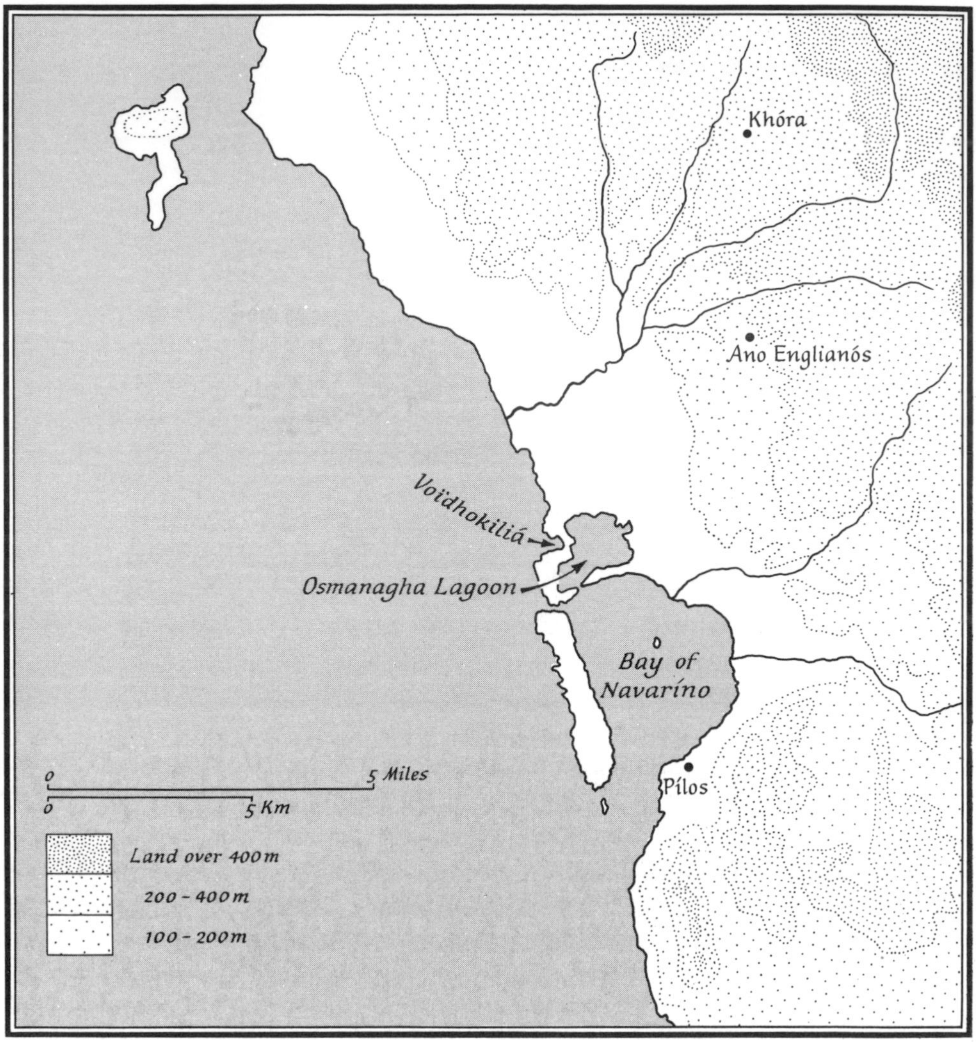

24 The Pylos (Englianós) area

yielded a large crop of habitation-sites to the patient research of the archaeologists. Moreover, these sites have the curious characteristic of being 'intervisible' – from any one you can see at least one other and often several – and the whole system seems to be dominated by the lofty hill of Kiparissía, crowned by a medieval castle, and no doubt the remains of more ancient fortifications beneath it. This valley offers the only other easy route to the great Messenian valley of the interior, the valley which extends northwards from the head of the Messenian gulf. We need to pursue our search still further, but not very far, for the northern limit of the Kiparissía river valley is formed by a wild, if not very high, region of mountain, which narrows the coastal plain to a pass just to the south of the river Nédha. This river valley, unlike that to the south, is apparently bare of Mycenaean sites, though they begin again a short distance to the north. Even today the area is sparsely inhabited, and it seems to be a natural no-man's land. Here at last is a suitable northern frontier. If we go still further to the north, we shall face the difficulty that the palace will occupy an eccentric position, and there would have been strong arguments for building it further north, since the frontier would then be over a day's march away. Can we confirm this view of the kingdom by reference to the written documents?

Fig. 25

The confirmation is far from easy. The documents contain no maps, and

25 Modern Kiparissía from the castle

although it is not difficult to deduce which words are place names, there is no way of identifying these with known sites. One name which appears repeatedly and from its use must surely indicate the principal town is *Pu-ro,* which would be the ordinary Mycenaean spelling for *Pulos* or Pylos. This can be confidently equated with the palace, for an ancient geographer tells us that the name, which in his day was applied to a site at the north of the Bay of Navaríno, had moved from an earlier site 'under mount Aigaleon', doubtless the modern Haghiá. It has now migrated even further south, and its modern form is here transcribed as *Pílos.*

But when we examine the lists of place names, they do not appear to match the classical geography or even the bare list of towns which Homer quotes for the realm of Nestor. We recognize a few names, like *Leuktron;* but if we seek this on the map, we find it three times in mainland Greece, the nearest site being away on the Máni, the central of the three southward prongs of the Peloponnese. Other places appear to be called *Erkhomenos* (later *Orkhomenos,* nearest site in Arcadia) and even *Korinthos,* which can hardly be the famous Corinth on the Isthmus. As in all countries and at all times, the same place names were repeated over and over again on the map of Mycenaean Greece.

In the early days of the decipherment scholars were willing to extend the kingdom of Pylos almost indefinitely, though most drew the line short of Corinth. I must confess to having contributed to this exaggerated view myself, for in 1955 Ventris and I had drawn attention to two names associated on the documents: *O-ru-ma-to* and *U-ru-pi-ja-jo.* These could be reconstructed linguistically as *Orumanthos* and *Ulumpiaioi,* which we compared with Mount *Erumanthos* north of the river Alpheios, and *Olumpiaioi,* the inhabitants of Olympia on that same river. Our enthusiasm now seems ill-founded: other reconstructions of these names are possible, and in view of the probability that the kingdom did not stretch so far to the north, it is plain we must abandon what now look less tempting identifications, for the vowel-changes we had to suppose have not received support from other examples. Unfortunately another important place name on the tablets appeared to lend colour to this theory. The name is spelt *Pi-*82,* where the second sign cannot be certainly identified. Some scholars favoured *Pi-sa*$_2$ and identified it with the classical Pisa in the neighbourhood of Olympia; one preferred *Pi-ja*$_2$ and suggested identifying it with the ancient name *Pheiai,* near the modern *Katákolo,* still further north. I now think the disputed sign is really *swa,* but although I accept the name *Piswa* as ancestral to classical *Pisa,* for *w* was lost from classical Greek, I think we must regard it as yet another example of a duplicated name. Indeed it would not seem impossible that some of the Mycenaean names later known from more distant parts of the Peloponnese may have been carried thither by migrants, who abandoned the south-west in the troubled times following the fall of Pylos.

Among the other names are some which are the ordinary Greek words for geographical features, like *Rhion* 'the promontory', *Kharadros* 'the ravine' and *Helos* 'the marsh'. The first of these names, however, is recorded as the ancient name of a site later known as *Asine* (and to make things more difficult, in medieval and modern times as Koróni, a famous Venetian fortress). This is on the far side of Cape Akrítas, on the west shore of the Messenian gulf, thus close enough to Pylos to merit consideration, if we can find other evidence that the kingdom extended beyond the mountains visible from the palace. And that evidence comes from the name *Nedwōn* on the tablets, which can hardly be other than the name *Nedōn* which survived as that of a river on the east side of the Messenian valley, flowing into the sea at what is now Kalamáta. Here at last we seem to be getting a fix.

There is one other place name which needs to be mentioned here: *Kuparissos*, the Greek name for the cypress-tree. I have already mentioned the modern name *Kiparissía*, and the ancient town on this site bore the same or a similar name; indeed Homer mentions another form of the same name (*Kyparissēeis*) as one of the chief towns in Nestor's kingdom. But as with other geographical names, it is perhaps dangerous to assume that it can be tied to any particular spot. Certainly cypresses still grow in abundance in the Kiparissía area, especially a little further south near Philiatrá. There is a resonable chance that the name is to be placed somewhere in this area.

But at this point our clue peters out. We must find another means of recreating the map of Mycenaean Messenia; we must see what the tablets can tell us about the location of the place names. First of all we can count them; in some cases of course it is doubtful whether or not they are place names, a fair estimate puts the number around two hundred. Archaeological surveys, which have been especially thorough here, put the number of Mycenaean sites round the same figure. But we must not assume that all the sites have been found, nor that all the places mentioned on the tablets are within the kingdom. For instance, we read in one place (An 1) of 'rowers bound for Pleuron'; might not a ship be going to foreign parts? We shall have other evidence of foreign names later.

Secondly, we have a number of internal clues to the distribution of the place names. We have three times (Jn 829, Cn 608, Vn 20), not to mention fragmentary examples, a list of nine place names always arranged in the same order. It runs as follows, adapting the actual case endings used in different lists, and quoting the figures (relating to cattle and wine respectively) attached to each name on two of the lists:

		Cn 608	Vn 20
1	*Pi-swa*	3	50
2	*Me-ta-pa*	3	50
3	*Pe-to-no*	6	100
4	*Pa-ki-ja-ne*	2	35
5	*A-pu*$_2$	2	35
6	*A-ke-re-wa*	2	30
7	*E-ra-to/Ro-u-so*	3	50
8	*Ka-ra-do-ro*	2	40
9	*Ri-jo*	2	20

In one case (Jn 829) the seventh name appears as *Ro-u-so,* and we must presume that this is an alternative name for *E-ra-to;* its form recalls the later Arcadian town *Lousoi,* which may be another example of a migrating name. It is clear that these are the nine principal towns and administrative districts of one part of the kingdom, since, as we shall see later, each has a local administrator or governor.

Now the consistent order might arise in several ways: it could be an order of importance, but the figures quoted in the table above show that the town with the highest figures (6 and 100) is not the first, and there is no sort of grading by magnitude. It might again be an 'alphabetical' order, if we imagine the Mycenaeans to have had a standard, if arbitrary, order for the syllabic signs, like our A B C...etc. The Japanese have such an order for their syllabary: *i ro ha*...etc. The two towns which begin with the same sign (*a*) stand together, but the theory breaks down on Jn 829, where the list is continued with a further seven names, and two of this second list begin with *e*, but do not stand together. The only likely solution therefore is that the order is geographical; but of course towns are disposed about the territory in two dimensions, and this has to be reduced to a single dimension to form a list, so some freedom must inevitably be allowed for.

At this point we must consider the seven extra names of Jn 829; these too are important towns or districts, and they recur elsewhere though not in a fixed order, since they are usually on isolated tablets, the original order of which is unknown. But from a battered document (On 300) which has the top line missing, it appears that the seven names belong to a province called *Pe-ra-a-ko-ra-i-ja* or the like, and this name is found elsewhere coupled with *De-we-ro-a*$_3$*-ko-ra-i-ja*. These must be compounds of an element *a₍₃₎-ko-ra-i-ja* with the prefixes *pera-* 'beyond' and *deuro-* 'on this side of'. Hence we can deduce that the kingdom is divided into two provinces, separated by some conspicuous feature. We have only to stand on the site of the palace and cast our eyes around to see what this is: the great chain of mountains mentioned at the beginning of this chapter, which runs roughly north and south down the peninsula and separates the western coastal strip from the great Messenian valley. It is an added bonus to discover that the classical name for this mountain was *Aigaleon* and the Mycenaean spelling may represent something like *Aigolaïa*, not a perfect match, but suspiciously close. It now follows that the nine towns lie in the western coastal strip, the seven over the mountains in the Messenian valley. This, one of the richest areas of the Peloponnese, will be described later; for the moment we must concentrate on the Hither Province.

The coastal strip makes it easy to reduce the two-dimensional distribution of the towns to the single dimension of a list; in principle we can be sure that the list must run along the line of the coast: north–south, or south–north, or possibly starting from the palace both northwards and southwards. It remains to see which of these possibilities fits best. Our first clue comes from the name *Pa-ki-ja-ne*, which is closely associated with Pylos (*Pu-ro*) on Tn 316, and also appears to be the location of various 'royal' craftsmen; for instance, the royal fuller has an estate there (En 74.3), and it is unlikely that men who served the king had their estates very far from the palace. So we can place the fourth district as that close to, perhaps including, the palace, for Pylos itself has a special status and does not figure on the lists of contributory towns.

Another clue is provided by *Ri-jo* (*Rhion* 'the promontory'), which as suggested above (p. 41) is likely to be on the site of the modern Koróni; that is to say, the list appears to end in the south with a name which takes us past the southernmost tip of the peninsula to the south-west shore of the Messenian gulf. It seems therefore that the order is probably north to south, and we can confirm that the first two names on the list, *Piswa* and *Metapa*, are in contact with the Further Province. This will make sense if we place them in the north, for there is a good route through the Kiparissía river valley to the Messenian valley. But how far north does the kingdom extend? A simple proportion suggests that if the palace is in the fourth district, there is less territory north than south of it. This should at least deter those who want to stretch the kingdom all the way up to the river Alpheios, tempting as it may be to equate *Piswa* with the later *Pisa* near Olympia. Ancient kingdoms, in the days before the existence of maps, were almost always bounded by natural features: mountain ranges, major rivers or other obstacles; and as we have seen, an excellent barrier of this

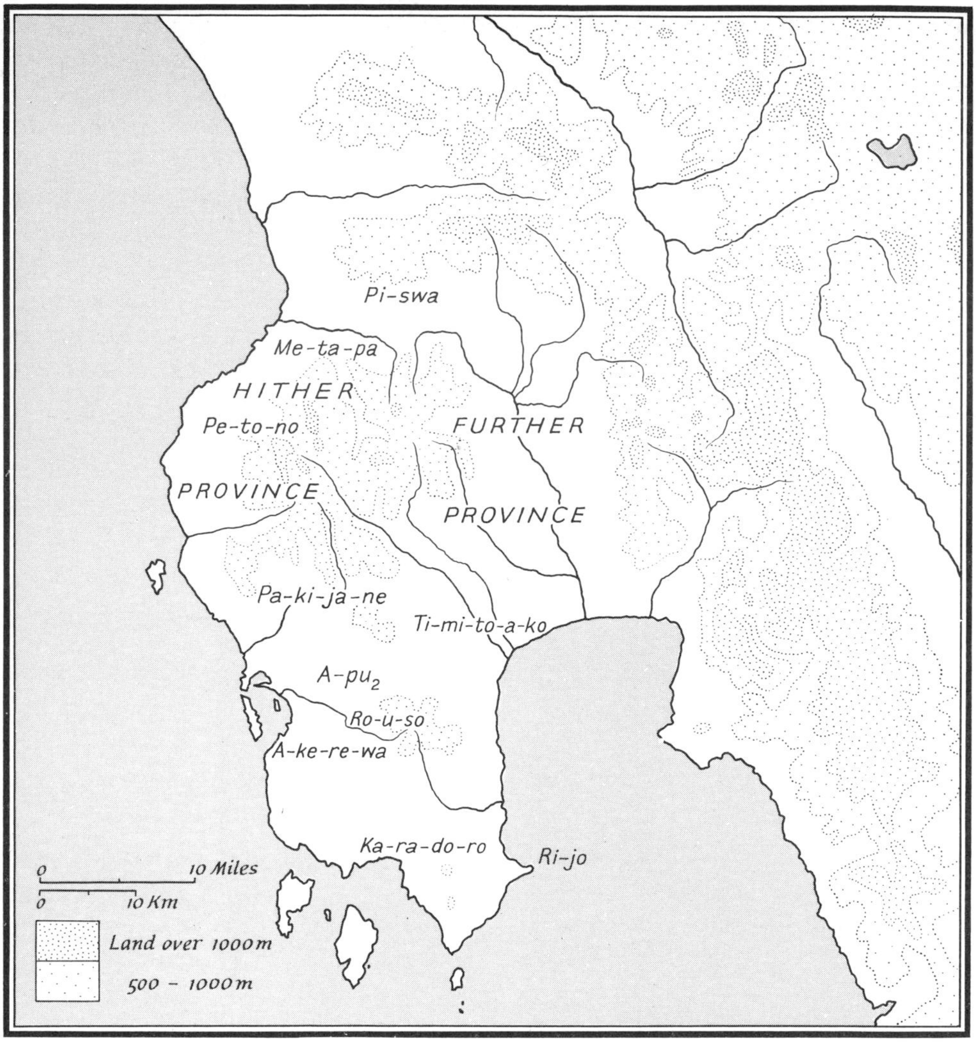

26 The Two Provinces

sort exists along the valley of the river Nédha and the Tetrázi mountains immediately to the south of it. There can be no doubt that the Nédha marks the northern frontier, and we may note here that the Mycenaean name of the river was almost certainly the same, since one of the prominent men of the northern area bears a name derived from it, *Nedwātās*.

Thus we have defined the northern and southern limits of the Hither Province, as we may call the coastal strip in which the palace lies. But the simple north to south order is of course a falsification, for not all the towns will lie on the coast or any continuous straight line; at the same time, geography dictates that the east–west spread must be restricted except at two points. At the northern end the Kiparissía river (also known as Peristéri) leads via the Soúlima valley to Mount Ithómi and the upper Messenian plain. It is therefore likely that the first two districts, which show contact with the Further Province, lie away from the sea in this valley; and Piswa in particular is an area rich in sheep. This accords well with the nature of the terrain, especially in the upper part of the valley. Similarly, south of the palace, on a level with the Bay of Navaríno, the country opens out again to the east, and we must expect some of the districts to lie inland.

Now it so happens that we possess another list of towns which, on the evidence of the list we have just discussed, must also run from north to south, but in this case all the places mentioned must be on or near the coast; this document will be discussed further in Chapter 9 (p. 175). For the moment all that need be said is that there is no reason to think that any of the towns are coastal until we reach the sixth on the standard list, *A-ke-re-wa*. We can also show that *Ka-ra-do-ro* and *Ri-jo* were on the coast.

Can we therefore begin to draw a rough map of the Hither Province? If we place *Pi-swa* well up towards the Soúlima valley, and *Me-ta-pa* nearer the coast to its west, this will satisfy all the details we know about these places. *Pe-to-no*, a large district to judge by the scale of its contributions to the palace, must lie between Kiparissía and the palace, and an important site has been located at Hághios Khristóphoros just inland from Philiatrá (McDonald and Rapp, 1972, 276). *Pa-ki-ja-ne* denotes the area in which the palace lies, and we know it is an important centre of religious cult; it may be significant that in a later age divine honours were accorded to Mycenaean tombs at Volimídhia on the outskirts of Khóra, a mere 3 km north of the palace.

To the south *A-pu₂* is more difficult. We began by thinking that this might be the Homeric *Aipu*, a name for which there is no firm location; it means 'steep'. But now that we understand better the rules governing the writing system, we can say that *pu₂* is never used in place of the ordinary sign for *pu* to represent Greek *pu*, but normally has the value *phu*. This place, which is not on the coast, probably lies in the hinterland of the Bay of Navaríno. *A-ke-re-wa* is a port of some consequence. The obvious location for it is on the Bay, not, however, at the north end, since it is apparently not the port for the palace. A location near modern Pílos at the south of the Bay therefore seems likely; no good site has been discovered here, though there are slight traces of Mycenaean occupation. The reason is probably that it was overbuilt in medieval and modern times, so that it is impossible to prove its earlier use without excavation. There are similar situations at both Kiparissía and Kalamáta, where the surface indications are too weak for the probable size of the site. *E-ra-to*, also called *Ro-u-so*, is not coastal, but is the home of wood-cutters; it must therefore be a wooded area (the woods, alas, have long since vanished), probably inland south-east of the Bay. This leaves us with only *Ka-ra-do-ro* to fit in before we reach *Ri-jo* at Koróni; it too is coastal, and there are only two likely sites for it on this stretch of coastline, Methóni and Phinikoús. Now the name *Ka-ra-do-ro* is instantly recognizable as a common Greek word, *kharadros*, meaning 'ravine' or 'gully'. Methóni stands on a small promontory at the south-west angle of the peninsula, and has no ravines in the vicinity. But the site of Phinikoús further east is dominated by two great ravines which meet almost above the Mycenaean site, and this leads me to suggest that the name may actually be (for the script is ambiguous) the dual form of the word: *Kharadrō* 'the two ravines'.

When we pass to the Further Province to the east of the mountains, it is more difficult to deal with the geography. This is partly because there is less information on the tablets, probably as a result of a measure of decentralization in the administration. A subsidiary archive dealing with local affairs may well have existed at the provincial capital, which we know was named *Re-u-ko-to-ro* or Leuktron. This is a common name in later Greek geography, but the nearest classical town of that name lies outside the probable limits of the Province. It is a pity we have no means of locating the site, for it might well repay excavation.

A further problem is created by the nature of the terrain. The Messenian valley is a broad, fertile plain, abundantly watered and hedged in by mountains on three sides. To the west lies the ridge which is so conspicuous seen from the palace site on the west coast, but which proves to have more depth on the other side, where the isolated height of Mount Ithómi (798 m) projects into the valley. To the north lies the high plateau of Arcadia, while on the eastern side the valley is shut in by the huge wall of Taïghetos, the rocky backbone of the Peloponnese with peaks as high as 2,400 m. To the south-east, beyond Kalamáta, lies a very rugged coast, along which communication has always been difficult by land, and a motor-road has only been constructed in the last few years. Until quite recently the inhabitants of the villages along this coast found it easier to take their produce by sea to markets on the opposite coast of the gulf.

We have in the coastguard tablets a valuable indication of the length of the coastline of the Further Province. Nine out of the ten sectors lie in the Hither Province, which, as we saw, extends into the western shore of the gulf at least as far as Koróni. Only one of the seven principal towns of the Further Province is known to be on or near the sea; and the other place name mentioned in this context is fortunately identifiable: *Nedwōn*, which must be the later (and modern) name *Nedōn*, the river on which Kalamáta stands. This appears to be the eastern frontier of the kingdom, so it follows that the east shore of the gulf, despite the presence of Mycenaean settlements there, did not fall under the control of Pylos. The boundary between the Hither and Further Provinces probably lay somewhere on the west coast of the gulf, between Koróni and the Mycenaean settlement at Nikhória, which has been excavated by an American team under the direction of W. A. McDonald between 1969 and 1973. It is tempting to equate this site with the coastal town known on the tablets as *Ti-mi-to-a-ko*.

The Further Province is thus located basically in the wide Messenian valley, and for a long time I could see no way of assigning the seven districts to their right place on the map. I owe the solution of this problem to the work of a brilliant young American scholar, Miss C. W. Shelmerdine. While she was studying with us at Cambridge, she presented a paper to our Mycenaean Seminar, the substance of which was subsequently published, together with an Appendix by myself (Shelmerdine, 1973). In this she demonstrated how a theory earlier proposed by another American, W. F. Wyatt, Jr (Wyatt, 1962) could be modified so as to demonstrate convincingly the administrative pattern into which these seven districts fall. They form four groups: (*a*) *Ra-wa-ra-ta*$_2$; (*b*) *E-sa-re-wi-ja*, *Za-ma-e-wi-ja*; (*c*) *A-sja-ta*$_2$, *Sa-ma-ra*, *Ti-mi-to-a-ko*; (*d*) *E-ra-te-re-we*, *A-te-re-wi-ja*. Groups (*a*) and (*b*) are paired, so are (*c*) and (*d*). The principle on which they are associated can hardly be other than geographical continuity; no one would bring together for taxation purposes two widely separated areas. Therefore we can look for a similar fourfold division of the territory.

Maps, as often, prove unhelpful, though they do show that the principal river, the Pámisos, with its tributary the Mavrozoúmenos, forms a division running roughly north and south; but viewed on the ground there is also a clear east–west line formed by a range of low hills around Skála. The two Fig. 27
intersecting lines neatly cut the province into four regions; we have then

only to determine which group corresponds to each region. We know that *Ti-mi-to-a-ko* in group (*c*) is near the coast and is likely to be close to the border with the other province: south-west is therefore the best choice for group (*c*). The same list (Jn 829) which establishes this also provides a linear list which must run from south to north, since the first name is known to be near the coast, though we must allow for the names being scattered to east and west of the Pámisos. *A-te-re-wi-ja* and *E-ra-te-re-we* can both be shown

27 The Skála ridge from the north; Mt Ithómi is at the right

to have connexions with the other province; group *(d)* should therefore be the north-west region, where there is an easy line of communication between the provinces. It then follows that (*a*) must be the south-east, (*b*) the north-east. The pairing of the regions is determined by the more prominent of the natural boundaries, the river system.

So far it appears dangerous to press further the identification of these names with actual sites. But *Ti-mi-to-a-ko* in the extreme south-west of the province may well be the Mycenaean name of the site at Nikhória as mentioned above. The picture which has thus emerged of Pylian geography at the time of the tablets gives us a firm background against which we can set the economic, social and military facts to be won from the documents.

Crete

Fig. 28 The king of Knossos did not enjoy such a good view of his domain as his colleague at Pylos. His palace was built upon a hill, but one lower than

28 The palace of Knossos

those surrounding it, so that his view was restricted to the valley in which it was situated. Only if he had climbed to the roof could he have seen, away to the north through a small gap in the hills, a glimpse of the sea. This is a striking difference between Mycenaean and Minoan sites; the Mycenaeans installed themselves in dominating positions, no doubt for strategic reasons. The Minoans of Crete had chosen merely pleasant and convenient sites, without bothering about their strategic importance; and of course the Mycenaeans of the mainland merely took over Knossos, with a certain amount of remodelling, because it was already there. Fig. 29

29 The view to the north from the roof of the palace of Knossos

30 Mount Ida from near Phaistos

Since Crete is an island, the first question we have to ask is whether there is anything to suggest that the king's dominions extended beyond it. The answer seems to be no, for there are no place names that can be identified as lying overseas. There is one reference to a flock of goats (C 914) which is being sent to *Akhaiwia* or Achaea, a name which occurs nowhere else on the tablets, but is reminiscent of the Hittite name for a kingdom with which they were in touch (*Aḫḫijawā*). There is still much dispute about its location, many scholars thinking it lies on or near the Turkish coast; it seems unlikely that Knossos would be sending goats overseas, and we may therefore suspect that it is really a place in Crete.

The archaeological evidence for Minoan colonies in the Aegean islands all dates to an earlier age, and there is no reason to suppose that by the end of the fifteenth century any of them were still controlled by Knossos. The replacement of Minoan by Mycenaean imports, which is documented for several sites, of course proves only that Greece replaced Crete as the dominant power in the Aegean at this time, a fact also apparently witnessed by the contemporary Egyptian monuments.

The second question then is how much of the island the king of Knossos ruled. We have more names at Knossos than at Pylos which we can recognize: Knossos itself, Amnisos its port, and the neighbouring site of

Tylisos all played a part in the decipherment (Chadwick, 1958, 63); and several more were clearly recognizable. At first sight they seem to cover most of the island, and we suggested that Knossos was, in this period, the capital of the island as a whole. But second thoughts have led me to reconsider the question.

Crete is a large island, as much as 260 km from east to west, but not more than 55 km wide at its widest point. Such statistics are easily gleaned from a map, but are quite misleading on the ground. Much of the land surface is above 300 m and there are three great mountain ranges with peaks between 2,000 and 2,500 m. Thus communications have never been easy between the different areas, and only now has the age of the bulldozer and the explosive charge made possible the creation of a good road-system. Those who have visited Crete recently will know that this system is still an unrealized potential, but progress has been rapid and parts of it are finished, other parts unfinished but in use, parts still in embryo. If we put ourselves back into the Bronze Age, with no road-making equipment but primitive tools and man-power, Crete readily falls apart into small areas.

If we start from Knossos, centrally placed near the north coast, we are in a large, fertile area, bounded by a region of moderately high but passable hills to the south and by the mountain ranges of Dikte and Ida to the

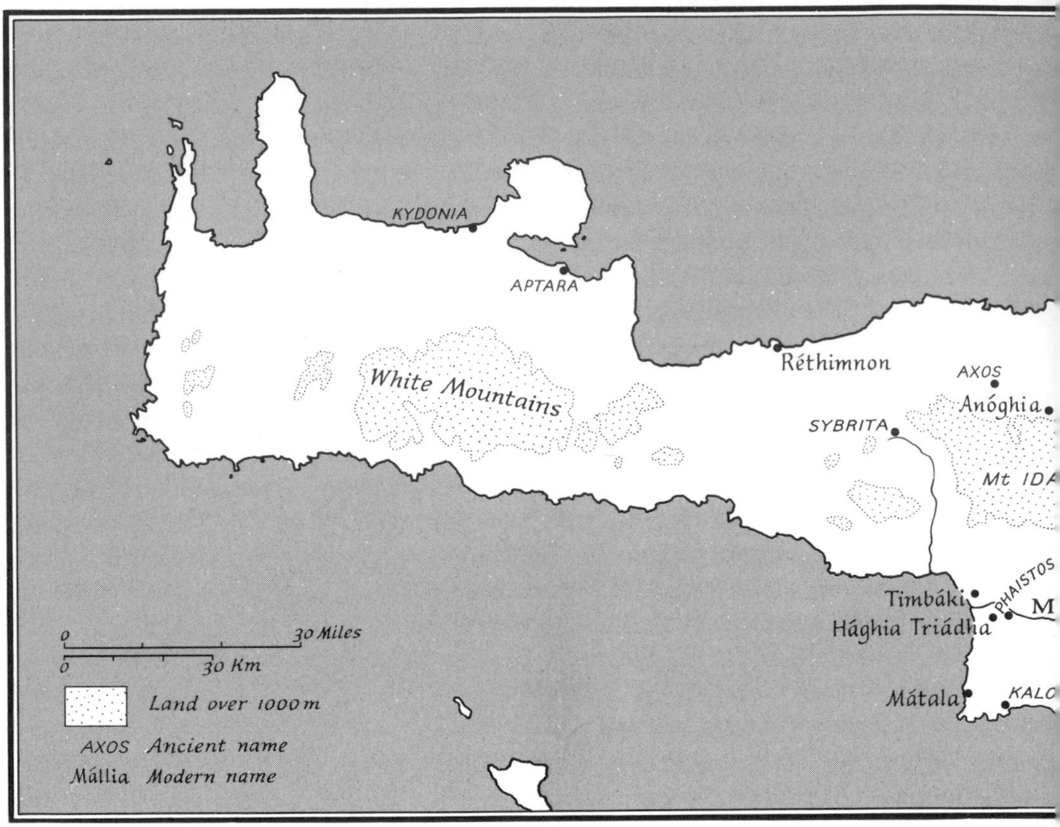

31 Crete

south-east and south-west. Eastwards along the coast there are no real obstacles, though low hills come down to the sea, opening up into a plain again around Mállia, the site of the third largest Minoan palace. Beyond this is another hilly region. All this territory must surely have been subject to Knossos; the names of Tylisos and Amnisos belong here, but we still do not know the classical, let alone Mycenaean, name of Mállia.

To the south of the watershed lies the one great plain of Crete, the one area likely to have produced a surplus of grain. This plain, now called the Messará, is bounded by high hills, or low mountains, to both north and south. The southern mountains drop steeply into the sea and offer poor shelter for shipping, as St Paul discovered when his ship was forced to put in at the tiny harbour of Kalí Liménes or Fair Havens. To the east is a region of broken, but not impassable, country; the west coast offers a good beach for ancient ships around modern Timbáki, where the sea may have retreated, and a useful bay at Mátala.

This area is dominated by the great Minoan palace of Phaistos (modern

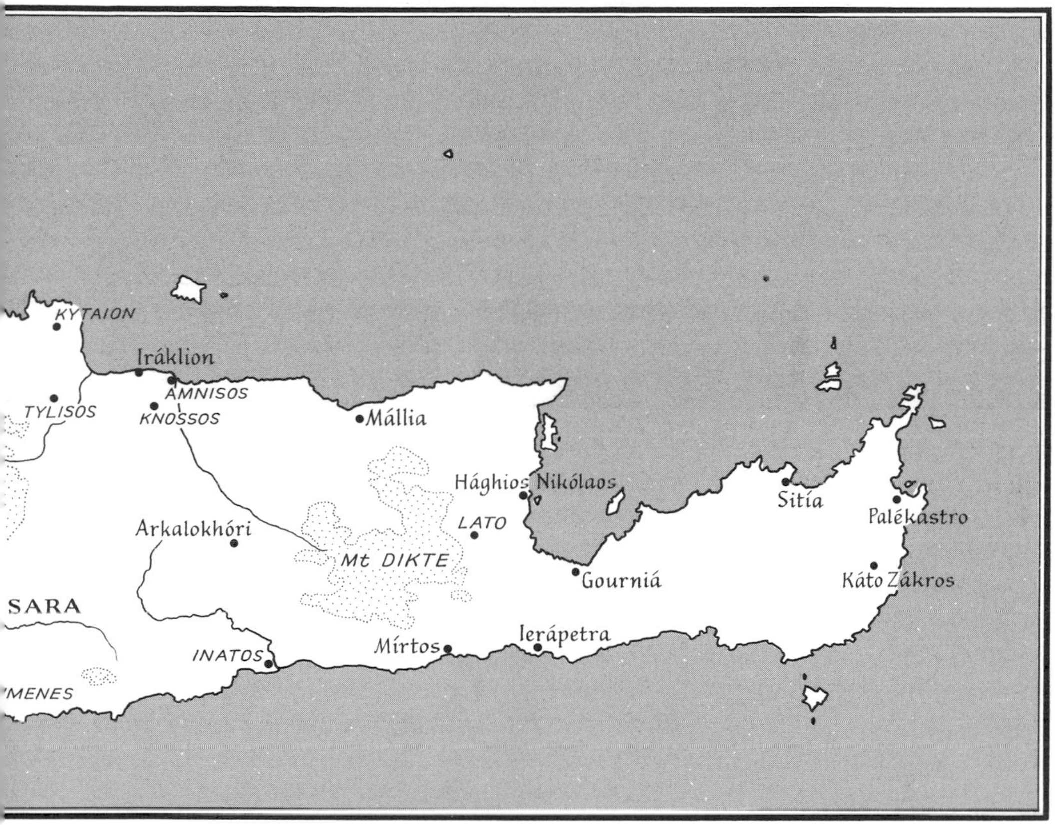

pronunciation *Phestós*), a name which figures prominently upon the Knossos tablets. There can be no doubt that Knossos controlled Phaistos, not merely as a superior power, but in all the petty details of administration, and the governor of Phaistos was a mere legate of the king of Knossos. It is not easy to reconcile this with the archaeological picture. The Minoan palace of Phaistos appears to have been destroyed, together with all the other Minoan centres, at the end of Late Minoan IB (around 1450 B.C.). Exactly what parts, if any, were re-occupied in LMII, the date of the Knossos tablets, is not clear. But there must have been a large and flourishing town near this site at this date. At a slightly later date we have good evidence for Mycenaean occupation at Hághia Triádha, the much smaller site which lies only three kilometres away at the other end of the same hill, and it is even possible that the name of Phaistos applied to this too – we have no knowledge of its ancient name. Its mere existence has puzzled archaeologists: why should the Minoan king of Phaistos have built a royal mansion so close to his palace? The most likely suggestion is that the

Fig. 32

Fig. 33

sea at this date came much closer to the hill, and Hághia Triádha was originally the harbour town for Phaistos.

But before we leave the Messará we must look at another name which occupies a prominent place on the Knossos tablets. It is spelt *Da-wo*, and does not answer to any name known in classical times, though it recalls the man's name *Daos* (Latinized as *Dauus*, so originally containing a *w* sound), which is often given to slaves. It is closely associated on the tablets with Phaistos, and in particular is known to be an enormous producer of wheat: we have its name (F 852.1) followed by an incomplete numeral which is not less than 10,000 units of wheat. Since the unit (see p. 108) is close to 100 litres, this gives the colossal figure of one million litres or about 775 tons of wheat as a minimum. There is only one place in Crete which is likely to have grown such an immense quantity of grain, and this is the Messará plain. Since *Da-wo* is a district separate from Phaistos, it must surely be located in the highly fertile eastern half of the plain, for although there is no obvious line of division on the ground, the eastern end is actually drained eastwards by a small river which now rejoices in the name Anapodháris or 'Upside-down' river, for it runs in the opposite direction to the main drainage of the area, and discharges its waters (when it contains any) through a gorge in the southern mountains into the Libyan sea.

It is not difficult to travel north-westwards from the Messará through either of two valleys leading up towards the north coast at Réthimnon. The northern ends of these valleys rise to high but penetrable hills, offering a practicable route for roads. At the upper end of the more easterly of these valleys, the Amári, is the classical site of a town variously named as Sybrita or Sybritos at the modern village of Thrónos: another apt name, for it is magnificently enthroned in a dominating position. There are reports of Minoan sherds on the site too, which has never been excavated, and it is unlikely that the Minoans would have neglected such a rich valley. Our interest in this site is due to the existence on the Knossos tablets of a name curiously reminiscent of Sybrita, *Su-ki-ri-ta*, which might stand for *Sugrita*. There are linguistic difficulties, but by no means insuperable ones, in accepting such an identification. Similar alternations of *b* and *g* occur rarely in other names of non-Greek origin.

If we penetrate the hills north of Sybrita, it is possible over a moderately difficult route to come out onto the narrow plain on the north coast which surrounds Réthimnon. The whole of the area from here eastwards seems to have been well settled at least in the LM III period, though LM I is still poorly recorded. This suggests that we should pursue our journey westwards from Knossos, passing through Tylisos and following a rather

32 Phaistos: the Minoan Palace

difficult pass, to reach the inland valley now dominated by Anóghia and containing the classical site of Axos, where LMIII pottery has been recorded. This name involves a problem, for it bears a strange resemblance to Mycenaean *E-ko-so*, a syllabic spelling for *Exos* since its derivative adjective is *E-ki-si-jo* = *Exios*. But although we might easily dismiss the variation in the vowel, a more serious obstacle exists, for the early alphabetic Cretan inscriptions show that *Axos* was previously *Waxos*, and although the loss of *w* is regular in later Greek, if it survived as late as the fifth century B.C., it must have been present in the Mycenaean form. I thought that this settled the question and that the similarity of the names was a mere coincidence, even though what we know of *Exos* fits the position of *Axos* well; it has 2,250 sheep (Dn 1092) and it is paired with *Sugrita*. But a visit to the site suggested to me another possibility. Most ancient Greek place names are meaningless in Greek, and wherever it happens that a population lives in an area covered with unintelligible place names, there is a tendency for these names to be modified to suit the language of the inhabitants. In Devonshire the Cornish *Pen-y-cum-gwik* ('head of the valley creek') has been changed into *Pennycomequick*, much as the Greek colony in Italy *Malowenta* 'rich in sheep' was misinterpreted by the Romans as *Maleuentum* 'ill-come' and therefore transformed into *Beneuentum* 'wel-come' (Livy 9.27.14). By the same principle the meaningless *Exos*, suggesting if anything 'outside', was perhaps transformed, not by the Mycenaeans, but their Dorian successors into *Waxos*, which may actually have been, and certainly suggests connexions with, a word meaning 'break' or 'cleft'; for the site is rather uncomfortably perched high up in a cleft of the mountain. If the blame for such a deformation can be placed on the broad shoulders of the Dorians, there is nothing to prevent us siting Mycenaean *Exos* at Axos. Its associations on the tablets certainly suggest that it lay in that general area.

To the north of this route the country is very undulating all the way to the coast; and here too we have another linguistic puzzle. A site near the coast not far west of Iráklion was in classical times called *Kutaion*; it lies in an area suitable for sheep but not otherwise very productive. The tablets show a site which is notable for its sheep but little else, in the general area of Knossos, with the name *Ku-ta-to* or *Ku-ta-i-to*; the variant spellings point to a form such as *Kutaiton*. Again, is it possible that this is the same as the later *Kutaion?* Here there is no easy explanation for the change, since neither form has a meaning; but there is a general tendency to reduce difficult-sounding words by omitting one of two similar sounds, as Connecticut in pronunciation loses one of its c's.

To the east of Knossos there must have been a settlement at Mállia, even

33 Hághia Triádha: the royal villa

if the Minoan palace was never rebuilt. Travelling further to the east we cross a fairly difficult pass to reach the Gulf of Merambéllou, now well known to the tourists who flock to the modern resort of Hághios Nikólaos. High on the hills overlooking this bay lies the classical site of *Lātō* (apparently the same name as the mother of Apollo and Artemis, though she is better known in her Ionian dress as *Lētō*). The Knossos tablets tell us of a place which has the same name; but no Minoan site has yet been found in the vicinity, and the name on the tablets may refer to a different site.

We have a single mention of *Winatos*, later *Inatos*, a small town on the south coast, now Tsoúdsouro. But many important sites which we know archaeologically are missing from this list, almost certainly because their Minoan and Mycenaean names did not survive into the classical period, so that we are as yet unable to identify them with the unlocated names of the tablets.

So far I have deliberately excluded the two ends of the island, the far east and the far west, for in both cases the settlements there would have been remote from Knossos, and geography makes land communications difficult. There are natural barriers to the west of Réthimnon and to the east of Sitía. Contact with these areas will have been easier by sea. Now there is a small group of place names which occur only in certain limited groups of tablets; the best example is the Co series, which lists at each place numbers of sheep, goats, pigs and cattle. The sheep are significant, because we have an enormous set of records by means of which Knossos controlled vast flocks all over central Crete. The absence of this special set of place names from these records therefore proves that these areas were not under the immediate control of Knossos, though of course a less direct control is still possible.

Two of the names in this class are readily identifiable. One is *Kudōniā*, well known as the ancient name of what is now the second largest city of Crete, Khaniá. It is mentioned by Homer indirectly, since he refers to its inhabitants, *Kudōnes*, the town itself having an unmetrical name. Very little has been known about Khaniá archaeologically until recently, since it is another of those tantalizing cases where a modern town overlies the ancient site, so that excavation has been perforce restricted to a few open spaces and hasty explorations of building sites. It was one of these which in October 1973 was investigated by the Greek archaeologist I. Papapostólou, and proved to contain the archive room of what must have been a Minoan palace, since numbers of fragments of tablets written in Linear A and a large collection of inscribed sealings and labels came from it. Other work had already disclosed jars bearing short inscriptions in Linear B, so it is now clear that this was an important town in both Minoan and Mycenaean times.

The other known name is *Aptarwā*, which in classical times was known as Aptara, or Aptera, the second being an excellent example of the deformation of an unfamiliar name into a meaningful word, for Aptera means 'wingless', and recalls the title of the goddess Victory (*Nikē Apteros*), for whom the Athenians built a small temple on the Akropolis. The site of the later Aptara is well known, high on the hills overlooking the entrance to Soúdha Bay.

None of the other four names on this group of tablets can be identified with later names. But there is a very curious fact about two of them. They occur again on some of the jars with Linear B inscriptions found at Thebes on the mainland, in one case at least six times. Two explanations were obviously possible: the names could be simply a coincidence, for we have already seen how names repeated on the map of Mycenaean Greece; or the jars in question might have been imported from Crete, presumably as the containers for some liquid. We might have dismissed them as due to mere coincidence, but for the fact that other jars, found elsewhere on the mainland, also had painted on them words which recur as place names on the Knossos tablets. One found at Eleusis in Attica has a Cretan place name which occurs frequently at Knossos: *Da-*22-to* (the phonetic value of the middle sign is still unknown, so it has to be transcribed by a numerical reference).

But here scientific archaeology has begun to lend a hand. Dr H. Catling, who was then at the Ashmolean Museum in Oxford, undertook an analysis of the clay of a number of Mycenaean vases. His method is to submit to spectroscopic analysis minute samples of the fabric of the vase, to determine what impurities were present in the clay of which it was made. All clays contain traces of other elements, often metals; and the clay of a particular region can be shown to have a characteristic pattern of impurities. Thus the analysis produces a kind of finger-print, which may determine the place of origin of the vase. The method certainly needs to be further developed, but it has already been shown to work in cases where the origin is not in doubt. Hence its application to the inscribed jars from Thebes might show whether or not they were of local manufacture. The results show that they do not match local clays, and, more remarkable, they do seem to match samples from Crete; but this method is perhaps not yet far enough advanced to give a clear answer. But that two independent lines of enquiry should both lead to Crete is a very remarkable coincidence, and encourages us to suppose that at a period rather later than the fall of Knossos, vases inscribed in Linear B were being exported from Cretan towns to the mainland. Further research may limit the areas of Crete from which they came; the earliest work (Catling and Millett, 1965) pointed to the extreme east of the island. But the connexions on the Knossos tablets point rather to the far west, and this may prove to be not inconsistent with the clay analysis. Thus the conclusion would be that the far west of Crete, the province of Khaniá, may have been outside the direct control of Knossos, though in some sense subject to its rule. The extreme east of the island too may have had a similar relationship, since geography suggests that communication with it by land would have been difficult.

We thought at one time we had identified a town in the far east; the tablets frequently mention a place called *Se-to-i-ja*, and it was tempting to equate this with classical *Sētaia*, modern Sitía. The linguistic difficulties were always recognized, and nothing has transpired to confirm the guess; on the other hand a great deal of evidence now suggests that it was located in central Crete, and we must abandon our early guess.

We have therefore a picture of Crete at this time consisting of a powerful monarchy, with a highly centralized administration at Knossos, controlling the island from Réthimnon to Ierápetra, but leaving the two ends under some other control, whether as autonomous but friendly states or as self-governing dependencies. It will be interesting to see whether later discoveries confirm this picture. At least it is clear from the existence of so many archives of Linear A tablets that in Minoan times the administration of the island was decentralized, though again we cannot decide between autonomous and dependent states outside the immediate area of Knossos. Clearly the ruler of Knossos was always the dominant power on the island. After the fall of the palace of Knossos it is likely that the island split up again into numerous small states, the condition in which we find it at the beginning of the historical period.

4 THE PEOPLE OF THE TABLETS

Despite a few hesitations, there can be no serious doubt that the language of the Linear B tablets was Greek; but were the people who wrote them Greeks? Greek of course at this date can have only one meaning: Greek-speaking, for the concept of nationality is an anachronism in the ancient world. It is hardly likely that speakers of another language would have kept their records in Greek; we surely do not have a situation parallel to the Latin of the medieval documents of England, where the vernacular was judged inadequate for the serious business of keeping official records. That situation could only arise where the language used had gained enormous prestige by its history, and survived as a medium of communication among the educated. We cannot envisage any similar situation in the courts of Mycenaean Greece, for the prestigious language would surely have been the Cretan recorded by Linear A; Linear B was a relatively new creation devised to meet the needs of the Greek language.

There is therefore a *prima facie* case for regarding the Mycenaeans as Greek-speakers. And we can offer a very strong confirmation: the large number of men and women on the tablets who bear Greek names, that is, names significant in Greek. Girls of many nationalities and hence speakers of many languages might today be named *Alexandra;* but when we find this name, which is significant in Greek, given to a woman of thirteenth-century Mycenae, her parents can hardly have been ignorant of its meaning. The literal meaning is rather surprising: 'she who repels men'; but we must remember that, if I may be forgiven such an illiberal sentiment, women's names are frequently merely derivatives of masculine types, and *Alexandrā* is simply a feminine pendant to *Alexandros* (Latinized as *Alexander*) 'he who repels men', a suitably martial appellation.

The Greek system of personal names, in Mycenaean as in classical times, differs radically from ours. Each individual has a single personal name, chosen from a much wider repertory than the customary first name of English-speakers. If it is necessary to distinguish him from others of the same name, this is usually done by giving his father's name as well. I was amused to find that for official purposes it is still the practice in Greece to qualify the first name with the father's first name as well as the surname; thus when I opened a bank account I found myself named 'John *tou* Fred', where *tou* serves to mean 'of', i.e. 'son of'. In some early Greek dialects and in Mycenaean the father's name is given not in the genitive but in an adjectival form, as *Kusamenios* – 'son of Kusamenos'. This method is, however, not often used on our documents and seems to be restricted to men of aristocratic family. For others it is possible to differentiate by specifying the man's home town or his occupation. We have no clear examples of women so particularized; there is a list of women's names (PY Vn 1191) in which each is preceded by a man's name in the genitive. Here we are most likely to have their husband's names, though the men might be their fathers, or if they were slaves, their masters. In the Greek system a woman bears her father's name in the genitive if she is unmarried, her husband's if married; it is still the custom in Greece today for a woman's surname to be in the genitive case.

It would not be surprising to find that during the latter part of the second millennium B.C. the population of Greece was not exclusively Greek-speaking. As the reconstruction of history I have sketched in Chapter 1 suggests, the conquest of Greece and the absorption of speakers of other languages will have been a slow process. We need only recall today, 600 years after the union of Wales with England, there are still many thousands of Welsh-speakers in Wales, even if the majority of the principality is English-speaking. Thus simply on *a priori* grounds, we should expect to find traces of languages other than Greek among the population of Mycenaean times.

Even in classical times there are several references in the historians to speakers of other languages, such as Pelasgian, which is a mere name to us; and in parts of eastern Crete as late as the fourth century B.C. inscriptions were still being put up in another language. In several parts of Greece we hear of subject classes, who will in all probability represent the descendants of the people subjugated by the ancestors of the later rulers. Although we are not told that any of them still spoke another language, some of them were no doubt descendants of non-Greeks. At Sparta there were actually two such depressed classes. A group of free but second-class citizens without political rights called *perioikoi* or 'dwellers round about' were very likely the pre-Dorian Greeks of Lakonia, the descendants of the Mycenaean population. A further population of serfs worked the land for their Spartan masters and these were called *heilōtes*, a name possibly meaning captives, and were presumably the subject class of Mycenaean times, a people of non-Greek origin. Even when a new language is adopted, people are very tenacious of personal names, as witness the Celtic

34 Fresco of warriors from Pylos

names still much affected by the English-speaking Welsh, Scots and Irish.

At least sixty per cent of the words recorded on Mycenaean documents are personal names. Thus it ought to be possible to use this material to estimate what percentage of the population had Greek names, though this is not in itself conclusive evidence that they all spoke nothing but Greek. But owing to the ambiguities inherent in the script, and the fact that there is no way that the meaning of a name can be verified, it is never safe to dismiss a name as non-Greek, just because we cannot see any likely Greek name behind the syllabic form. But we can at least feel confident that some are so transparently Greek that it would be absurd to challenge them. The woman's name *Alexandrā*, already quoted, is a good example, and the same tablet gives us *Theodōrā*. Among men's names we may instance *Amphimēdēs, Eumenēs, Euruptolemos, Opilimnios, Philowergos.* All of these are not only readily recognizable as Greek; they are of a special type, what are called compound names, so that each name can be decomposed into two significant parts. This type is so wide-spread in the Indo-European language that it is hard to believe it is not a common inheritance. But it is also found elsewhere, and many Japanese surnames are rather similar. On the other hand the Romans invented or borrowed a totally different system. Thus the appearance of compound names in Mycenaean Greek is evidence of a long-standing tradition, even if many of the elements of which they are composed are not found outside Greek. It is hard to believe that people who chose such names for their children were doing anything but following a traditional Greek custom, and consequently we may regard them as Greek-speaking. There is nothing particularly aristocratic about such names, for the lists of shepherds at Knossos include examples, and they were presumably not men of the highest rank.

Many more names are of another familiar Greek type, derivatives of common nouns. Sometimes a vocabulary word may be itself used as a name: *Glaukos* 'grey-eyed', is a name familiar also from Homer; there is a shepherd called *Ekhinos* 'sea-urchin' (was he a prickly character?), and even one called *Poimēn* 'Shepherd', just as there is a bronzesmith who rejoices in the name *Khalkeus* 'Smith'. In these cases of course the argument might be stood on its head; these transparent names might have been conferred not by parents on their children, but by Greek-speaking masters who could not get their tongues around an unintelligible foreign name. We may certainly suspect this process where we get simple descriptive names like *Eruthros* 'Red' or *Poliwos* 'Gray'. A few names appear to be downright uncomplimentary, if not frankly obscene. But it is hard to judge the limits of what is acceptable as a name; in classical times too uncomplimentary names are not unknown, and we may guess that they began as nicknames, and having once become accepted, went on being used by later generations with no thought for their meaning.

More often the name is distinguished from the common noun by the addition of a suffix. A familiar classical example is the name *Sīmōn*, derived from *sīmos* 'snub-nosed', but apparently never regarded as opprobrious. In Mycenaean Greek we have many examples: *Tripodiskos* has the diminutive suffix *-iskos* attached to the name of the tripod-cauldron, 'Little Threefoot'; *Makhāwōn* is formed from *makhā* 'battle', *Argurios* from *arguros* 'silver', *Pomnios* from *poimnā* 'flock', *Plouteus* from *ploutos* 'wealth'. Some of these suffixes are also found with the compound type: *Opilimnios* is an adjective in form derived from *opi* (classical *epi*) 'on' and *limnā* 'lake', or *Guowaxeus* from *guous* (later *bous*) 'ox' and *agō* 'I lead'.

One of the commonest means of forming a derivative name in classical Greek is with the suffix *-idēs* or *-adēs* meaning 'son', exactly like the English surnames which end in *-son*. This seems to be wholly absent from Mycenaean names, and this is not so surprising seeing that Homer too has no personal names of this type, though he does use such formations as adjectives, meaning 'the son of'.

If we imagine the situation in which a small Greek ruling class dominates a larger non-Greek population, and succeeds in imposing its language, we might expect the descendants of the non-Greeks to continue to use their old names, though some parents may have liked to curry favour with the rulers by adopting Greek names for their children. Thus it would not be surprising if we found a number of non-Greek names alongside the Greek ones, especially among the humbler folk. Yet we must not forget that Greek must have been spoken in the Pylos area for centuries before the date of the tablets, so that evidence of a foreign name must not be taken as proof that a foreign language was still spoken there. We face too the difficulty that a Greek name is often self-evident even in its ambiguous spelling, but we have no means of recognizing a foreign one, since we do not know to what language it may belong. But some Mycenaean names, especially at Knossos, have an uncouth look to Greek eyes, and it is hard to believe that they are anything but foreign. In a few cases it is possible to add a less subjective proof: on the Knossos tablets a number of names appear which are repeated more or less exactly on the Linear A tablets from Crete before the Greek invasion. For instance, *Di-de-ro* and *A-ra-na-ro* are very likely to be hellenized forms of the names *Di-de-ru* and *A-ra-na-re* found on Linear A tablets from Hághia Triádha. A small group of names at Knossos begin with *Piya-*, a common element meaning 'giving' in Hittite names, but surprisingly no one so far has been able to identify a language which will account for any large number of these non-Greek names.

It is difficult to decide where to classify the names derived from non-Greek place names. If a man bears the name *Lampsakos*, known much later as that of a Greek colony near the Dardanelles, is this to be classed as Greek or not? *Tulisios*, the adjective of the Cretan town *Tulisos*, occurs as a man's name at Pylos; similarly we have a woman called *Korinsiā* from *Korinthos*, Corinth, but there seems to have been another place of this name within the territory of Pylos. Some names, however, do suggest contacts with distant lands: *Aiguptios* at Knossos must be 'the Egyptian', so perhaps *Lukios* is the man from Lycia (S.W. Anatolia), *Turios* the man from Tyre (in the modern Lebanon).

One theory we can fairly certainly reject is that the Greeks were not the dominant people of Mycenaean Greece, but only a class of scribes employed by non-Greek rulers to keep their accounts. It is unfortunate that we are never directly told the names of the kings of Pylos or Knossos (but see below p. 71); for if they had unmistakably Greek names, this would prove the point. But there are lists of important officials, for instance the 'Followers', *e-qe-ta*, of the king of Pylos, who must belong to the ruling class, and these lists can be shown to contain typically Greek names, such as *Alektruōn* son of *Etewoklewēs*, the later Eteokles (An 654.8). His brother has one of the many names in *-eus* which are typical of the early legends, like *Akhilleus, Odysseus;* in some cases it appears that these represent a shortening of a longer name.

Although not a single one of the characters of the Homeric epics can be identified on the tablets, it is quite clear that many of the people of the tablets have Homeric names. If a subordinate officer at Pylos (An 657.3) has the name of Agamemnon's son *Orestes*, does this imply that the content of the epics was already known to the Mycenaeans of Pylos? If there is at both Pylos and Knossos a man called *Akhilleus*, does this imply that the story of the *Iliad* was already famous? The answer to this question is emerging as we get to know more about the names Mycenaeans bore, for it is becoming clear that the number of names in use was not unlimited. Not only is it possible to show that the same name at the same site may refer to two different people, but the number of names found at two or more sites is now considerable. Every new access of material seems to add to these examples. It would therefore seem likely that Homer was able to draw on a tradition that contained genuine Mycenaean names. But the strange fact emerges that many of these Mycenaean names are those given in the epic to Trojans. Long ago the ingenious theory was invented that the alternative name of the Trojan prince Paris, *Alexandros*, which is patently Greek, was no more than a Greek corruption of a name which appears in Hittite documents as *Alakshandush*. The evidence that the feminine form,

Alexandrā, was already in use in the thirteenth century at least proves that *Alexandros* could be a genuine Mycenaean name, and it may be the Hittite form which is corrupt, if indeed it is the same name at all. But since not only *Hektōr* but even the mythical founder of Troy, *Trōs*, appear as names at Pylos, it is hard to resist the conclusion that Trojan names too are taken from the common Mycenaean stock. It does not of course follow that the Trojans were Greek-speakers; Homer may ignore linguistic problems and allow Greeks and Trojans to converse freely in Greek, just as film-producers today make foreigners converse in heavily accented English.

The stock of Homeric names thus matches the sample of the Mycenaean names which happens to have come down to us. Homer does not apparently use types which were unknown in Mycenaean Greece, and the frequency of names in *-eus* is proved to be a correct piece of archaizing. There is no evidence to confirm any of the names of the Homeric tradition, but at least we can be sure that Homer uses names which might have been in use in Mycenaean times.

Apart from the great wealth of personal names, there are a few names describing groups of people which do not appear to be simply the adjectival formations from the towns where they lived. There is in particular a group of eight names describing men employed on coastguard duties in Pylos (see p. 175). One or two of these names could be given a Greek etymology, but others are probably of non-Greek origin; yet there is never a mention of a place which could serve as their home town. It would therefore seem possible that these are the names of tribes which maintained their identity down to the date of the tablets. Their names suggest a non-Greek origin, and it would have been prudent to employ these people only on non-combatant duties to provide a coastguard force under Greek officers. This theory may also explain why some of their names reappear in the records of flax production (see Chapter 8).

Population

It would obviously tell us a great deal if we knew the size of the population in a Mycenaean kingdom; and since the documents contain so much numerical information, it is tempting to try to devise a method of estimating this. But the tablets are very far from being a census return; they record only figures of direct interest to the palace, and the number of mouths to be fed is of interest only to those who must provide the food. The figure of approximately 750 female slaves directly controlled by the palace at Pylos, together with a similar number of children, at least imposes some sort of standard. The 1,000 women and children actually located at

Pylos surely imply that the total population of the town, as opposed to the excavated palace, was not less than 2,500 and may well have been much larger.

The number of place names on the Pylos tablets amounts to around two hundred, and the archaeological survey of Messenia located a similar number of settlements. Some of these were perhaps tiny hamlets, but others, such as the administrative centres of the local districts, would have been small towns. If we guess at an average size of around 250 persons per settlement, this would suggest a figure of 50,000 for the whole kingdom. McDonald and Hope Simpson (McDonald and Rapp, 1972, 141) made very cautious estimates along these lines, arriving at the conclusion that 50,000 was a minimum figure.

There is one place for which the information on the tablets offers a chance of calculation. We know two facts at the regional centre in the Further Province called Asiatia: the smiths are excused a contribution which is one twelfth of the region's total assessment (Ma 397); and the smiths can be shown (Jn 750) to number twenty-one, though this figure includes four without an allocation of bronze. If we assume that the smiths normally contributed in proportion to their numerical strength, then the total contributory population must be 252, or 204 if the unemployed are not counted. If we assume further that the productive work-force is a quarter of the total population, this will put the size of this town at 800 to 1,000 persons. But there is a further ambiguity here: the document which records the rebate for the smiths probably refers not to the town alone, but the district of which it is the centre. But the list of smiths is likely to be more specific, and there could have been other smiths located within the region, though not at its chief town. Thus it must not be supposed that we can safely extrapolate from these figures, though they may give a fair estimate of the size of the average market-town.

5 THE SOCIAL STRUCTURE AND THE ADMINISTRATIVE SYSTEM

36 Carl W. Blegen

35 Sir Arthur Evans from a portrait in the Ashmolean Museum, Oxford

When the archaeologists discover a large building constructed of well-worked masonry and decorated with frescoes, containing many rooms, some of them large, and surrounded by numerous magazines and store-rooms, they talk justifiably of a palace. They presume rightly that access to the wealth needed to create such a structure implies that its owner was able to control a large enough population to support such luxury. Hence neither Evans at Knossos nor Blegen at Pylos scrupled to talk of palaces, though it might have been more scientific to resist the temptation to give them such romantic names as 'the Palace of Minos' or 'the Palace of Nestor'. Although the great palaces are easily distinguished and we can

Figs. 35, 36

confidently so name the major complexes of buildings at Knossos, Phaistos or Mállia, at Mycenae, Tiryns or Pylos, it is not so clear how small a palace can be. Káto Zákros certainly has a palace; but has Hághia Triádha a royal palace or only a nobleman's mansion? What of the principal building at Gourniá? Are the structures at Gla in Boeotia a palace or not?

It is hardly possible to answer these questions purely on the basis of archaeological evidence. What we can infer from the palace buildings is that these are administrative centres, and in the Mycenaean period administration demanded written documents. The existence of an archive proves the presence of a palace in the sense of a major administrative centre. The recent discovery (1973) of Linear A tablets in Khaniá proves, without any architectural finds, the existence of a palace, for nowhere else is there likely to have been such a large group of administrative documents. In this sense too the archive of Linear A tablets from Hághia Triádha proves that this ranked as a centre of administration.

Any administrator needs an office to work from, and in an unsophisticated society his office is likely to be also his main residence. Thus each centre of administration implies an administrator, whether he be an independent monarch, a semi-autonomous prince, or a local baron owing allegiance to a superior ruler. Such details escape the spade of the archaeologist, but the documents can cast some light on the processes of administration.

It was no surprise to find that the ruler of a Mycenaean state was called *wanax*, since this, with the regular omission of *w*, is one of the Homeric words for 'king'. What was more surprising was the fact that *guasileus*, the ancestral form to *basileus*, the other word for 'king' in Homer and the only classical term, had a less exalted meaning to the Mycenaeans, and seems to have been used for the 'chief' of any group, even the head of a group of smiths. Traces of this use can still be found in Homer, for we read of many *basilēes* in Ithaka (*Od.* 1.394–5), and Alkinoos the Phaeacian king mentions twelve *basilēes*, not counting himself, among his people (*Od.* 8.390–1).

But there is a problem over the use of *wanax* on the tablets. No one can seriously doubt that in most cases the word refers to the human ruler; when, for instance, we read of a list made 'when the king appointed Augewas to be *da-mo-ko-ro* (an offical title)', this is plainly a human action. Yet in other cases we are left wondering whether 'king' is not applied as a divine title, since in this usage the word continued to be employed in classical Greek. The clearest example is in a series of tablets at Pylos (Fr), which records quantities of perfumed oil and unguent distributed to various deities. It would be a little odd to find 'the king' included here among the deities. But it is also noticeable that the entry here is never simply 'for the king'; the term is combined with another name which functions as an address. This was perhaps enough to show that here the human ruler was not meant.

The only document which offers us any real information about the king is one from Pylos (Er 312) which records the size of various estates. Here we have listed 'the king's estate', 'the estate of the *Lāwāgetās*' and the lands of three officials called *telestai*. The interesting fact here is the size of these estates: that of the king is three times that of the *Lāwāgetās*, and the three *telestai* together have lands of the same size as the king. This would appear to set him apart as a privileged person; but the tablet presumably refers only to his estate at one particular place, and he must have owned other land as well. The adjective meaning 'of the king', 'royal' is applied to craftsmen: we meet at Pylos a royal fuller (En 74.3), a royal potter (Eo 371), and another whose trade is obscure (En 609.5). At Knossos textiles are described as 'royal', presumably ornamented or coloured in a manner peculiar to royalty, like the imperial purple of later ages. Beyond this there is little that can be said about the king. His title has not yet been mentioned on any of the few documents from Mycenae; at Thebes we can confirm only the existence of the word.

But although the king at Pylos is never named, there is a man named *E-ke-ra$_2$-wo* (perhaps something like Enkhelyāwōn, but we cannot be sure of the reconstruction), whose position in the hierarchy seems so exalted that it is hard to believe he is not the *wanax*. A tablet listing offerings to Poseidon (Un 718) shows, like the list of estates mentioned above, four donors: two are given the same title, but *E-ke-ra$_2$-wo* appears in place of the king, and the *dāmos* in place of the *telestai*. If we assume that *E-ke-ra$_2$-wo* is the king, then the addition of such facts as are known about him enables us to fill out the picture a little. He has forty men serving as rowers in the fleet (An 610), and he seems to possess an enormous estate totalling 94 units (Er 880), that is, more than three times the size of the king's *temenos*; it is planted with over a thousand vines and a similar number of fig-trees. It is hard to see how such an important person could be fitted into Pylian society, unless he stands at its head. We have evidence elsewhere that a man might be referred to either by his name or his title; by combining the two we get a much more satisfactory picture of the king's possessions.

The title *Lāwāgetās* is found at both Pylos and Knossos, and means literally 'the leader of the people'. Since the word translated 'people' frequently refers in later Greek, especially in the *Iliad*, to 'the people arrayed for battle, the war-host', some have assumed that the Mycenaean title designates the commander of the army. But this cannot be confirmed by anything the tablets tell us about him. We know that at Pylos his estate was one third the size of the king's, but was no bigger than the average of the three *telestai*. His contribution to Poseidon (Un 718) consists of two rams and quantities of flour and wine. By contrast, King *E-ke-ra₂-wo* contributes more than six times as much grain, four and a half times as much wine, a quantity of honey, ten cheeses, one ox and a sheepskin. Like the king, the *Lāwāgetās* has tradesmen allocated to his service: perhaps a wheel-wright (Ea 421) and another whose trade is obscure (Na 245); and two other men are described as belonging to him, but in what sense we cannot tell. The title recurs in its derivative form at Knossos, but only in such fragmentary contexts that there is little to be learnt from them; one tablet (E 1569) may give us the size of his estate, for it matches closely that of the *Lāwāgetās* of Pylos, but it could equally refer to a quantity of grain.

An ingenious suggestion has been made by a Swedish scholar, Dr Margareta Lindgren (1973, II, 134–6), that the name of the *Lāwāgetās* at Pylos is *Wedaneus*. Certainly, Wedaneus is a man of great importance, who receives offerings of grain in the same context as Poseidon (Es), has twenty men serving as rowers in the fleet (An 610), and seems to be the owner of many flocks of sheep.

In societies of this type the king needs a group of nobles to act as his delegates and to enable him to impose his rule throughout his kingdom. This need is generally met by a class of aristocrats, often kin to the royal house, who provide the senior officers of the administration; they also form the élite troops of the army and command the levies of infantry. This class is represented in Mycenaean society by the *hequetai* or 'Followers.' The name is not to be taken too literally, for royal courts have always been full of officials whose duties do not correspond to their strange-sounding titles; but one of their duties must surely have been to follow the king and attend on him, both in peace and war. There is an obvious parallel to 'Follower' in the words for 'companion' often used of the king's table-companions and intimate friends; the Latin *comes* has the same meaning, and is the word from which English *count* is derived.

Confirmation of the high status of the Followers comes from a number of indications. A Follower may possess slaves (PY Ed 847), and one of the important land-holders listed at Pylos, Amphimēdēs, has been acutely identified by Lejeune (1966, 260) as the Follower mentioned in the summary of this series (Ed 317). Many of the Followers mentioned on the coastguard tablets of Pylos (see pp. 173–9) are known by their father's name in addition to their own names, a kind of aristocratic dignity which does not seem to be conferred on humbler folk, though the telegraphic style of the tablets can always be blamed for the omission of honorific titles. At Knossos there is a much damaged list headed 'Knossian Follower(s)'

(B 1055), and we meet a Follower from one of the other towns of the kingdom (Exos, Am 821).

Three different things are described by the adjective derived from the title of Follower: slaves, clothes and wheels. The existence of slaves owned by private individuals is guaranteed elsewhere on the tablets, though it is rare except in the case of bronzesmiths. Probably their apparent rarity is due to the fact that they are not usually listed. The mention of textiles at Knossos (Ld tablets) indicates that the Followers wore a distinctive form of dress, no doubt a uniform – it may have had white tufts or fringes. The wheels are meant for chariots, so we can assume that the Followers had chariots, presumably with wheels of a distinctive pattern. All of this is consistent with their high status; but the chariots suggest that they may also have had military functions. Since there is evidence that Knossos possessed a force of about two hundred chariots, while that at Pylos may have been rather smaller (pp. 167, 170), we may speculate whether the Followers were in fact the only troops who rode into battle. Their chief function will presumably have been to act as officers for the infantry; as suggested later (p. 176), the Pylian army may have had eleven regiments each commanded by a Follower. But they could also have been used as élite troops, capable of being moved rapidly wherever the ground or roads permitted, and, relying on their heavy armour, able to hold at bay a much larger force of lightly armed troops.

The local administration

Alongside the nobles making up the royal court and administration, it is not uncommon to find a second class of grandees, who include the major holders of land. While the nobles too must possess land, either in virtue of their office or privately owned, there is ordinarily a much larger class of land-holders who supply the local administration outside the capital. These two upper classes serve also the useful purpose of forming a check on each other. Any attempt by the local upper class to break away from the central authority can be countered by the use of the companions; while any companion who is tempted to usurp the royal prerogative can be checked by the power of the territorial nobility.

How far we are justified in fitting the Mycenaean titles into this framework may be disputed; but I propose here to allow it to impose a pattern which is otherwise lacking in the Mycenaean titles. The kingdom of Pylos was divided into sixteen administrative districts, each of which was controlled by a governor called *ko-re-te* and a deputy called *po-ro-ko-re-te* (Jn 829). The reconstruction of these titles is uncertain and they will here be called *koretēr* and *prokoretēr* without implying that these are the exact renderings. There is a problem in the long heading to the list of contributions imposed on these officers, for although the main body of the text specifies only a *koretēr* and a *prokoretēr* in each district, four other titles appear coupled with them in the heading. The most likely solution to this problem is that the others are alternative titles which can all be subsumed under the two headings of *koretēr* and *prokoretēr*; in other words the *koretēr* of one district may have been called *dumar*, a word which elsewhere means 'superintendant' or the like. The other titles for the junior office are curious. One is *klāwiphoros* or 'key-bearer', a title which occurs elsewhere; there is a woman with this title named Karpathia on the Sphagiānes land tablets, who exceptionally has two plots (Eb 338, Ep 704.7), and it recurs next to a priestess on a damaged tablet (Un 6) dealing with religious offerings. The impression is that the title is mainly a religious one, and can, if not must, be held by a woman. The combination of secular and religious office should cause no surprise; in later times the same person was often magistrate and priest, and the separation of the religious from secular powers is a relatively modern phenomenon. But it would be very surprising if the deputy governor of a district could be a woman. Since the Greek word for 'key-bearer' can be used equally of men and women, there is no difficulty in supposing that the title can be borne by either sex. In classical Greece the Mycenaean 'key-bearer' becomes more often a 'key-holder' *(kleidoukhos)*; but the word continues to be a synonym for priestess, though we know from inscriptions that the title might also be held by men.

It is clear from this same text that the *koretēr* and his deputy in each district were responsible for extraordinary contributions of bronze, which will be discussed further in Chapter 8 (p. 141). We find the same titles in a damaged tablet from Pylos (Jo 438), which lists contributions of gold (see p. 144). Here the contributors are sometimes listed by their titles of *koretēr* and *prokoretēr*; in other cases we have only the name of the district, or the name of the official himself. This makes it probable that the men who are named here are of this rank.

Much the same picture emerges from another important document consisting of two tablets (Aq 64 and 218). Here too there is a tantalizing gap which has lost us all of the introductory formula except the end of the last word, but this suggests that it is a list of people performing some sort of official function. Two of the men named are given also the title of *koretēr* of a district; one of the districts belongs to the seven of the Further Province (p. 42), but the other is unknown except for its appearance on the list of gold contributions discussed above. But we find here a new title, *mo-ro-qa*, which has been interpreted as *moroqquās*, literally 'shareholder'; but as always it is dangerous to attempt to guess the function of a title from its etymology. This document proves that *moroqquās* is a rank rather than an office, like *koretēr*, since one man is described as both: Klumenos the *moroqquās*, *koretēr* of Iterewa, who is also known to us as the commander of one sector of the coastguard. The second-in-command of another coastguard sector (An 519.2) is also given this title. But three other men on the list under discussion (Aq 64) have the title *moroqquās* without further qualification. It would seem that it is a high rank, though there is no reason to connect it specifically with the royal court. The word occurs at Knossos too, but could there be merely a personal name.

Various theories have been proposed to explain the list, but although certain facts emerge the general picture is far from clear. The second paragraph (Aq 64.12–16) lists holders of plots of land; the third (Aq 218.1–6) men under obligation to do something which is unclear, the fourth (Aq 218.9–16) men who have no plots of land. All the men except those of the third paragraph have an entry 'one pair', but of what is left unspecified, and various suggestions have been made, including a tempting theory that the word for 'pair' is here used for a measure of land; unfortunately the men who are called 'without plots' also have the entry 'one pair', though one can avoid this difficulty by supposing that the document relates to a future distribution of land. It should also be added that wherever land is recorded it is measured by a different system, which will be discussed in Chapter 7. There is also a subsidiary entry in the first two paragraphs: an unclear ideogram and a number between 3 and 12 and always a multiple of 3; and this entry correlates with a phrase in the text which translates: 'this year he will take (or he took) as follows'. The two entries without the obscure ideogram have the words: 'and he will not (did not) take'. The verb I have rendered 'take' probably has some more specific meaning. It originally seems to have meant 'catch' and it is associated with the word for hunting; but in some dialects it acquired a more general meaning. It is also unfortunate that the defective system of spelling does not enable us to distinguish in this case between a past and future tense; the ambiguity would have been no obstacle to the clerks who handled these documents, but for us it is an additional problem.

The five men of the third paragraph, who do not have the entry 'one pair', are interesting, because three of them are Followers named on the coastguard tablets, though here they are not given that title. There can be no doubt that they are the same men, because they are again given their father's name as additional identification. The other two men in this paragraph are simply named as 'the priest' of such and such a place; one has a further entry which is also probably a title of some kind.

At this point we must take up another much disputed problem: the status of the title *telestās*. The document which lists the estates of the king and the Lāwāgetās (Er 312, p. 71) also refers to the estates of the three *telestai*, which are together equal in size to that of the king. They are clearly major holders of land, but exactly how they fit into the hierarchy is unclear. I now think the easiest solution is to assume that they stood in the same relation to the district governor as the Followers did to the king; that is to say, they were the most important people in the local districts after the governor and his deputy, who may have been chosen from their ranks.

In proposing this I am partially going back on a view which I held earlier, that, since the word *telestēs* in later Greek had associations with cult and ritual, its meaning in Mycenaean times too might have lain in the religious sphere. If I now abandon this view, it is not simply that I think religious associations were lacking, but that, as explained above, the separation of religious and secular office cannot be assumed at this date. But the theoretical pattern which I have followed requires a class of local land-holders, and there is good reason for seeing these in the *telestai*, whatever other function they may have had to serve.

The title occurs almost exclusively on documents dealing with holdings of land. Their numbers are relatively large; the district of Sphagiānes at Pylos had originally fourteen, though the holding of one seems to have been deleted. We know of their existence at four places in Crete, and at one of these (Aptarwa in the west of the island) they numbered no less than forty-five. The size of their holdings is often large, and the term *ktoinookhos* 'plot-holder' may be used as a synonym. The title appears to be derived from a verb expressing their function: we are told (PY Eb 149) that 'one *telestās* is under obligation to — but does not —', where the blank is the related verb. This suggests that the title may be not so much a permanent label as a description of the man's function in a particular context, just as a doctor, a lawyer and a schoolmaster may all be described as 'householders' in an appropriate context.

At Pylos we also have references to the *dāmos*, the word which in its later Greek form *dēmos* is the ordinary term for the people collectively (hence our *democracy*). But in Attica it has also the special sense of a local administrative district of the same sort of size as the English parish. Since we know that the Pylian kingdom was divided for administrative purposes into sixteen districts, it is tempting to suppose that these were already called 'demes', and that the term could thus be used for the people of the district collectively. This will then explain why a list of porkers (PY Cn 608), which are being fattened up by the *opidāmioi* or officials of the demes, are enumerated under the names of the nine districts of the Hither Province.

At Sphagiānes and elsewhere communal land is held from or at the hands of the *dāmos*. In one passage (Ep 704.5) the *dāmos* makes a statement contesting ownership of certain lands claimed by the priestess Eritha on behalf of her deity (p. 114). The interesting point here is that this is from the edited version, but the preliminary draft which we also possess (Eb 297) appears to substitute for the *dāmos* 'the plot-holders'. This implies that the collective voice of the district was expressed by the major land-holders. This seems to be confirmed by the parallel discussed above between the list of estates (Er 312) and the offerings to Poseidon (Un 718); for here the *dāmos* takes the place of the three *telestai*. Thus we seem to establish that these three terms are in practice synonymous.

Here too we must mention the official called *da-mo-ko-ro*, who is recorded both at Pylos and Knossos. The long description of valuable furniture at Pylos (p. 147) was written 'when the king made Augewās *dāmokoros*'. Thus we know that it was a royal appointment. It is likely to be a compound of *dāmos*, perhaps with the same root as gave *koretēr*. But what was the distinction it is not easy to see. He is mentioned at the end of a mutilated list of *koretēres* (PY On 300.7) of the Hither Province, but no deduction can be safely drawn from this, since we still do not understand the purpose of this document; as so often, the heading has been lost.

The lower classes

It is very hard from our records to form a picture of the ordinary people and imagine what sort of lives they led. One has the impression that the royal administration concerned itself mainly with nobles and land-holders on the one hand, and with its dependants and slaves on the other; and between these two classes must have existed the large mass of the working population. In the district of Sphagiānes we have listed the sub-tenants as well as the major land-holders; a few are royal tradesmen, but the majority are qualified as 'servant of the deity', though exactly what this title implies is not yet clear. When major construction works were required, some kind of *corvée* system of labour must have been applied. But there is nothing in our documents which can be interpreted in this way. The largest bodies of men recorded at Pylos are the 800-odd who form the coastguard (p. 175) and the 500–600 who are apparently serving as rowers in the fleet (An 610). There is a Knossos tablet (B 807) which refers to 237 men of the town of Utanos; this sounds like a census of the available adult males.

There is a list of masons at four different places, but the numbers are small, and presumably these are craftsmen, not the labouring force (see p. 138). The second half of this tablet seems to record a commercial transaction for the purchase by barter of alum, and it is difficult to see what connexion this could have with the list of masons. More often we have tablets listing payments in barley to various groups of tradesmen; but the size of these groups is not specified, and only in a few cases can it be deduced (see p. 118).

The names of special trades listed imply an impressive division of labour; we are not in the crude period where any man might be by turns farmer, builder, carpenter, and so forth. This is a period when you had an expert at hand, whether it was an ordinary cup or a piece of furniture inlaid with precious materials that you wanted. A trade such as 'maker of blue glass paste' argues a degree of luxury, for by no stretch of the imagination could such a trade be called necessary; perhaps it is significant that that trade is known only from Mycenae. One of our problems here is that many trade names did not survive into classical Greece, and are thus impossible for us to interpret. There are notable absentees from the list of trades: such as the word for 'farmer' (or any more specialized agricultural activity) or 'scribe' (or perhaps we should say 'clerk').

At the bottom end of the social scale we have the slaves. It must be remembered that the classical dichotomy of human beings into slave and free was not always as clear cut as the ancients liked to pretend, and in any case it only makes much sense in a society in which the free men are, to some extent and however small their numbers, the masters of their own destiny. In classical Athens the free citizens had political rights and duties, the slaves none. But in an autocratic society ruled by a monarch, it is hard to say that any man but the king is truly free. Freedom and slavery are then relative concepts, and the word which in classical Greek means 'slave' ought perhaps in Mycenaean to be translated 'servant'. What is clear is that slaves, at least of the female sex, existed in some numbers, and that their status was lowly, whatever their exact social rank or political rights.

Individuals could possess slaves, though presumably the owners of slaves were of a relatively high class. We have already met slaves of the Follower, and a few other named individuals possess them. The most numerous privately owned slaves we hear of are those belonging to smiths at Pylos, who were equally craftsmen with their masters. At least thirteen are mentioned on surviving tablets (Jn series), and a damaged section (Jn 431.25–26) seems to imply the listing of 36 men as slaves. Allowing for the fact that nearly a third of the tablets in this series appear to be missing, it would seem that the real total is somewhat higher.

At Knossos the word meaning 'he bought' (*qi-ri-ja-to*) occurs four times on tablets listing men and women, and in some cases the word for 'slave' appears in the same context. It would seem probable that small numbers of slaves were acquired by purchase, though from whom must remain obscure. Here too individuals can possess slaves (Ap 628.1, Ai 824).

But the majority of slaves listed on the tablets are not specifically so called, and although their status is undoubtedly humble it may be questioned whether they were in quite the same situation as the slaves of classical Greece. The Knossos tablets show large groups of women engaged on textile production at a number of the principal towns (p. 151); and a large series of parallel documents from Pylos shows that the reason for this census is the issue of rations. In both cases the women are accompanied by children, but have no husbands. Girls outnumber boys, but at Pylos there is a separate series of tablets enumerating groups of men who are described simply as 'the sons of such-and-such a group of women'. These must presumably be young men who were now too old to go on being classed as boys and allowed to remain with their mothers; a few boys are sometimes attached to these groups, probably the older boys who were approaching the age at which they could be classed as adult.

It is hard to imagine women and children in this situation, fed and presumably housed by the palace, unless their status was effectively that of slaves. The situation in Crete may have been slightly different, since here the women are most often described as 'women of Phaistos', 'women of Dawos' and so forth, and it can be shown that they were actually living in these towns, and were not women from these places who had been brought to Knossos. The fact that in all cases they have their children with them argues against any system of *corvée* labour; for if the women were required to do so many days' work a year for the palace, and were fed by the palace only for that period, it is surely incredible that they would have brought their children and drawn rations for them too. A community will always ensure that the old women look after the children in their mothers' absence, apart from babes in arms. It is thus most likely that these women were permanently dependent upon the palace, and whether they were actually known as 'slaves' then matters little. The groups of young men mentioned above would hardly have had such a curious description, unless they are the sons of slaves.

The absence of male slaves, apart from these, is some confirmation of their status. It is one of the facts of ancient life that it requires a high degree of social organization to keep men in a state of permanent slavery. Thus on capturing a town or conducting a slaving raid, it was customary to put to death all adult males, and to take captive only the women and children. In due course the male children will grow up, and if their numbers are large it will be difficult to keep them in a state of slavery. The special designation of the young men no doubt reflects the unusual situation in which adult male slaves exist in any numbers. In one case (Ad 684) there is a cryptic note added that five youths and one boy are the sons of some rowers, as well as of a group of female weavers, but it is difficult to see what this means.

The groups of women at Pylos are described in two ways: by an occupational term, such as corn-grinders, bath attendants, flax-workers, spinners and so forth; or by a geographical term, which, since their location is indicated separately, must refer to their origin. The trades enumerated, so far as the words are understood, are all humble; some are domestic workers, but the greater number are concerned with the manufacture of textiles, and these will be discussed further in Chapter 8, p. 151.

The geographical terms are very surprising, for three of the places are familiar names, but they are all on the far side of the Aegean; and although, as we have seen, place names were frequently repeated in different areas, it would be a strange coincidence if all three belonged to the same area. 'Women of Milātos' would prove nothing, since there was in classical times a town of this name in Crete; but the more famous one is that in Ionia, known in later times as *Milētos* (Miletus). It has long been known that Miletus was an important Mycenaean settlement, and may be the town mentioned by the Hittites under the name of Millawanda, though this involves some linguistic difficulties. But we have also 'women of Knidos', another Ionian town 100 km south of Miletus; and 'women of Lāmnos (Lēmnos)', a large island in the north-east Aegean. In addition to these we find women who are called *A-swi-ja* (*Aswiai*) from Asia, probably the area later known as Lydia, but referred to in Hittite documents as *Aššuva;* and women of Zephyros, where Zephyria is recorded as an old name of the Halikarnassos area. Four of the five names are on the Asiatic coast of the Aegean, and the other is an off-shore island. The conclusion seems inescapable that these women came from a distant part of the Mycenaean world.

But how were women from such a distant area brought to Pylos? They might be the product of piratical raids by the ships of Pylos; but one of the groups is specifically called 'captives', and this implies that the remainder were not. Moreover, it is hardly likely that the Mycenaean Greeks would have raided other Mycenaean settlements, and we know that Miletus at least was one; the evidence of Mycenaean pottery in a cemetery near Halikarnassos also suggests a Mycenaean outpost there. It thus seems more likely that these places were Mycenaean trading posts, through which the luxuries produced in Greece were traded for Anatolian products such as slaves. It might be worth exploring the peninsula of Knidos (now called Reşadiye Yarımadası in Turkish) and the island of Lemnos for signs of Mycenaean trading activity. Very little is still known about Bronze Age settlements on the Turkish coast, though the Greek colonies of the Iron Age are well known. It is interesting that the Greeks thought it worth while to keep these groups of foreign women and their children together; probably not for humanitarian reasons so much as to exploit any special skills they may have possessed, and to make them more content with their lot. One of the most repulsive features of the eighteenth-century African slave trade was the way in which children were torn from their mothers on arrival in the New World.

Since each group of women may be mentioned three times, it is possible to make some estimate of the completeness of the records. The best list is the Aa series, which divides into two parts, each written by a different scribe; these parts correspond to the two Provinces. The Ab series contains no tablets for the Further Province and is thus incomplete, possibly because the information for this had not yet arrived in Pylos. Thus the groups in the Hither Province should each be represented on three tablets (Aa, Ab, Ad); those from the Further Province on only two (Aa, Ad). There are forty-nine groups known to us, and it is unlikely that any of the Hither Province are not represented by one or other of the three sources, though there is a chance that among the records of the Further Province one or even two groups might have been totally lost.

Each tablet of the Aa series lists a number of women, a number of girls and a number of boys. There follows optionally either or both of the entries *DA* 1 and *TA* 1; these are abbreviations which will be discussed below. The Ab series is like the Aa, but no figures follow *DA* or *TA*, and the text ends with a record of a quantity of wheat and an equal quantity of figs, presumably their rations. The Ad series lists men and boys, whose only qualification is that they are the sons of one of the groups of women known from the other series; clearly grown men would have been given a separate designation, so they must be youths just old enough to be classified as men (perhaps from the age of 15 upwards), and the boys will be the older boys who can usefully be attached to working groups of young men rather than to the groups in which their mothers work. The number of boys listed in the women's groups is less than that of girls, and the deficiency will be accounted for by this transference.

The numbers of women in each group vary from one to thirty-eight. The children are on average roughly equal to the number of women, which is not so surprising when we remember that some classed as women will be too old for child-bearing; and there are more girls than boys for the reason given above. The total number of women, making allowance for missing tablets, is of the order of 750, with about the same number of children. Of these about 450 are at Pylos, thus proving that the name refers to the whole area, not merely the excavated palace; for the excavators proved the existence of a large complex of buildings on the lower ground surrounding the hill on which the palace stood. Another 100 or so women are at other places in the Hither Province, about 200 in the Further Province, over half of them at Leuktron, the important royal establishment which may have functioned as the capital of the Further Province. The work-groups of young men amount to around 275, allowing for missing figures, plus 100 boys; again about two thirds of the total are located at Pylos.

The determination of the rations of the Pylos slave women makes an interesting story. It was obvious that the size of the ration was roughly proportional to the number of women and children, but no simple formula seemed to work, although it was hardly likely that arbitrary scales were used for different groups. The first break into the system came from my discovery that if we assumed a basic ration of two tenths of a unit for each woman, and one tenth for each child, no group received less than this basic minimum. But most groups received a little more, and it looked as though the mysterious *DA* and *TA* were in some way connected with the supplements.

One of the obstacles to further investigation was the inaccuracy of some of the readings of the figures on the tablets, and these were improved by a revised version by their chief editor (Bennett, 1957). This enabled two scholars independently to take the next step: L. R. Palmer (1959) and H. Ota (1959) in an article published in Japanese and not seen in Europe until later, both proposed the following scheme of correlations (all figures to be read as tenths of a major unit): *TA* = 2, *DA* = 5, *TA DA* = 7 or 9. This implies that *TA DA* may stand either for 1 *TA*+1 *DA* = 7, or 2 *TA*+1 *DA* = 9; and although this 2 is never specified, a remarkably similar series of tablets from Knossos (Ak) in fact shows the expected *DA* 1 *TA* 2 entries, though here the rations are not calculated. Palmer explained the mysterious abbreviations *TA* and *DA* as supervisory personnel, *TA* being a woman, for whom he postulated the same ration as a working woman, *DA* a man paid at a much higher scale. He then produced evidence purporting to show that men had a ration equivalent to 2½ times that of women. The fallacy in this argument will be discussed in Chapter 7.

I therefore proposed a slight modification in the idea: it would be remarkable if the ideograms for man and woman were not used, if the total strength of the group was in fact one, two or three persons larger than appeared. Moreover, one woman (Ab 388, cf. Aa 785) would appear to have a female supervisor all to herself. But if we suppose that the supervisors are all female and are counted in the total already given, we have only to emend the theory by allowing junior supervisors to be paid at the rate of four (instead of two) tenths, senior supervisors at seven tenths. All the figures then make sense, for we should expect supervisory staff to get more than their charges; and we may even go on to conjecture that *DA* is an abbreviation of the word written *da-ma* or *du-ma*, which we already know means superintendant (of either sex?), and that *TA* stands for the word *tamiā*, later found in Homer for 'female superintendant', 'housekeeper'.

There is one blemish on the final theory, a tablet (Ab 555) which shows a supplement of 45 tenths instead of the maximum of 9 observed elsewhere. There can be now no doubt that this is a simple error, and Palmer (1963, 117) ingeniously suggested how the error may have occurred: the scribe may, at some stage in his working, have simply omitted the sign for 'tenths', which should have preceded the last four unit strokes, so that he wrote 16 in place of 12.4. Whatever the cause of the error, it would be interesting to know whether the book-keeping error was translated into fact and the lucky group received its extra rations. The actual size of the rations is a matter we must leave for discussion later (p. 107).

One document from Pylos (An 607) would be of paramount importance in our understanding of Mycenaean slavery, if only we could be sure of its interpretation. It lists a total of thirteen women, but even that fact is not wholly certain, so incompetent was its author; he seems to have changed his mind about the number half way through, and in any case has failed to observe the normal rule about starting each entry on a new line. But the interesting fact is that the tablet records their fathers and mothers. The women are divided into four groups, which are presumably families: one consists of six women, two of three, and one entry has only one woman. Since her parentage is expressed in the same formula as that employed for one of the other families, there would be no point in making a separate entry unless the father and mother were different individuals. The names of the parents are not given, but their status is variously described. It would appear that in every family one or other of the parents is a slave, and the thirteen women are collectively called slaves. It would thus be easy to jump to the conclusion that the child of any union between a slave and a free person was a slave; but there are too many unknown factors to allow us to treat this as more than a likely guess.

What causes some of the difficulty is that one of the parents is the slave of a deity. Slaves (or servants) of a deity are often to be found at Pylos, and it is clear that they are not slaves in the ordinary sense of the term.

6 RELIGION

The difficulty of interpreting the dumb finds of the archaeologists is nowhere greater than in the field of religion. There is no lack in any museum concerned with the Bronze Age of objects given a religious character. Any human figure is liable to be interpreted as a divine image; any awkward-looking vessel is likely to be called 'ritual'; and an inexplicable architectural feature can always be labelled a temple or ceremonial room.

Now it is perfectly true that the world's religions have produced a vast number of representations of divine figures in human guise, many peculiar artifacts whose use would be hard to conjecture from their appearance, and highly specialized forms of building. So long as we know from other sources about the religion which produced them, there is no problem in interpreting the material remains. But suppose we had to infer the content of Christianity from the sculpture, decoration, furnishings and plan of a few churches, with no help at all from written texts; it will at once be plain how dangerous it is to attempt this solely from material remains. Yet up to a few years ago this has been the only way of approaching the subject of Mycenaean religion. The only other approach has been the attempt to uncover the prehistory of classical Greek religion by conjecturing its origins and guessing the meaning of its myths.

The danger of treating myths as history should not really need to be emphasized, were it not for the numerous attempts of this kind still being made. One of the most pitiful is to be found in the notes attached by Robert Graves (1958) to his admirable narration of *The Greek Myths.* But the idea that myth is a primitive kind of history dies hard. The trouble arises partly through a failure to define what a myth is; the name is applied indiscriminately to stories about the gods and about men, to accounts of the origin of the world and to explanations of natural phenomena. The one thing that they all have in common is that they cannot be regarded as literally true. But the test applied is apparently plausibility. If the walls of Troy were built by superhuman labour, this is dismissed as fiction, or at least a gross exaggeration; but if Troy was sacked by men, this must be accepted as historical fact. It does not seem to have occurred to anyone that we have no right to pick and choose which myths to believe and which to reject. I cannot help feeling that the function of myths has little to do with history; but this is a subject I must not pursue now.

One of the obvious and almost inevitable consequences of the archaeological approach to religion has been the confusion of Minoan and Mycenaean; indeed a famous book was entitled *The Minoan-Mycenaean Religion* (Nilsson, 1927). Yet looked at in the light of what we now know about the history of the Aegean world in the second millennium B.C., it is plain that, however much the end product was a fusion, there were here in origin two separate traditions, which we can characterize as the Minoan of Crete and the Mycenaean of the mainland. Even the Mycenaean is hardly likely to have been homogeneous. Early peoples rarely felt confident enough, like the Jews, to reject outright their neighbours' gods; almost always they took over and absorbed into their own system other religious systems with which they came into contact, either syncretizing the foreign deity with one of their own with similar attributes, or inserting the newcomer into the existing roll of deities. If we could feel certain that the pre-hellenic inhabitants of Greece and Crete each practised a single, uniform religion, then the fusion would be of only two elements; but in fact we must be ready to recognize the possibility of a threefold origin for the classical data.

The analysis of classical religion has easily yielded the separation of two strands: alongside the so-called Olympian deities, who are placed not so much upon the actual Mount Olympus in northern Greece as in a remote area of the sky, stands another less prepossessing group known to experts as chthonic, who were thought of as located within or below the surface of the earth; their technical name means simply 'earthy'. It is a reasonable hypothesis that the chthonic element represents the religion of the pre-hellenic people, the Olympian element the religion of the proto-Greek newcomers. But even this view is probably an oversimplification, and there is a vital piece of linguistic evidence here which is all too often overlooked.

There were traditionally twelve Olympian deities: Zeus, Poseidon, Hermes, Ares, Apollo, Hephaistos, Dionysos; Hera, Artemis, Aphrodite, Athena, Demeter. Of these Demeter is probably a latecomer to this group, being in origin a realization of the Earth-goddess; and Dionysos had always been considered a very late introduction, until the revelation of his name on two Pylos tablets upset this comfortable belief. The linguistic fact concerns the names of the deities. If these cults went back to the time before the Indo-European peoples had broken up, we should expect to find that the names of the gods were paralleled in other languages.

In fact only one name is found elsewhere. Zeus is a regular Greek development of a form which we can restore as **Dyēus*, and the associations of his name show that he was conceived as the god of the clear sky. He is known in the Vedas as *Dyaus pitar*, exactly as *Iuppiter* in Latin, incorporating the word for 'father'. There can be no doubt that this name was brought to Greece by the ancestors of the Greeks; Zeus has an impeccable ancestry. It is rather a shock to find that none of the other Olympians share this respectability, for wherever their names reappear outside Greek, this may be due to borrowing.

Of course enormous efforts have been made by scholars anxious to supply the other names with etymologies. Every handbook on Greek religion devotes a good deal of space to explaining the names; but a little research soon shows that there are several different and mutually contradictory explanations of each. For some reason this fact does not arouse the suspicions of the experts on religion; they still cheerfully found their theories upon the supposed original meaning of the name. The trained linguist, however, is well aware of a flaw which invalidates any conclusions of this sort. An etymology is not just a guess that two superficially similar words have a common origin; it is a cardinal principle that the words compared must have either identical meanings or at least meanings close enough for it to be plausibly shown how one has developed from the other. But a proper name has, *ipso facto*, no meaning, other than its specific reference. There is thus no way in which the alleged etymologies of the divine names can be checked, if they are not, like Zeus, inherited by a number of cognate languages. All we can do is to judge whether the alleged meaning of the name is plausible; if it is not, we can reject the proposed explanation; but if it is, this does not prove it is correct. Any account of a god which begins from an explanation of the meaning of his name ought to be treated with grave suspicion.

Let us examine briefly the name of Poseidon, the god of the sea, of earthquakes and of horses, since this is the one with the strongest claim to Indo-European origin. The form of the name varies in the ancient Greek dialects. Homer has *Poseidāōn*, which we now know to be the Mycenaean form; in other dialects it is often of the type *Poteidān*, and this enables us to postulate an original **Poteidāōn*. We can then analyse it as a compound of **potis* (classical Greek *posis* 'husband', cf. Sanskrit *patis* 'lord', Latin *potis* an adjective meaning 'able'). The second syllable offers a surprising diphthong, but this can be explained as a vocative (*Potei* 'O Lord'), since such forms are sometimes subsequently treated as invariable; this is probably the case with Latin *Iuppiter*. The second element was found in the syllable *dā*, *-ōn* being a common termination of men's names. This *dā* was alleged to be a word for 'earth', so that the whole name meant 'the lord (or husband) of the earth'. Yet this word occurs in the whole of Greek literature only in ejaculations, such as the famous passage in Aeschylus' play *Agamemnon*, where Kassandra breaks a long silence with the alarming cry: *otototototoi popoi da*! Neither of the first two words are known to the Greek vocabulary; they are plainly meaningless cries, like the *op-op-op-op-op* still to be heard in Greece today as a cry of surprise. It is curious to be told that Aeschylus intended *da* to be an invocation of the earth, for Kassandra was the priestess of the Olympian god Apollo.

There is but one other source for this mysterious word, another of the same set of names, *Dēmētēr*, or in its earlier form *Dāmātēr*. Since Demeter is beyond question the earth-goddess, and *mātēr* is the Greek word for 'mother', *dā* must mean 'earth'; Q.E.D. This is of course a circular argument, though it has taken in most of the experts on Greek religion. You cannot defend your analysis of one divine name by breaking up another to produce the confirmation. Every Greek was aware of the maternal functions of Demeter; if her name bore the slightest resemblance to the Greek word for 'mother', it would inevitably have been deformed to emphasize that resemblance. Yet if the first element were thought to mean 'earth', how did it escape transformation into **Gāmātēr*, a name transparent to any Greek speaker?

Some readers may wonder why I find this pair of etymologies unconvincing. I can only answer that my experience of the way languages work makes me very suspicious, for words that are not understood are constantly deformed to give them meanings. Mere resemblance is of course nearly always deceptive; linguistic history is full of amazing parallels, like Latin *habeo* and German *habe*, identical in meaning, which cannot possibly be related.

The other divine names are even less amenable to etymology. Some theories can be easily disproved; Hermes has nothing to do with cairns (*hermata*), because this word has originally initial *w*-, but Hermes (Mycenaean *Hermahās*) has not. Hera is not the Saviouress (cf. Latin *seruāre*) for a similar reason; her name may be connected with *hērōs* 'hero', but that is no help, since it too is etymologically obscure. Apollo is not the destroyer, though the Greeks liked to pun on the verb *apollūmi* 'I destroy'. Aphrodite has probably no connexion with *aphros* 'foam', despite romantic pictures of her emerging from the foaming breakers. *Dionysos* is likely to contain the name of his father, Zeus (genitive *Dios*), since Mycenaean now confirms the expected *w*, *Diwo*-; but the second member of the compound remains opaque. Names like *Hēphaistos* and *Athēnā* show patterns observable in place names of pre-Greek origin.

We must not forget that at least 600 years lie between the arrival of the ancestors of the Greeks in Greece and the earliest of our Mycenaean texts. It is no wonder that whatever religious beliefs they brought with them had been transformed out of all recognition by the time we can perceive a few facets of their religious life; nor is it surprising that much changed too in the following 600 years, before we get the fuller picture of classical religion.

When we turn to the documents for enlightenment on the gods, we are faced with a major disappointment. There are no theological texts or even hymns, no temple dedications, not even the brief inscriptions which the Minoans sometimes placed on dedicated objects. The gods appear only as the recipients of some of the stores issued by the palace administrators. They do not even write the name of a god in any special way, so that we are sometimes in doubt whether a name belongs to a man or a god. All we can do is to identify certain of the names as corresponding to classical divine names, and then, proceeding by analogy, identify some of the unfamiliar ones as also divine.

One of the first texts which attracted my attention in 1952, when I began applying Ventris's tentative values for the Linear B signs to the Knossos tablets, was V 52. It was a small, two-line tablet (fig. 37), broken at the right,

37 Knossos tablet V 52 showing the names of four Greek deities

but with a small fragment giving a continuation of the bottom line. Transcribed it read:

a-ta-na-po-ti-ni-ja 1 [

e-nu-wa-ri-jo 1 *pa-ja-wo*[ ]*po-se-da*[

No Greek scholar could read the first word without dividing it *Athānā potnia* 'Mistress Athena', almost echoing the Homeric form: *potni(a) Athēnaiē*. Yet whether this is really the right interpretation is still in doubt, as will become clear when we discuss Potnia in more detail. *E-nu-wa-ri-jo* is plainly the name *Enualios*, which is used frequently in Greek literature as an alternative for Ares, the god of war, though in some cases the name is given to a separate deity, said to be the son of Ares. *Pa-ja-wo* suggested Homeric *Paiēōn*, which earlier would have been *Paiāwōn*, later *Paiān*, an alternative name of Apollo, if not again a separate god. *Po-se-da*[could be completed as *po-se-da-o*, a form already familiar from the Pylos tablets, which transcribes as *Poseidāōn*. Here then were four well known Greek gods. Any one might have been an illusion, but four in one list were too much for coincidence.

Subsequently a small fragment was found which joins the two pieces and fills the gap in the bottom line. This reveals that *pa-ja-wo*[is really *pa-ja-wo-ne*, the dative case, and the other entries may be in the same case. Thus it appears to be a record of something issued, one apiece, to these four deities. But there is no indication on the tablet what the numeral 1 refers to; perhaps this was shown on the missing portion, but this seems unlikely. It is perhaps more significant that the tablet belongs to a curious group which may be scribal exercises rather than true records (see p. 169).

Another document (Tn 316) which was plainly religious in character soon appeared among the Pylos texts, for it contained the names of Zeus and Hera and what must be the Mycenaean form of Hermes, three more Olympians. But it has taken a long time to arrive at a probable explanation Fig. 38

38 Record of a major religious rite at Pylos: Tn 316 (both sides)

of it, and there are still a lot of unsolved problems. Not only is it an isolated document, with no similar ones to match it; it is also the most disgraceful piece of handwriting to have come down to us. It is a large tablet with writing on both sides, though each ends with blank lines; it bears traces of frequent erasure and re-writing; the signs are hastily formed; in at least two places the scribe has omitted a sign by mistake; and in places the resulting text is so confused as to be illegible. So far from carefully planning his tablet with lines corresponding to days of the month, as has been suggested, it would seem that the writer had no clear idea of his text when he began to write. It looks as if he began on one side, became dissatisfied, erased all he had written, turned the tablet over and began again on the back. After completing less than half the text, although he had drawn rules for the next paragraph, he turned it over again and continued on the other (now erased) side. This too ends with blank lines as if more was to follow. The easiest explanation of this muddle is that the writer was trying to record the decisions of an unusually stormy meeting. But why did he not subsequently make a fair copy for storage in the archives and consign this rough draft to oblivion? The most likely answer is that he had no time; and that would make sense if the tablet were written within the last few days, perhaps the last few hours, of the existence of the palace. As we shall see later, this supposition fits well with what little we know about the fall of Pylos.

The text begins with what may well be the name of a month: *po-ro-wi-to-jo*. We have other tablets, and these are often of a religious nature, which record the date by a month name in the genitive case; unfortunately the word for 'month' does not here accompany it, and although its use elsewhere fits the theory, it is not entirely certain that this is the right interpretation. L. R. Palmer (1955, 11) offered an excellent suggestion, that the month was called *Plowistos*, which would mean 'the month of sailing'. The Greeks were scared of navigation in the stormy winter months and resumed sailing towards the end of March; so a month so named would fall around that date in our calendar. Greek months were of course lunar – it was the Romans who eventually divorced the month from the moon – and the sign of the crescent moon is employed on the tablets to denote month.

Then follows at the left of each paragraph the two signs for the name PYLOS written in signs about three times the normal size. There can be no doubt that the text concerns the capital city. But another place name is mentioned in the adjacent text; the action of the first paragraph takes place at one of the chief districts, *Pa-ki-ja-ne*. This name cannot be certainly restored but has been transcribed in this book as *Sphagiānes*. The apparent contradiction is explained by the fact that Pylos is not itself the chief town of one of the nine districts; but there are other indications that *Sphagiānes* was the name of the district in which the palace lay (see p. 45). It is tempting to place it near the modern town of Khóra, just north of the palace, for the discovery here of Mycenaean tombs which became the site of a religious cult at a later date suggests that its reputation as a religious centre survived the Mycenaean collapse.

39 Gold bowl from Dhendrá in the Argolid

The formula which begins each paragraph has been disputed, and the first word cannot be satisfactorily explained on the basis of later Greek; but the best suggestion (Palmer, 1963, 265) is that it refers to some religious ceremony. The formula continues with a reference to the carrying of gifts and the bringing of *po-re-na*. This too is a word missing from the later Greek vocabulary, but the verb translated 'bring' implies that it means something which could walk. Then follows the entry: '(for) Potnia: one gold vessel, one woman'. After this come four more names, presumably also deities, each receiving a gold vessel and in two cases a woman. This pattern is repeated in the other paragraphs with different names of deities; in two cases, where the deity is male, a man is substituted for a woman.

It is impossible to resist the conclusion that the obscure word *po-re-na* in the introductory formula refers to the human beings, and, despite initial reluctance to accept the unpalatable fact, that these unfortunate people were to become sacrificial victims. The same word has now appeared again, in the dative plural, on a new tablet from Thebes (Of 26) indicating recipients of wool, but in a religious context. Since sacrificial victims in Greek ritual were frequently decked out with wool, this is some slight confirmation of the meaning of the word.

Some finds of human bones outside Mycenaean tombs have been interpreted as implying human sacrifice, though the evidence is apparently not wholly unambiguous. Yet in view of the widespread Greek tradition there is no reason to reject such an idea; though the Greeks of the classical age disapproved of the practice, they were familiar with it from Homer, and it forms an essential element in the plot of many tragedies. If this interpretation of the Pylos tablet is correct, it is further confirmation that the occasion of this ceremony was a very special one, for human sacrifice is unlikely to have been a regular feature of the religious calendar. Nor is even a wealthy king likely to have dedicated thirteen gold vessels to religious purposes as a matter of annual ritual.

We must now turn our attention to the deities listed on this unique document. In the first paragraph, located at the place *Sphagiānes,* we have *Potnia,* the title we have already met at Knossos apparently with *Athena.* But here she is a goddess in her own right. The title is an inherited Greek word meaning 'Mistress', 'Lady', often used of queens, and it is exactly matched in form and meaning by the Sanskrit *patnī*; hence it has an Indo-European origin, and is not a pre-hellenic borrowing. But although the word is genuine Greek, its use as a divine title may well be a translation of a pre-hellenic term of similar meaning, just as 'Our Lady' is an English appellation familiar to Christians and in other countries is translated by names of similar meaning.

When we assemble all the other references on the tablets to Potnia a remarkable fact emerges. In all but two or three cases the word does not stand alone, as it does here, but is qualified by a preceding or following word. This is often a genitive, sometimes actually written as one word with *potnia;* for instance, at Pylos we meet three times the form *u-po-jo po-ti-ni-ja. U-po-jo* is plainly a genitive, but of what is obscure. At Knossos we have *da-pu$_2$-ri-to-jo po-ti-ni-ja* (Gg 702), and *da-pu$_2$-ri-to* bears a strong resemblance to *laburinthos*, our 'labyrinth'; now this is not a pure Greek word but a pre-hellenic borrowing, as the *-nthos* suffix shows, and *d* and *l* are sometimes confused in such words; a parallel case may be *Oluseus* found in Greek dialects for *Odusseus*, and with other modifications in the form in which Latin borrowed the name, *Ulixes* or *Ulysses*. In other cases *Potnia* is accompanied by epithets: *Aswia* (PY Fr 1206) 'of Asia', *i-qe-ja* (PY An 1281) 'horsy', 'of horses'. Or another sort of word such as *wa-na-so-i* (PY Fr 1235) or *di-pi-si-jo-i* (Fr 1231), which appear to be either places or festivals, may be added to characterize her. It is very much like the Christian (Roman Catholic) habit of qualifying 'Our Lady' by an epithet of place or function. Thus the mention of the place *Sphagiānes* in Tn 316 may serve to define which 'Lady' is meant. A new tablet from Thebes speaks of a dedication 'to the house of Potnia' without further qualification; here it may be relevant that in later times there was a district just outside Thebes called *Potniai*, 'Ladies' in the plural.

These *Potniai* were understood by the classical Greeks as Demeter and her daughter Persephone, who became the Queen of Hades; that is to say, they continued, in different aspects, the pre-hellenic cult of the Earth Mother, which is so abundantly attested by figurines and pictures of all kinds throughout the Bronze Age. There can be no doubt that from Early Helladic times onwards the cult of the Earth Mother dominated religious life all over the Aegean world; and this continued into the classical period under a variety of names. The conclusion that *Potnia* was the Mycenaean name for this figure is inescapable. That her name would appear prominently among the lists of dedications on the tablets is certain, and no other female deity is even half as well attested.

One of the interesting features of Mycenaean Potnia is that an adjective derived from her name is used to describe flocks of sheep at Knossos, and bronzesmiths at Pylos. The sheep were doubtless assigned to the goddess to provide an income for her shrines and attendants. But the association with smiths requires comment. In this aspect Potnia is probably the predecessor of Athena, though Hephaistos too can claim a share as the smith of the gods. Professor Marinátos dug several Cretan caves which were venerated in Minoan times; and at Arkalokhóri to the south of Knossos he observed that the finds indicated that the cave was used as a workshop by bronzesmiths as well as for cult purposes. The link is not so surprising if we remember the religious basis of many medieval craftsmen's guilds. An interesting confirmation of this came from the house inside the Citadel at Mycenae dug by Lord William Taylour in 1968, where in a room adjoining a metal workshop was found a fresco of a female figure. I believe she can be none other than Potnia herself. It would Fig. 40

40 Fresco showing a large female figure, perhaps Potnia, from the Citadel House at Mycenae

seem likely that communities of smiths dedicated to this goddess were dispersed over Greece following the Minoan collapse of the fifteenth century. Their descendants might well have maintained their cult, however much hellenized themselves.

The next entry is a gold vessel and a woman for *Ma-na-sa*. This name does not appear elsewhere and cannot be reconstructed to fit any known Greek goddess. It is followed at once by a similar entry for *Po-si-da-e-ja*, and although no such goddess is known in classical times, it is clear that she is *Posidaeia*, a feminine derivative of Poseidon. It is curious that although the next paragraph mentions a precinct of Poseidon, no offering on this tablet is directed to Poseidon himself, though, as we shall see, he was evidently an important deity at Pylos.

The last line of this paragraph has offerings of gold vessels, but no human beings; the two recipients are named as *Tris-hērōs* and *Do-po-ta*. The first name is a compound of the familiar *hērōs*, a term used in later Greek of demi-gods and local deities, and *tris* 'thrice', but no such compound is known there. He reappears on the list of recipients of perfumed oil (see below p. 96). *Do-po-ta* might be a dialect form of the Greek word for 'master' (classical *despotēs*), but this is very uncertain. The conclusion from these five entries is clear; the cults of *Sphagiānes* were of local, and very likely pre-Greek, origin, since even when the names are Greek they sound like translations.

The second paragraph, the first on the reverse, refers to a place *Posidaïon,* which means 'belonging to Poseidon'; since again PYLOS precedes, it is probably not a geographical term, but a building or precinct in the vicinity of the capital. The first entry specifies a gold vessel and two women; but here the name of the deity is missing from its usual place in the formula. Instead two names have been inserted after the formula, and here the bad handwriting impedes us, for some word may have separated them; but the names are *Qo-wi-ja* (= *Guōwiā* 'she of the cow'?) and *Komāwenteia* (a name apparently formed as feminine derivative of a male name meaning 'long-haired'). The two female victims presuppose two goddesses, so despite the irregularity in the order these must surely be their names. 'Cow-eyed' is a regular Homeric epithet of Hera, and also of other goddesses and women; it is not of course insulting. *Komāwenteia* has now reappeared in the Thebes tablets (Of 35) where again she might be a goddess, though there is no proof of this.

The next paragraph refers to 'the precincts (?) of *Pe-re-swa, Iphemedeia* and *Diwya*' and each of these goddesses receives an offering. *Iphemedeia* receives only a gold vessel, each of the others a gold vessel and a woman. *Pe-re-swa* is mentioned on another Pylos tablet (Un 6), where she receives along with Poseidon, an offering of a cow, a ewe, a boar and a sow, the same three species of animal sacrificed in the old Roman ritual of the *Suouetaurilia.* Her name might be reconstructed as *Preswā* which vaguely recalls the first element of *Persephone,* the Queen of Hades. *Iphimedeia,* with a slightly different spelling probably due to a popular etymology ('she who rules by strength'), is known from Homer (*Od.* 11.305) as a mythical figure who had two sons by Poseidon; but it is remarkable to find her worshipped as a goddess at Pylos. *Diwya* is another goddess whose name is found elsewhere on the tablets. At Pylos she has male and female servants (Cn 1287, An 607), and her name is mentioned at Knossos (Xd 97). She would appear to be a female counterpart to Zeus, as Posidaeia is to Poseidon, perhaps a sky-goddess. At the end of this paragraph comes the first offering of a man, for Hermes Areias. The significance of *Areias* is unknown, although it resembles the name of Ares, god of war; but it is used as a cult title of Zeus, Enyalios and Athena in an Arcadian inscription of the fourth century.

The last paragraph deals with 'the precinct (?) of Zeus'. Here the offerings are to Zeus and Hera, and a certain *di-ri-mi-jo* (*Drimios?*), not otherwise known, who is called 'the (uncertain word) of Zeus'. There is reason to think the uncertain word may mean 'son', though it is not the classical word; if so, we have another unknown god. It is also possible that the word is wrongly spelt and a syllable is missing, as happens elsewhere on this shockingly badly written document; this would enable us to read it as 'priest'. The offering here is a gold vessel, and since all the other figures would seem to be divine, it is perhaps safer to place this too in the same category, though the human servants of deities appear elsewhere as recipients of offerings.

To sum up, the document is a hastily compiled record of an unprecedented group of offerings, thirteen gold vessels and ten human beings to three groups of deities. Zeus, Hera and Hermes are the only names which are instantly recognizable as major figures in the classical pantheon, unless we allow the equation of Potnia with the later Demeter. Do the unfamiliar names conceal familiar figures, or were the gods of Mycenaean Greece very different from their successors? The temptation is to concentrate on what we recognize and to dismiss the other names as representing local cults. But this document at least proves the importance assigned to these local figures.

Perhaps the most extraordinary omission is the name of Poseidon, although his feminine counterpart is represented, and his precinct is mentioned, apparently occupied by two minor goddesses. Yet elsewhere on the Pylos tablets he is an important figure; indeed we should conclude, even without the Homeric reference to a festival of King Poseidon at Pylos (*Od.* 3.43), that he was the most important of the gods here. He is the only major god listed as receiving annual contributions of grain; in the Es tablets a group of thirteen land-holders are taxed for contributions of wheat to Poseidon and three other obscure figures, but Poseidon's are by far the largest, amounting to about 1,075 litres (see p. 116). He is the recipient too of long lists of offerings including oxen, sheep, goats, pigs, wheat, wine, honey, unguent, wool and cloth (Un 718, 853, cf. Un 6). He is also represented prominently on another important series of tablets (Fr), which deal with allocations of perfumed oil, sometimes unguents; since the recipients seem to be largely deities, this series needs to be discussed in detail.

The certainly divine figures are Poseidon, who appears three times, on each occasion with a different epithet or annotation; Potnia four times, with three different epithets, and where the epithet is repeated a location is given to distinguish the entry. Twice we have simply 'the gods', though in the only complete text this is qualified by a location. Once each we have the 'Divine Mother' (perhaps to be rendered 'Mother of the Gods', a title given to Rhea, another of the manifestations of the Mother-Goddess); the Thrice-Hero, who has already been discussed on the human-sacrifice tablet; and the Attendants, who may be attendant divinities or perhaps more likely the human ministrants of the god. More difficult to analyse are the four references to 'the King'; each time he has an epithet, which probably distinguishes him from the human king of Pylos, who has none. Three times the epithet is the same, though slightly different in form; once it is different. Since Potnia is a word for 'mistress', but undoubtedly refers to goddesses variously particularized, it would seem that 'King' too is here a divine title, though I think it would be rash to infer from Homer's use of 'King Poseidon' that they were one and the same; but this remains a possibility.

This list, however, does not exhaust the recipients of perfumed oil, for in some cases no deity is specifically mentioned, the name of a place (e.g. the precinct of Zeus, Fr 1230) or a festival serving instead. Two festivals have intelligible names, though as usual there are ambiguities. One, which is once associated with the name of Poseidon, is 'the spreading of couches'; this has been interpreted as a 'sacred marriage', but might also refer to a divine banquet at which images of the gods were displayed on couches and food was served to them. The other is most likely to mean 'the holding of thrones' though it is possible to extract other meanings from the compound, given a motive. The locations stated are often at *Sphagiānes* (five times), but obviously when a deity had only one shrine it was unnecessary to specify the place. There are two references to 'the Lousian territory', which may be the area east of the Bay of Navaríno. None of the offerings seem to be sent to the more remote parts of the kingdom.

Now this series of tablets is closely parallel to the Fp series at Knossos. Here too the commodity is olive oil, though we are not specifically told that it was perfumed. Most of these tablets carry a month name; six or possibly seven month names are represented, which may indicate that the palace was destroyed in the seventh month of the current year, though unfortunately in Greek calendars the year did not always begin at the winter solstice. The names of months in later Greek calendars varied from one city to another, and this seems to be true of Knossos and Pylos, for none of the known month names recur at the other site.

Most of the tablets are short, but the one long one (Fp 1) will do as a specimen to discuss. After the initial line reading 'in the month of Deukios', each entry occupies a single line. The first is a familiar name: 'for Diktaian Zeus'. This is a well known title of Zeus in classical times; it is generally believed to be the result of mixing the Greek Zeus with a pre-Greek Cretan deity, with rather different characteristics. Dikte is the great mountain range to the south-east of Knossos, and several caves used as cult-places are known in the area. The second entry is 'to the Daidaleion'; the story of Daidalos, chief engineer to King Minos, is too well known to need repeating. What the Daidaleion was, we have no means of knowing, but it does not follow that Daidalos was worshipped as a god; the derivative might mean no more than the structure erected by Daidalos. Since traditionally this was a labyrinth, and we have already met the Lady of the Labyrinth (p. 92), it may possibly be another name for her shrine. The next entry, *pa-de*, is obscure; it resembles the Greek word for 'child' but it is fairly certain that this is an illusion. Then we have 'for all the gods', an entry frequently repeated in this series of tablets. Again we have an unfamiliar type of dedication for Greek ritual. Then another strange name, *qe-ra-si-ja*. At this point a new heading is introduced and perhaps applies to all the following entries; it is the town of Amnisos, the port just north of Knossos. The entry here is again 'for all the gods', so it is clear that there were at least two shrines with this dedication. Then comes a surprising figure: *Erinus*, the later name, usually in the plural, for the Furies or avenging spirits believed to pursue murderers. The same name has now been deciphered on the edge of the famous list of Greek gods at Knossos (V 52) with which I began this chapter. Then after another obscure entry, apparently another place, comes 'for the priestess of the winds'; here again cults of the winds were little known in later Greece and so no parallel can be quoted. Other tablets of this series mention the priestess of the winds; one locates her at the town of *U-ta-no*.

Some of the other tablets dealing with olive oil may bear divine names, but here we have clearly also human beings and trade groups, so it is dangerous to draw inferences about unfamiliar names. Here we have another reference to *Erinus* (Fh 390) and an entry 'to Dikte' written above a broken word which is perhaps 'shrine' (Fh 5467).

Another group of documents at Knossos with religious associations are the honey tablets (Gg). They are not well preserved but we cannot fail to recognize 'the Lady of the Labyrinth' (Gg 702, see above), 'all the gods' (Gg 702, 705, 717) and at Amnisos *Eleuthia* (Gg 705), who also receives wool (Od 714, 715, 716). Now *Eleuthia* is a known dialect form of a name variously written in alphabetic Greek, but most familiar in its Homeric form, *Eileithuia*, the goddess of child-birth; for Homer (*Od.* 19.188) speaks of 'Amnisos where is the cave of Eileithuia', and the actual site on the hill behind the port has been excavated. It was continuously used from Minoan down to Roman times.

Another entry in this series has recently proved to have religious associations. Gg 713 reads 'for Marineus, (for) the female servant', which might be appropriate even if Marineus (if this is the right reconstruction of his name) were a man. But a list of men (As 1519, an improved reading) ends with the note 'to the house of Marineus, so many men: 10' and the same word for 'house' is used at Thebes (Of 36) of 'the house (i.e. shrine) of Potnia'; and a group of women there (Of 25, 35) are called by a derivative of the same name, Marineus. It would be an odd coincidence if men of this name at both sites had such clear religious connexions; it would be easily explained if he were a god.

An interesting link with later religion emerges from this group of tablets at Thebes which record disbursements of wool. One consignment (Of 25) is addressed to Amarynthos. This is known in classical times as a town on the west coast of the island of Euboea, thus although not in Boeotia it is still not too far distant from Thebes; on the other hand, as we have seen in other cases, it is possible that there was another town of this name in Boeotia. But we know that classical Amarynthos had a famous temple of Artemis, and the site was certainly occupied in Mycenaean times. Since some at least of the consignments of this series have a religious background, it seems reasonable to assume that the cult of Artemis at Amarynthos may have already been established. Artemis is definitely mentioned by name at Pylos, (Eb 650.5) where a man is described as 'the servant of Artemis' (*a-te-mi-to do-e-ro*). It is less certain whether the spelling *a-ti-mi-te* in PY Un 219.5 is the dative 'for Artemis', but in view of the presence of Potnia and Hermes in the same list, it would seem probable. The fluctuation of spelling between *e* and *i* is found in other words and names which are probably borrowed from a pre-Greek language, and it may be relevant that the goddess apears in a Lydian inscription as *Artimul.*

Ares has appeared already under the name of Enyalios, if indeed this is to be regarded as the same god. But there are two examples at Knossos of the spelling *a-re*, one of which is in a religious context (Fp 14); it looks very much like *Arēs.* The real difficulty is that we should expect here a dative, probably therefore *a-re-i*, but this is not insuperable. At least the men's names *Areios* and *Areimenēs* must be derived from *Arēs*, so we can add this to the list of Mycenaean gods.

A similar deduction is possible in the case of *Hēphaistos*, the smith of the gods. There is a man's name *A-pa-i-ti-jo* at Knossos which is likely to be *Hāphaistios* or *Hāphaistiōn.* Apollo is mentioned only if he is to be identified with *Paiāwōn.* There is no trace of Aphrodite. But Dionysos surprisingly appears twice at Pylos, in the form *Diwonusos*, both times irritatingly enough on fragments, so that we have no means of verifying his divinity.

41 Sacrificial scene from the Hághia Triádha sarcophagus

One of these (Xa 1419) has on the reverse an obscure word which may be a compound of the word for 'wine'; this has been hailed as proof that the connexion of Dionysos with wine is already established for Mycenaean times. Caution demands that we reserve judgement here.

Finally, in addition to those already mentioned, there remain a number of obscure names which are likely to be divinities of some sort. Names like *qe-ra-si-ja*, *pi-pi-tu-na*, *a-ju-ma-na-ke*, *a-ro-do-ro-o* at Knossos fall into this class. It has been pointed out that *pi-pi-tu-na* may have the same suffix as the Cretan goddess *Diktunnā*, but she remains totally unknown. We can conclude that, as might be expected, the Greek take-over in Crete left intact the old Minoan gods, and this is confirmed by a number of religious shrines which show continuity from Minoan times into the LM III period.

A Pylos tablet (Un 2) has an intriguing heading which can be interpreted as a record of an initiation ceremony. As usual, such events are not directly recorded, but the issue of goods for use as offerings requires an entry in the accounts ledger. The scene is again Sphagiānes, which we know was a most important cult centre. The key phrase is not by any means certain, but could mean 'on the initiation of the king'. The word for 'initiate' is not in exactly the classical form, but parallels exist for the presumed development. The word order too is surprising; but it remains the most plausible interpretation. The list of goods is impressive: 1,574 litres of barley, 14½ litres of cyperus, 115 litres of flour, 307 litres of olives, 19 litres of honey, 96 litres of figs, 1 ox, 26 rams, 6 ewes, 2 he-goats, 2 she-goats, 1 fattened pig, 6 sows, 585½ litres of wine, not to mention three commodities which are listed by unknown abbreviations or ideograms. The barley alone

would provide rations for 43 people for a month. But if the ceremony really were a royal initiation, these offerings are not by any means excessive.

This pattern of mixed offerings is repeated on other tablets; that to Poseidon (Un 718, cf. Un 853) has already been mentioned (p. 96). Unfortunately, unless the heading of a large tablet is preserved it is impossible to judge whether the list is for religious purposes or not. Similarly at Knossos a group of tablets (Fs), which may well be religious offerings since one is addressed to *pa-de* (see p. 98), lists quantities of barley, figs, olive oil, flour and wine; but here the quantities are much smaller, for only once does the amount of barley exceed 10 litres.

The offerings of single commodities seem to be olive oil (often, if not always, perfumed), honey, grain and wool. Classical ritual made use of wool too, but the indications are that some of the wool was woven into cloth, and textiles appear on lists which may be offerings. It is hard to judge whether Mycenaean, like classical, gods were adorned with robes, but it would seem likely. Stone sculptures as cult figures are unknown, but there are several cases of terracotta figures on a considerable scale. But surely the cult-images were most commonly made of wood and have therefore not survived. There are in classical times many references to wooden statues of very great antiquity known as *xoana;* is it impossible that some of these were not, as has usually been assumed, of the archaic period, but actually Mycenaean? It is by no means impossible for wood, if carefully looked after, to last for a thousand years.

7 AGRICULTURE

Weights and measures

Before we go any further we must turn to the subject of weights and measures. As explained in the Preface (p. xiv), the units of the metric systems, for which there were doubtless words, are represented in the script by special signs. In some cases we can guess what these words were, but since they are never written out syllabically we have no way of verifying these guesses. The way in which these signs are used differs from that found in the Minoan Linear A script, since there smaller amounts than whole units are described by a complicated system of fractional signs. In Linear B the signs (in some cases clearly the same signs) represent smaller units, which are of course specified fractions of the major unit. But despite the difference of usage, it would not be surprising to learn that the basic units were the same, and we shall see a remarkable point of agreement later on.

The weights are relatively simple, though we have too little evidence to complete the lower end of the scale. The largest weight, used of things like

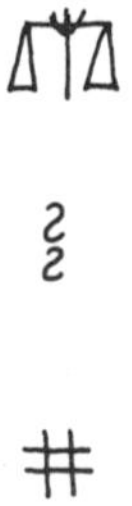

$= \text{L}$

$= \text{M} = \frac{1}{30}\text{L}$

$= \text{N} = \frac{1}{4}\text{M}$

42 The Mycenaean signs for weights

bronze, is a sign representing a balance, transcribed conventionally as L (see fig. 42). The largest unit of weight in use in the classical period was called *talanton* (Latin *talentum*, hence our *talent*), and since this name too means a balance, there can be little doubt that it was also the name of the Mycenaean unit. This is divided into 30 M, the classical talent into 60 *minae;*

but since the Mycenaean sign is plainly double we can safely call this a double-mina (*dimnaion*, a word which remained in use as a monetary unit in Cyprus in classical times). The word *mna* (Latinized as *mina*) is Semitic, and the sexagesimal system, based on 60 parts to a unit, is also clearly of Near Eastern origin.

The double-mina was then divided into quarters (N), and this in turn probably into twelfths (P); the doubt is due to the fact that we find P 12 and P 20, but these are perhaps not reduced to the higher unit (as we often quote a weight in pounds, and not as so many hundredweight, quarters, etc.). There is at least one smaller weight, used to give quantities of saffron, which cannot be certainly fitted to the system. The smaller weights are also used for gold. The smaller weights of the classical system do not appear to match: the *drachma* is one hundredth of the *mina*, the *obol* one sixth of the *drachma*.

The classical weights are very difficult to compare because there were two quite different standards: on one the talent weighed 25.86 kg, on the other 37.80 kg. There is no obvious way of judging whether the Mycenaean talent approximated to one or other of these standards, or fell between them, but at least these figures set reasonable limits for our discussion. A collection of bronze ingots from Hághia Triádha have an average weight of just over 29 kg, which is likely to be a little lower than the original values; this might well approximate to the talent.

The ideal way of solving the problem would be to identify a series of contemporary weights; though here too we must tread warily, since metal weights tend to become lighter through corrosion, chemical reaction or mechanical damage. Evans devised a method of compensating for the last by making a plaster cast which he then restored and so calculated the volume lost. But weights from this period are still very rare, and it so happens that most of them are from Crete or at least the Minoan sphere of influence in the Aegean.

Evans (1935, 550–656) found at Knossos a number of weights, the largest of which is a block of gypsum with octopus decoration. It has been Fig. 43
disputed whether this is really a weight; if it is, its weight, quoted by Evans at 29 kg, must be a talent. The more certain examples are flattish cylinders, sometimes with markings on the top. A large one is marked with two large circles flanked on each side by two small ones, and Evans plausibly suggested that this was a notation for 24 units. This gave a unit of approximately 65.5 g, and other weights could then be shown to fit this: one with what is probably meant to be five circles weighs 327.02 g ($65.5 \times 5 = 327.5$), and another weighing 68 g is not far from the supposed unit.

43 A stone block with octopus decoration from Knossos, possibly a talent weight

J. L. Caskey (1970) in his most instructive dig on Keos (or Kéa) in the Cyclades found, again in a Minoan context, a number of lead weights. These too appear to fit the Knossos unit: one with two dots weighs 121.3 g (if its original weight was 131 g this would represent two units), another with eight dots weighs 517 g (8×65.5 = 524), and there is an unmarked example weighing 648.5 g, or close to ten times the unit.

The difficulty comes when we try to fit this unit of 65.5 g into a place on the Mycenaean scale. The only plausible value for it would have to be P 3, since this is one four hundred and eightieth of a talent: thus 65.5×480 = 31,440 g. The multiples would then represent the following weights in Mycenaean units.

1 = P 3
2 = P 6
5 = N 1 P 3 (i.e. N 1¼)
8 = N 2
10 = N 2 P 6 (i.e. N 2½)
24 = M 1 N 2 (i.e. M 1½)

If we look for examples of P 1 and P 2 (21.8 and 43.6 g), we can certainly find plausible examples at Keos; but the smaller the weight, the greater the uncertainties due to losses, and it is certain that many of the weights found in Minoan sites do not fit this series at all. It is hard to resist the conclusion that the 65.5 g unit is only one of a number of competing systems current in the Minoan world, and it may not have been the one selected by the Mycenaeans as their standard. As the difference between Linear A and Linear B in the method of expressing weight shows, the units in the system were probably rearranged, even if the basis remained constant, just as when Britain introduced decimal coinage in 1972 the pound was kept, but its relationship to the penny was changed.

Anything which could be poured, not only liquids but particulate solids like grain or seed, was measured not by weight but by volume. It is not too easy to equate these two systems, since the volume occupied by a given weight of wheat or barley will depend not only on the condition of the grain (whether husked or winnowed thoroughly) but also on its age, variety, etc.

The basic unit of volume is the cup, for there is now no doubt that this is what the sign transcribed z in fig. 44 stands for. It is almost certain that the

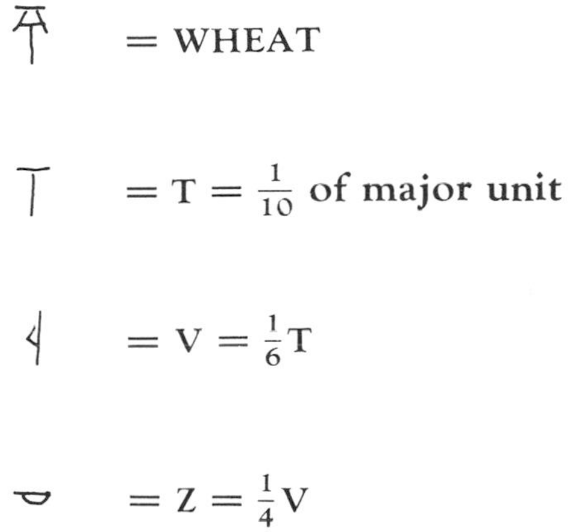

44 The Mycenaean signs for dry measure

classical word was already in use as the name of this unit: *kotylē*. Indeed, the word is still not dead in Greek, for although it is now only a learned word, Professor Marinátos once described to me how, when a dipper or scoop was found in his dig at Thera, his foreman immediately identified it as what at home in Arcadia he called *koutoúli*, clearly a dialect form of this same word.

In the classical system four *kotylai* make one *khoinix*, and since this exactly agrees with the ratio of z to v, it seems likely that v = *khoinix*. But above this level the systems differ: eight *khoinikes* make one *modios*, and six *modioi* one *medimnos*. Thus the *khoinix* is 1/48 of the major classical unit, but 1/60 of the major Mycenaean unit.

As in the case of weights, the classical values may give us at least a clue to the limits within which we ought to place the Mycenaean unit. There are again two standards, so that the *kotylē* ranges from 270 to 388 cc, the *medimnos* from 51.84 to 74.5 litres. If the *kotylē* rather than the *medimnos* continues an ancient tradition, the major Mycenaean unit will be as much as twenty-five per cent larger than the classical *medimnos* (i.e. up to 93.1 litres).

The system for liquid measure is partly the same and partly different. This is like the British 'Imperial' system which has *pint* and *quart* common to both dry and liquid measure, but thereafter distinguishes *gallon* (liquid)

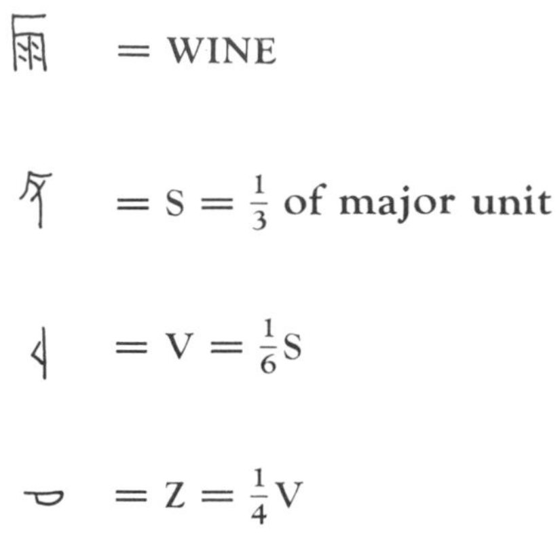

45 The Mycenaean signs for liquid measure

from *bushel* (dry). The signs transcribed V and Z in fig. 45 are identical with those in fig. 44 and must be presumed to have the same value. It therefore follows that the major unit of liquid measure has only thirty per cent of the volume of the major unit of dry measure; it contains 72 Z instead of 240 Z. The reason for this discrepancy is no doubt to be sought in the relative weights: a litre of water weighs 1 kg, but a litre of grain only about 630 g. In other words, the weight an average man can carry will represent one and a half times as much grain as liquid, and we may hazard the conjecture that if the talent (L) is a convenient load, the major units of dry and liquid measure also are probably based upon the same human standard.

In fact the attempt to give explicit values to these metric signs has been very difficult. There are to date no recognized measuring vessels found on Mycenaean sites; it is not impossible that they used wooden vessels for this purpose, since it is easy to hollow out a wooden vessel to the exact volume required, but impossible to shape a pot so accurately. Professor Marinátos, however, found what he took to be measuring vessels, in association with mills, at Thera. It may be dangerous to argue from Minoan to Mycenaean units, but these vessels are said to have volumes of about 200 and 800 cc.

In spite of the inevitable inaccuracy of hand-made pottery, especially when thrown on a wheel, it is likely that the potters will tend to concentrate on sizes appropriate to units in the system of measurement, at least for the large pots. Professor Mabel Lang (1964) carefully measured the capacity of all the intact pots recovered from the excavation of Pylos, to see if any regularity emerged. The results are not very convincing; but among the larger vessels there is some sign of clustering around the values of 2.4 l and 3.2 l. If this is not due to accident, it would appear that a figure of 0.8 l (= 800 cc) plays some part in the system of measurement. The coincidence with the figures from Thera is so close that it seems unlikely to be fortuitous.

The smallest unit in the system is unlikely to be larger than 500, nor smaller than 200 cc. This range is dictated both by practical considerations and the parallel of similar systems with known values. If 800 cc represents a significant step, it can therefore be fitted in at two levels: either 800 cc = V 1, and Z 1 then = 200 cc; or 800 cc = Z 2, and Z 1 then = 400 cc. Both of these solutions have been proposed, the first by Miss Lang and supported by Professor L. R. Palmer; the second is my modification of the value Z 1 = 500 cc originally proposed by Ventris and myself as a very rough guide in 1955. The choice between them is still not easy.

There is one useful piece of internal evidence: a Pylos tablet (Fr 1184) which specifies that Eumedes received from Kokalos 18 units of olive oil, and from Ipsewas 38 jars. The word for jar is quite certainly, in view of the drawing which accompanies it elsewhere, the Mycenaean term for what archaeologists call a 'stirrup jar' (or false-necked jar), the standard container for olive oil. It seems hard to resist the conclusion that the 38 jars were intended to hold 18 units of oil. Thus the average content of a stirrup-jar must be just under half a unit.

The rival theories, if the deduction made above is correct, give the volume of the average stirrup-jar as 6.8 l (Miss Lang) or 13.6 l (my own). But it is still not easy to choose; for stirrup-jars come in varying sizes; the large ones, which are usually thought of as containers for oil, often hold between 12 and 14 l, but there is a smaller type holding 6–7 l, examples of which were recovered from Pylos. But I think my figure on this basis is slightly the more likely.

The other argument which can be used is based upon the ration figures (see pp. 82–3). The basic ration, which is often exceeded but never reduced, is 2 T of wheat or 3¾ T of barley per month. Calculating on a month of 30 days (a reasonable approximation to the actual value of 29½ days in a lunar month), the barley ration is exactly 3 Z per day; the wheat ration is not an integer reduced to the z units, but comes out at 1.6 z per day. If we convert these according to the two theories, we have the choice of 1.2 l of barley equivalent to 0.64 l of wheat; or on Miss Lang's figures 0.6 l of barley or 0.32 l of wheat. Now it is very hard to calculate how many calories each of these rations contains, since much depends upon the type of wheat, and how the grain is prepared for eating. But I have grave doubts whether a third of a litre of wheat is an adequate daily ration for a working man, though here again we cannot be sure whether it was the only food available. In the case of Pylos slave-women, it was supplemented with an equal quantity of figs.

There is a further problem concerned with the size of plots of land, which are measured by a volume of seed-corn (see p. 110). Here too, the higher figures appear to give a more likely answer, though even they yield ridiculously small plots if the basis of our calculation is correct; the lower figures would very much increase the difficulty. Against this it must be admitted that the measuring vessels from Thera are more likely to represent 1 z than ½ z, and 1 v than ½ v. But here the fact that they belong to the Minoan civilization of Crete and not to mainland Greece ought perhaps to be taken into account. No final answer will be possible until a recognizable set of measuring vessels is found on the mainland; but for the present it seems preferable to accept the larger figures, while bearing in mind the possibility that they ought to be halved.

If the suggestion made above that the major unit of each system is a convenient human load, then the figure of 28.8 litres for the major liquid measure will be equivalent to the same number of kilograms, which, allowing for the container, brings us close to the figure of *c.* 30 kg for the talent. Unfortunately grain does not weigh as little as one third as much as water, so that the major dry unit (96 litres) must weigh considerably more than 30 kg. Perhaps this is due to the fact that a sack full of grain is easier to carry than a much smaller container full of liquid, and it is not impossible to handle sacks holding a hundredweight (= 51 kg), if they contain something that allows them to conform to the back of the carrier.

Throughout this book the larger values have been adopted.

Cereals

It is obvious that a society of any age before the Industrial Revolution was based on agriculture. But when we come to ask what sort of agriculture the Mycenaeans practised, we must remember that what we possess are not the account books of a small farmer, but the administrative records of a royal palace. We must not expect to find there records of every crop, only those which were of special concern to the king. Nor do we learn anything of how the crops were produced; the king was interested in the contributions of his dependencies, but not, it seems, in how they were produced.

We can of course supplement our meagre documentary information by archaeology. Animal bones and carbonized seeds can bear witness to the diet on which a people lived; but such finds are relatively rare and the evidence is patchy.

The tablets demonstrate that at both Knossos and Pylos there were two principal food-grains. It seemed obvious that these must be wheat and barley, which were the staple foods of classical Greece. But it is curious that during historical times the cultivation of wheat seems to have been increasing at the expense of barley, so that if we extrapolate from this trend we should expect to find that barley was the main crop of the Bronze Age. On the contrary, the Mycenaean evidence shows that the two grains were about equally plentiful; though it is not just a matter of adding up all the available figures, as will appear presently.

The identity of the two grains was guessed at an early stage, but confirmation has been slow. They are invariably recorded by means of ideograms (see fig. 46), and these are only described by the generic term *sītos* 'grain', never by the specific words for 'wheat' and 'barley'.

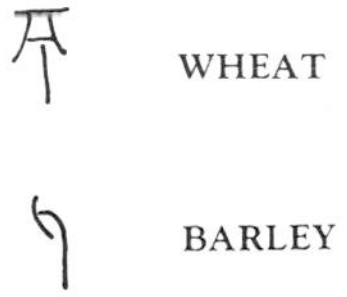

46 The ideograms for grain

Arguments have been drawn from the shape of the ideograms, for although in their Linear B forms they have become stylized, their ancestral forms of Linear A bear a little more resemblance to plants, but even so it is hard to choose between them.

The solution to this problem came from the discovery that a ration of one grain is almost double that in the other grain. There is a text (PY An 128) in which a sum in one seems to have been converted into the other by multiplying by two, though unfortunately the details are obscure and other interpretations are possible. But it is quite certain that the basic ration is 2 T units per month in one, 3¾ T units in the other. This has important consequences, for we must suppose that the nutritional value of these two rations is approximately the same. Since therefore one is nearly twice as nutritive as the other, this must be wheat; and, more important, the wheat was presumably of the 'free-threshing' type, if it yields more flour for a given volume of grain than barley. We can therefore regard these values as certain, though it does not necessarily follow that because a ration was calculated in wheat it was always paid in that grain, since there may have been a convention that two measures of barley could always replace one of wheat. Similar provisions for rations are known much later in the Roman army.

The main problem which remains to be tackled concerning grain is the use of the ideogram for 'wheat' in contexts which plainly refer to land. All through the long series of documents at Pylos which list the estates of named individuals, their size is quoted as: 'so much seed: x units of wheat'. That this is not in fact an issue of seed corn is evident from some contexts; as for instance when we are given the figures for the royal holding (Er 312), or where the land in question appears to be bearing vines and fig-trees (Er 880).

The practice of measuring land by the quantity of seed required for a sowing is well known in antiquity and has survived up to the present in some Mediterranean countries; I was told of a man in the Greek island of Naxos who owned 'two bushels of vines', i.e. a plot of land covered with vines which would have needed two bushels of seed if put down to grain. The advantage of such a measurement is that it allows for the difference in productivity of different types of land. A piece of stony hillside will be less productive, and hence sown at a lower rate, than rich valley bottom; hence there is probably no constant by which seed-measures can be converted into superficial area, except by way of average. Similarly the Greek peasant today still measures distance in terms of the time needed to cover the route; two hours' march may represent a short distance on the map if it involves much climbing and descending mountain trails, but a much longer distance across a plain.

When we come to examine the actual size of the plots described, we find that they vary between the king's estate at 30 full units (= 2,880 litres of wheat) and 1 V unit (= 1/60 unit = 1.6 litres). At any normal seeding ratio this minimum plot must be no more than garden-sized; and we must bear in mind that even this figure would be halved, if we adopted the lower value of the metric units which has been proposed (see p. 107). On the other hand, if we adopt a very low seeding ratio, then the king's estate will be very large – at all events the relationship between the maximum and minimum is fixed at a ratio of 1,800:1. It need not, however, follow that the minimum size of plot is equal to the total holding of the man concerned. We know of cases where a man holds two or more plots.

The one area for which our records are likely to be complete is the district of Sphagiānes, apparently the district within which the palace lay. For this district we have not only a complete land-register, but the same information in two separate redactions. But the area concerned is not large, and we must perhaps distinguish between the wider administrative district called Sphagiānes and the lands immediately adjacent to the settlement of that name. The first set of documents was compiled piecemeal, as the information came in; it was then copied on to larger tablets with some editing, but fortunately for us the first version was not then destroyed, and gaps in one version can often be made good from the other. The land is never described and we have no account of its exact location; the register is of tenants-in-chief and sub-tenants.

This terminology is borrowed from the feudal system of medieval Europe, and in what follows I am using as a parallel the famous English land-survey called the 'Domesday Book', which was compiled in A.D. 1086 by King William I. We must not press the parallel too far. We have no way of telling what kind of obligations were imposed in return for grants of land, nor do we know who was its ultimate owner. But the listing of the estates of important nobles, followed by lists of their tenants, follows so closely the pattern of the Mycenaean documents that conditions cannot have been totally different. The parallel will be discussed further below (p. 114).

The land is basically of two types, represented by the terms *ko-to-na ki-ti-me-na* and *ko-to-na ke-ke-me-na; ko-to-na* is *ktoinā*, a word for a piece of land which was more or less obsolete in classical Greece, though it survived with religious associations in Rhodes. The term *ktimenā* is related to words which in classical Greek mean 'to reside on' or 'settle (land)', and this etymological value accords well with the fact that such land is held partly by major land-owners in their own right, and partly by tenants. The effective value of the term is thus 'privately owned', though we must allow for the possibility that, as in Norman England, the king was the real owner, and the apparent land-owners held their fiefs at his pleasure. The other term, *ke-ke-me-na*, is more obscure; etymologically it may mean 'abandoned', 'left out of the distribution', and this would fit its effective sense, which must by contrast be 'public'. In all cases *ke-ke-me-na* land is owned by the *dāmos*, and is leased to individual holders. The word *dāmos* (classical *dēmos*) appears in this context to mean a collective body of men representing the local district; *hundred* and *shire* are so used in Domesday Book.

The public and private sectors are both treated alike in that a series of small preparatory documents was written listing individual holdings; these were then used as the basis of a revised version on two series of large tablets. The private sector is represented by the documents in the following table:

Estate owner	Preparatory	Final
Wa-na-ta-jo	Eo 211	En 609
A-ma-ru-ta	Eo 224	
*Ru-*83*	Eo 276	
A_3*-ti-jo-qo*	Eo 247	En 74
Pi-ke-re-u	Eo 160	
Qe-re-qo-ta	Eo 444	
A-da-ma-jo	Eo 351	
A-i-qe-u	Eo 471	En 659
Ra-ku-ro	Eo 281	
A-ka-ta-jo	Eo 269	
Ti-qa-jo	Eo 278	
Po-te-u	Eo 268	En 467
Pi-ri-ta-wo	Eo 371	

Thus the thirteen preparatory documents, giving in each case the tenant-in-chief and his sub-tenants (if any), were replaced by four large documents. These are not exact copies, though so far as they are preserved the figures are reproduced exactly; but spellings of names have sometimes been changed and the formulas regularized. For instance, in the estate of *Qe-re-qo-ta*, Eo 444 lists five sub-tenancies, En 659 only four; it seems likely that Eo 444 listed two holdings of one man separately, and they have been combined into a single entry in the revised version. En 609 must be the first tablet of the second version, since it has added a general heading: 'Sphagiāniā: so many *da-ma-te: DA* 40; and so many *telestai* are included: 14 men.' The trouble is that, as the table above shows, there are actually only thirteen tenants-in-chief. Either a document listing the fourteenth is missing from each series; or the broken documents have been incorrectly matched. But if the fourteenth Eo tablet were deliberately suppressed before the second version was completed, this would account more naturally for the facts. What is extraordinary about this change of fourteen to thirteen, is that in another series of documents listing land-holdings and charges upon them, exactly the same thing seems to have happened: Es 650 lists fourteen names, Es 644 and the thirteen other Es tablets have only thirteen. It is of course conceivable that in the course of a year one member of a group of fourteen might die; that the same thing should happen in two different groups is a strange coincidence. And why is the number fourteen in the two cases?

There is, however, a further complication. In each of the preparatory (Eo) tablets, the tenant is specified as holding his tenancy from (or at the hands of) the land-owner named at the head of the tablet. This superfluous verbiage is pruned away by the compiler of the revised version. But on Eo 224, the estate of *A-ma-ru-ta*, only four of the tenants hold their land from him; two hold from *Pa-ra-ko*, one from *Ta-ta-ro*, and this is ignored in the revised version. *Pa-ra-ko* recurs on the other group of documents dealing with 'public' land, and is in one place (Ep 613.11) described as a land-holder. *Ta-ta-ro* equally reappears as a tenant on 'public' land (Ep 301.6). But if we count both, the total rises to fifteen; perhaps only *Pa-ra-ko* was counted, since he alone was a 'land-holder'.

The entry 'so many *da-ma-te: DA* 40' is also puzzling. If we count not tenancies, but tenants, it appears that there are twenty-seven, but one of them is already counted as a tenant-in-chief; thus the total number of persons holding land in this series of documents is thirty-nine, and since we have just seen that the thirteen *telestai* are in fact reckoned as fourteen, this gives the total as forty. But why are the tenants counted as *DA*, not as persons? The word *da-ma-te* looks as if it must be a plural noun, and, if so, the word for 'so many' is feminine: there is only one feminine noun known to later Greek which in the plural would fit this spelling: it is *damartes*, but unfortunately it means not 'parcels of land' but 'wives'. This seems an unlikely development of sense, though perhaps it is not entirely to be excluded.

The second set of documents (Ep, preparatory texts Eb) relates to 'public' land, and this is said to be held 'from the community (*dāmos*)'. The size of the individual holdings is small, though some larger estates are listed under the title *ka-ma*. The word obviously relates to some special sort of holding, but both its exact form and its meaning remain obscure. Its holders, who include persons of some importance, are apparently under obligation to perform some sort of service, and, although this is not expressly stated, it is reasonable to assume that this service is in return for their holding of lands. Unfortunately the nature of the service is a matter of dispute, and no satisfactory solution has been proposed. There are three verbs used to describe it, one of which is apparently the generic term for all such acts; this is *wo-ze*, the etymological meaning of which is roughly 'works', but it obviously does not refer to cultivation of the land. The classical words from this root (*rezō*, *erdō*) have also the specialized meaning 'sacrifice', and the related noun *orgas* was used for a piece of sacred land. It is therefore tempting to suppose that the obligations imposed upon these land-holders were of a religious nature; similar holdings associated with religious duties are known in classical Greece.

There is a list of holders of public land (Ep 301) who are specifically called 'plot-holders' and this includes a number of the 'tenants-in-chief' of the private land. But the majority of tenants in this class are the 'servants of the deity', both men and women who seem to be the dominant class in this area of Sphagiānes. Of those persons given titles, the great majority are religious, though they include one or two tradesmen and some servants of Amphimedes, who seems to be a Follower. One of the largest estates is held by the priestess Eritha, and this is of particular interest since it is the subject of a dispute.

The entry as usual exists in two versions which differ slightly in wording. The preparatory text (Eb 297) runs: 'The Priestess holds and claims that the deity holds the (obscure word), but the holders of plots [claim] that he [or she] holds leases of public plots.' The final version (Ep 704.5–6) runs: 'Eritha the Priestess holds and claims that the deity holds the (obscure word), but the community says that he [or she] holds a lease of public plots.' There is no way of telling whether the deity is male or female, but there is a general rule in later Greece that gods are served primarily by a priest, goddesses by a priestess; hence we may assume that the deity is here a goddess. The obscure word is clearly some special kind of property right, which is also held by Amphimedes the Follower; it is tempting to continue with the modern parallel and suggest a meaning 'freehold'. But it must not be forgotten that these translations are at best very loose approximations to the real values, which we have little means of making more precise. None the less, the fact in dispute is whether the land is subject to a 'lease', and this term too, though we cannot define it accurately, suggests that land so held involved the holder in some obligation.

However, no attempt seems to be made to resolve the dispute; the king's agent responsible for compiling the record is content to record the fact. Now we can obtain some enlightenment by comparing this whole set of Mycenaean documents with the English Domesday Book compiled by the agents of King William I, shortly after his conquest of England. In the year A.D. 1086, he sent commissioners throughout the length and breadth of England to prepare a detailed report on the amount of land in each locality, how it was farmed, and who held it. Studies of these vastly longer and more detailed records show that it was compiled by a series of itinerant commissions, which held sessions in all the principal towns, and recorded in Latin the evidence given by the land-holders. At least one series of preparatory documents was made, and these were then edited and copied into ledgers by the court officials at Winchester. We shall hardly be wrong in seeing in the Mycenaean documents the work of a royal commissioner performing a very similar service at Sphagiānes. Indeed some linguistic peculiarities of the preliminary version, such as an apparently redundant 'and' following the tenant's name, may well reflect the original deposition by the tenant himself: 'I am So-and-so the such-and-such, *and* I hold...' This appears in the record as: 'So-and-so the such-and-such, *and* he holds...' But by the time of the final redaction this has been altered and the 'and' is dropped from the formula, except for some cases where it has been carelessly carried over from the preliminary version.

Now it is by no means unusual for the Domesday Book to record disputes about ownership, and in strikingly similar language. For instance at one point we read, translating the Latin: 'The Viscount's officers say that this half hide [a measure of land] belongs to the King's estate, but the Hundred [the local community] and the Shire [the wider community] say that King Edward gave it to this man and they have his seal on it.' Another quotation will illustrate even better the processes involved in making such a register: 'Count Godwin bought it from Azor and gave it to his wife, so that she could live off it so long as she remained at Berkeley. For he was unwilling to consume anything from the manor itself to avoid the destruction of the Abbacy. Edward holds this land in the estate of Wiltshire, unjustly as the County alleges, because it does not belong to any estate. No one gave an account of this manor to the King's commissioners, nor did any of them come to this session.' Here too we have the technical language of feudal land-holding with terms like hide (*hida* in Latin), estate (*firma*), manor (*manerium*), Hundred (*hundreda*), Shire (*scira*) and County (*comitatus*). If we had as little other evidence as we have for the Mycenaean documents, we would certainly be arguing about the exact meaning of these terms, just as we are about the Mycenaean ones. The holdings of *e to ni jo* (freehold?), *ka ma*, *ko-to-na* (plot), *o-na-to* ('lease'), and so on clearly had specific meanings for the Mycenaean officials, hard though they are for us to reconstruct. Equally Domesday Book lists men in several different categories and the task of establishing their rank and functions has so far defeated scholars.

There are several other series of tablets dealing with land, but in these cases the scribes gave even less information about the area with which they deal. One of these (Ea) seems to have been divided into two parts for filing, but both seem to deal with the same individuals and hence presumably the same area. The persons listed here are predominantly tradesmen: we meet sewing-men (tailors or saddlers?), a messenger, a wheelwright, an unguent-maker (perfumer?), a priest, and men in the service of the *Lāwāgetās*. It would seem to follow that these estates must have been close to the palace. It is curious that while many of the estates of Sphagiānes were held by women with religious titles, here none of the holders can be shown to have been female, and very likely they were all men. It would seem that only in the sphere of religion had women achieved independent status.

Another sort of land-register is again concerned with religion (Es). There is no indication of place, and most of the names do not occur elsewhere; if the *Alektruōn* of this list is the Follower of that name, the son of *Etewoklewēs,* he is attached to one of the northern sectors of the coastguards (see p. 176), and there is another name on the list which seems to have associations with northern areas. But neither of these are firm evidence. The basic list of holdings (Es 650) enumerates fourteen estates, of very different sizes; the largest is more than twenty times the size of the smallest.

In the remaining lists the total of fourteen land-holders is reduced to thirteen by the omission of the last name on the list; the amount of his holding has been deleted on the basic list. Each list specifies contributions: in one case these are said to be annual, but the recipient is not named, in the other no indication of frequency is given, but the same four recipients of the contribution are listed. Of the four recipients Poseidon gets the lion's share; the other three get equal shares which are never more than an eighth of Poseidon's and usually much less. Of these three two were undoubtedly high officials; the third is a group, since it is in the plural, and might be either human or divine. Since it comes before the two high officials, perhaps it is a group of cult servants, possibly in the cult of Poseidon. The curious thing about these various assessments is that although the holders of the large estates contribute more than the small holders, there is no observable regularity in the figures. It is rather like a list of donations to a charity; the wealthy of course give more, but some of the poor are proportionately more generous. Since Mycenaean tax-collectors were certainly able to perform complicated sums to distribute totals according to a regular pattern of proportions, it is strange that they did not do so here.

The fact that some land is registered in the palace archives presumably means that the king had some sort of interest in it, but he is never quoted as the owner, though in a monarchical society all property is ultimately held by others at the king's pleasure. But we have one document (Er 312) which lists 'the royal demesne', using a different word for 'estate' (*temenos*) which to the classical Greeks was restricted to estates owned by a deity. The size is large (30 units), but even more interesting is what follows. The demesne of the *Lāwāgetās* is listed next at 10 units; then land of the *telestai* at 30 units with the note that there are three *telestai,* each therefore has an estate of the same order of magnitude as the *Lāwāgetās,* which is one third the size of the king's. Finally we have the waste (uncultivated land?) called *Wo-ro-ki-jo-ne-jo* (a place-name?) amounting to 6 units.

This document must clearly be read with another (Un 718) which is a list of offerings to Poseidon and has already been discussed in Chapter 5 (see p. 72). The four contributors in this are *E-ke-ra*$_2$*-wo,* the community (*dāmos*), the *Lāwāgetās*, and the *ka-ma Wo-ro-ki-jo-ne-jo*, which can hardly be anything but the 'waste' of the other document. The three *telestai* may well constitute the Community of this district; and, as shown in Chapter 5 (see p. 71), *E-ke-ra*$_2$*-wo* may be the name of the king himself. If so, we have the same four parties involved in a contribution to Poseidon on a scale somewhat similar to the land-holders of the Es series discussed above.

A second tablet (Er 880) is badly damaged, but the heading can be plausibly restored to translate: '*E-ke-ra*$_2$*-wo* has as private property the planted estate of *Sa-ra-pe-do*.' This place name is the same as that quoted on the offering tablet Un 718. Then follow two lines giving the size of two very large estates, but their descriptions are missing and the figures are incomplete; fortunately at the end we have the entry 'total 94 units', which must be the sum of these two estates. The two intervening entries apparently give the number of plants, in one case possibly vines, in the other certainly fig-trees. The numbers are incomplete but neither is less than 1,100. It is curious that the total should be 94 units, for the same figure emerges from the addition of five estates apparently inspected by a high official on Eq 213. For comparison the total at Sphagiānes seems to be around 102 units.

At Knossos there is nothing similar to the Pylos tablets of the E series which we have been discussing, though some of the terminology of land-tenure reappears there; the same can now be said of Tiryns on the basis of two recently discovered fragments. Thus while there was doubtless some special reason for the surveys of certain areas at Pylos, it is quite likely that the unrecorded situation at Knossos was similar. There is a list of persons (Uf) who are apparently recorded as holding estates at various places in Crete, and some of these may be orchards or the like.

We do, however, have some records which must relate to the grain harvest, though the series is so fragmentary that we cannot form any clear picture from it. One of the few complete tablets runs: 'Men of Lyktos 246.7 units of wheat; men of Tylisos 261 units of wheat; men of Lato 30.5 units of wheat.' Assuming that the size of the unit is correctly calculated in the discussion at the beginning of this chapter, this would represent a figure of around 19 tons for Tylisos; it is impossible to calculate the land required for this crop accurately, but this amount might be produced on less than 10 hectares; even if half the land were fallow each year, the total is still perfectly reasonable. Other towns are recorded as producing olives as well as grain; this combination may reflect the practice, still be seen in Greece, of growing grain on the land between the olive-trees. But the most extraordinary figure for wheat is for the area called *Dawos*, which we have good reason to think was in the fertile plain of the Messará in the south of the island. Here the tablet is broken so that the numeral is incomplete, but it unquestionably began with 10,000 units. Even assuming that no further figures followed, this would amount to some 775 tons. In modern times the central area of Crete, which includes all the places we are discussing, produces more than 10,000 tons of wheat, so these figures, though high, are not by any means surprising.

The absence of any record of the grain harvest at Pylos is doubtless due to the time of the year at which the destruction of the archives occurred (see p. 191). But we can infer something about the scale of production from the rations issued to the slave-women (see p. 82). A broken tablet (Fg 253) is probably a total of the rations issued each month to these women; it gives a figure of 192.7 units of wheat, or around 14 tons. This implies the need for an annual production of about 170 tons for this purpose alone. The modern figure for wheat in Messenia, roughly the same area as the kingdom of Pylos, about 22,000 tons.

There are also a number of documents giving rations, or perhaps rather payments, in barley. At Knossos the rations are quoted (Am 819) for a work-group composed of 18 men and 8 boys as 97.5 units of barley. Now it is of course impossible to solve an equation containing two unknowns on the basis of a single sum like this. But in practice certain restraints can be predicted: each of the rations must be an integer when expressed in the smallest unit in the metric system (Z = 1/240 of a unit); the proportion between a man's and a boy's ration must be reasonable (e.g. the man's ration will hardly be more than five times the boy's), and the boy's must not be greater than the man's. The result of some simple calculations shows that there is only one plausible solution: the whole group receives the same ration, namely Z 90 = T 3¾. This has the useful quality that it permits the issue of the rations on a daily basis (Z 3), since the lunar month of 29½ days will presumably be counted as 30 days for this purpose.

Some of the Pylos barley lists seem to imply rations as small as Z 3, so that these are presumably daily rations. Others have larger amounts: some demand V 1 (= Z 4), while others may rise as high as V 5, but we are not told the period for which they are reckoned. If the documents were better preserved, it would be easier to see the basis of the calculation. The ration of V 5 emerges from the figures on Fn 79, and it is likely that three other fragments belong to one or more similar lists. The rations when converted to V units, all fall into the following series: 5, 10, 15, 30, 40, 105; the only common factor is 5. There is one apparent exception where T 5 V 1 would give V 31; but closer inspection shows that the last stroke of the 5 is dubious, and T 4 V 1 would give 25, another multiple of 5. If V 5 were a daily ration, this would give a monthly ration of T 25, which is hardly probable, if the basic ration can be as low as T 3¾. It is difficult to see any other solution than that this group is rationed for a 5-day period on the scale of V 1 (= Z 4) per day.

Spices

The cereal diet which formed the staple food of the Mycenaeans would have been very dull, if it could not be enhanced by the addition of flavouring. It is therefore not surprising that the documents refer frequently to substances which seem basically to be spices, flavouring ingredients added to food. We must note, however, that some of them are also aromatic, and these may have been used also for their perfume. This is one of the few subjects which is recorded in our small archive of tablets from Mycenae, and it may be convenient to go through the list recorded there, adding comments on the use of these substances at the other sites.

Some of these names are familiar to us from classical Greek; others are doubtful or completely obscure. In several cases it is easy enough to identify the Greek word, but impossible to be sure which of the many varieties, often even species, covered by the word in later Greek is meant here. It is possible that some may have been imported from overseas; but where the quantities are large they must surely have been locally grown. In Crete a considerable amount of land seems to have been devoted to the cultivation of these luxuries.

One of the most common spices is coriander, that is, the seeds of an umbelliferous plant which are still used today in cookery. The Mycenaean form of the name is slightly different from the classical, but there can be no doubt it is the same word: if it is to be reconstructed as *koriadnon*, it has a pattern curiously similar to the name of Minos' daughter *Ariadnē*, and it is plain how this might be corrupted later to *koriannon* or *koriandron*. At Mycenae it appears to be required (if that is the right interpretation of the Ge series) in amounts of about 19 litres per person. Much larger figures appear at Knossos, and the total of coriander issued amounts to more than 7,500 litres; the receipts recorded are much smaller than this, and we cannot tell how the books were balanced. If such large quantities were required it must have been grown on a considerable scale. The one clear reference at Pylos records 6 units, or 576 litres, among a list of produce given by a senior official to a perfume-maker; this was presumably used for its aromatic property, though the smell of coriander is not attractive to us now. There are probably other amounts listed under the abbreviation *ko*.

Cumin is easily recognized, for it is unchanged in the classical form; the word is alleged to be Semitic. The quantities are much smaller, and it is not mentioned at either of the two main sites.

Fennel again is clear, for it differs from one of the classical forms only by the addition of a *w* (*marathwon*); it is the plant which gave its name to the plain of Marathon in Attica, though I have not seen any fennel growing there now. At Mycenae it is abbreviated to *ma*, and the same sign is used at Knossos in a context which suggests we may be dealing with a spice (Ga 953); but there is a complication because the sign *ma* is almost identical with the sign for 'wool', and the two are sometimes confused. It occurs again at Pylos (Un 219) but in an unverifiable context.

Sesame is a plant well known in Greece today, for its pounded seeds are used to make the sweet called *halvá*. The name is another Semitic word.

Celery is clear enough, but since the quantities are weighed, it must be the seeds that are meant; as much as 2 kg is recorded.

Mint is counted by means of a abbreviation, so that it is hard to guess in what form it was used.

Garden cress appears to get one mention; the seeds of this too were used as a condiment.

A mention of pennyroyal now seems to be due to a wrong reading, and ought perhaps to be withdrawn, though it would not be surprising in such a list.

The Greek word for safflower occurs a number of times and is distinguished into two sorts; white, which is measured, and red, which is weighed. The explanation is that there are two parts of the plant which can be used; the pale seeds and the red florets. The florets have been used to make a dye, hence the Latin name *Carthamus tinctorius;* but there is ancient evidence that they were also used as a relish. The oil, extracted from the seeds, is also known to have been used for culinary purposes.

More difficult is the mention of rush, since there are a number of plants known by this name, and in one place (MY Ge 602.5) the entry reads 'both rushes' suggesting that there were two varieties even to the Mycenaeans. Another epithet applied to it cannot be certainly identified. The best suggestion is that it is sweet rush or gingergrass.

Some plants not found in the Mycenae lists must be added. At both Knossos and Pylos we have references to a plant name which continues in use in the form *Cyperus*, but this is a broad term botanically covering a number of plants; it is probably the fragrant *Cyperus rotundus* which is meant, as its chief use, at least at Pylos, is as an aromatic for the making of perfumed oil.

Another plant called *ki-ta-no* was obscure until a young Spanish scholar, J. L. Melena, called attention to an entry in an ancient lexicon which showed that *kritanos* was another name for the turpentine tree, and the Mycenaean spelling could represent a variant form of this word. The tree is strictly *Pistacia terebinthus*, but the name may cover others of the *Pistacia* family; it is a member of the family (*Pistacia Vera*) which produces the pistachio nuts which are still widely eaten in Greece. If the enormous quantities of *ki-ta-no* mentioned in the Knossos tablets refer to the actual nuts, not just the edible kernels, this will be readily intelligible.

Finally there is an item, again recorded only at Knossos, which can be reconstructed as the Greek word *phoinikion*. But its meaning is not easy to guess. One meaning is 'Phoenician'; but were the Phoenicians of Syria, later such adventurous traders, already so called? And what was this product which the Cretans called by their name? It can hardly have been imported from there since the records show that it was grown in certain areas of Crete. The word was also used to mean 'dark red'; but this too offers no clue. The noun *phoinix* also means a palm-tree, and it seems to be so used in the description of furniture (see p. 148). Dates therefore seemed a possible identification of the product; but unfortunately although date-palms may grow in Crete, the climate does not allow the fruit to ripen. *Phoinikion* thus remains a mystery.

Olives

The domesticated olive-tree is still today one of the staples of Greek agriculture. Its origins are unknown, but olive pollen was identified in samples from the western Peloponnese dating back as far as the twentieth century B.C. Surprisingly the palaeobotanical records showed a great increase in the proportion of olive pollen after this date, reaching a peak around the tenth century. There has been much argument over the interpretation of this fact, but it must not be forgotten that these analyses are conducted on a percentage basis. During the Mycenaean period the pollen of weeds associated with grain cultivation was increasing; the grains themselves do not unfortunately leave a trace in the pollen record. The sudden drop in population after the thirteenth century will have automatically reduced the amount of land under annual cultivation, so these weeds will have died out as the land reverted to natural vegetation. But the olive-tree is very long-lived, and the olive orchards will thus have continued to produce fruit for some centuries with the minimum of attention, for this tree has the advantage that its labour requirement is very small, except for the short season of the harvesting of the crop.

The main disadvantage of the olive is that the size of the crop varies very much from year to year, since not only does a tree bear heavy crops only in alternate years, but the trees of a whole district seem regularly to be in phase. On the other hand the fruit can easily be stored in jars, and the expressed oil keeps well. It can be used for cooking, lighting and washing. There is some archaeological evidence for lamps, and we may assume culinary use. But in the absence of soap the ancient world made much use of olive oil for the toilet, and it was a normal practice to anoint the body with oil after exercise.

There are two different types of olives recorded on the Knossos tablets, where the abbreviations *a* and *ti* are attached to the olive ideogram. It is tempting to suggest that these represent Greek words for 'wild' (*agrios*) and 'cultivated' (*tithasos*), but the fruit of the wild olive is of such poor quality that it seems unlikely to have been harvested in quantity, and the *a* type accounts for the majority of the olives recorded. Whatever the words so abbreviated, they must refer to different sorts of olive, or possibly to olives picked at different stages of ripeness. Dawos, the area in southern Crete which produces such large amounts of wheat, also produces about 9,000 litres of olives, in the proportion of 7 of *a* type to 2 of *ti* type. Olives are sometimes listed along with figs or barley, which again suggests that they are for eating.

Figs

The fig is another popular crop in Greece, and we have ample evidence of its importance in the Mycenaean diet. The rations of the Pylos slave-women include a volume of figs equal to that of wheat; and since fresh figs would have been available for only a short season, while the rations are calculated on a monthly basis, it seems likely that these figs were dried and used all the year round. At Knossos small quantities of figs are issued for what are apparently religious offerings, along with barley, olive oil and wine (Fs). Larger quantities, such as 7,200 litres, must represent deliveries of fruit. A badly damaged tablet (Gv 862) refers to 1,770 fig-trees. An official at Pylos appears to have a title (*opisukos*) which must mean something like 'overseer of figs'; but the contexts in which this title appears do not suggest that his duties were restricted to figs. Official titles all too often conceal the real function of the holder.

Wine

The vine is a native plant of the Aegean basin, though the date of its domestication cannot easily be fixed, since it is hard to distinguish wild and cultivated varieties on the basis of such botanical specimens as are known. The Greek name, in Mycenaean *woinos*, is a member of a group of words

47 Olive trees near Phaistos

for 'wine' widely spread over the Mediterranean and Near East; the name for the vine, *ampelos*, not directly attested in Mycenaean, though a personal name may be derived from it, is also believed to be a borrowing from some Mediterranean language. Wine is usually represented by an ideogram (see fig. 48), which is thought to represent a vine growing upon a wooden frame. There is another word in Mycenaean for vines, which we should

48 The ideogram for wine

not have understood, but for the fact that it is quoted by an ancient dictionary. A Knossos tablet (Gv 863) refers to 420 vines and 104 fig-trees, and a special ideogram associated with the vines occurs elsewhere. A damaged tablet at Pylos (Er 880) also refers to at least 1,100 vines, and again the next entry is fig-trees.

Wine does not figure in the ordinary ration lists and may have been something of a luxury. But we do have a document from Pylos (Gn 428) which records the issue of small quantities; the highest figure is 48 litres, issued to an individual, though he may of course be the representative of a group. Two other groups receive quantities as small as 9.6 litres each. A large building in the palace complex at Áno Englianós containing large jars was identified by the excavators as a wine-store, and this was confirmed by the presence of sealings bearing the ideogram for wine; one of these also bears the word 'honeyed'.

At Knossos a broken tablet (Gm 840) probably gives stores or receipts from the last vintage, since the figures are large: the highest is about 4,800 litres, and the total of the four entries amount to over 14,000 litres. These figures would not have been much reduced by the issues of wine on the Fs tablets, where the amounts are small. We can assume that much of the wine was drunk at Knossos. The area south of Knossos is today one of the chief wine-growing areas in Crete.

Bee-keeping

One of the familar sights in Greece is the collections of bee-hives, often painted light blue, to be found on uncultivated mountain slopes wherever there is an abundance of thyme or other wild plants which can supply nectar. The honey of Hymettos is justly famous. It is no surprise therefore to find evidence of bee-keeping among the Mycenaeans. The title 'bee-keeper' appears among the Pylos land-tenure documents (Ea series), and several people are said to hold leases from him. His description is not exactly in the classical form, for it is derived from the word for 'honey', not

49 Vineyards near Knossos

the word for 'bee'. But there is no reason to doubt that he was a person of some importance, perhaps really an official in charge of honey production. Some similar significance must be borne by another title (*me-ri-da-ma-te*), which combines the word for 'honey' with another meaning something like 'chief', 'overseer'; as many as five of these officials are mentioned at one place, so this cannot be an exalted rank.

The chief context in which honey appears in our documents is religious. A series at Knossos (Gg) shows large jars of honey being sent as offerings to various deities, amongst whom is Eleuthia of Amnisos (see p. 98). Another series (Fs), which may well have a religious purpose, records small quantities of barley, figs, oil, flour and wine, and then on the reverse many tablets have an entry of honey, usually in very small amounts. The religious association is confirmed by the only tablet at Pylos which directly mentions honey (Un 718); here a quantity of 4.8 litres figures among the offerings of *E-ke-ra$_2$-wo* to Poseidon. The 'honeyed' wine of Pylos has already been mentioned (p. 124).

Livestock

The horse seems to have been one of the innovations brought into Greece by the proto-Greeks, but one must remember it was a small breed more like a modern pony. Our knowledge of horses derives almost entirely from their appearance on documents dealing with chariots (see pp. 164–71). There is no evidence of the sources from which these horses were drawn, though a small tablet from Knossos (Ca 895) shows foals associated with

50 Knossos tablet (Ca 895) showing horses, asses and their foals

mares and stallions, and the equivalents for asses. At Pylos we read of a man who held various large parcels of land, one of them 'on account of the horse' (Ea 59.5); but we are left in total ignorance of the connexion between the horse and the holding, and we can only speculate that he was an official in charge of horse-breeding. A quantity of cyperus is also attributed to 'horse' (Fa 16); perhaps in this context it means galingale, which is eaten by horses in Homer. It does not seem necessary to follow L. R. Palmer's suggestion that 'Horse' is here the name of a god.

Oxen are not recorded on the tablets in large numbers, though a casual reference at Pylos to 90 oxherds may give a better idea of the numbers. Since they were the only domesticated animal which could be employed on heavy work, such as ploughing, we are probably justified in assuming that every community kept an adequate supply, but that these did not appear in the royal archives. It is possible to make an indirect estimate of the number in the kingdom of Pylos by noting that each of the sixteen administrative districts were assessed for a contribution of ox-hides (Ma tablets). The total number required annually by the palace is 234 hides. It follows that the kingdom must have contained at least 1,200 head of cattle to permit such a tribute, and the number may well have been much higher, for some skins must surely have been left in private hands to supply leather.

At Knossos we meet working oxen, and at Pylos men called 'yoke-men', who are presumably drivers of ox-teams. But a truly remarkable series of documents from Knossos (Ch) lists the names of individual ox-drivers and the names of their two oxen. What is important about this is that most of the names are clearly intelligible as Greek words: Dapple, Dusky, Noisy, Whitefoot are rough equivalents of some of the words used. This fact establishes beyond any serious doubt that the ordinary farmers of Mycenaean Crete spoke Greek; for although there are many personal names on the Knossos tablets which appear not to be of the Greek type, as might be expected if a considerable population of Minoan origin survived, the fact that oxen are named in Greek proves that the Greeks in Crete were not merely a small aristocracy dominating a non-Greek peasantry.

In the late 1950s J. T. Killen (see p. 21) began work as a research student in Cambridge under my direction. The subject which he tackled was a big one, though I did not appreciate how important his work would turn out to be until it was well advanced. He set out to study the great collection of tablets from Knossos which deal with sheep; there are over 800 tablets in this series, though each one deals with no more than a single flock. Still it is evident from even a cursory study that the total of sheep listed runs to close on 100,000.

We had long since established that the sheep were divided into rams and Fig 51
ewes, since the ideogram for sheep is normally given the special marks

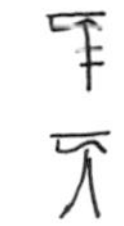
RAM
EWE

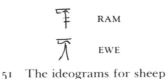

51 The ideograms for sheep

which indicate male or female sex. But we were alarmed by the preponderance of rams, which, as any sheep farmer will tell you, is nonsense for actual flocks. There were also a number of other types of sheep indexed, which we could not identify. It is to Killen's credit that he discovered the solution to this puzzle, and in so doing revealed one of the important sources of wealth in the Mycenaean kingdom of Crete.

The problem of the excessive rams was really very simple, once you know something about how sheep-farming was practised before modern times. Rams were kept only for breeding purposes, and did not need to be numerous; but for wool-production the males were castrated and these wethers, as they are then called, formed the bulk of the flocks. It was clear that the Mycenaean scribes had no separate sign for castrated male, and the mark of masculinity was applied to wethers, just as it is applied to bulls who are said to be 'workers' – i.e. oxen. Further imbalance between the sexes was also caused by the habit of totalling male and female as male: a common enough practice at the grammatical level, where 'men' is often construed to include women, but we were not prepared for it when applied to ideograms.

On this basis Killen (1964) was able to construct a rational explanation of the records. For if the main wool-producing flocks were wethers, there would need to be separate breeding flocks to provide replacements. These Killen identified from lists of ewes accompanied by sheep qualified by an abbreviation *ki;* whatever the word so abbreviated, their numbers and the way they are subordinated to the ewe entries prove that *ki* sheep must in fact be lambs. Moreover, in order to manage the flocks of wethers efficiently, the central authority must annually be informed of the numbers needed to bring the flock up to notional strength, and it is useful to have an idea of the age of the sheep in the flock; in particular the manager needs to know how many old sheep there are, and how many are young animals, of this or the previous year. The mysterious abbreviations were thus solved by Killen as words meaning 'old', 'young', 'this year's' and 'last year's'. Like all convincing solutions it looks very easy when you see it; it was a brilliant piece of deduction to have arrived at this result.

Now among the vast set of records, by which the administration at Knossos controlled its flocks spread out over much of central Crete, is a series of tablets dealing with sheep and wool. Wool is measured by a special unit, but fortunately the unit is divided into three sub-units, and the sub-unit is written with the sign of the weight series (M) which has the approximate value of 1 kg. The unit therefore has a value of around 3 kg. The tablets record both the target figure for the flock and the actual performance. The target is one unit of wool for every four sheep, i.e. about

750 g per sheep; this agrees well with the quantity expected from sheep in medieval times, when farming conditions were similar. But the breeding flocks also yielded wool, though here the ratio is very different, namely one unit of wool for every ten sheep, and this will also fit well with the actual yield, for the lambs will produce no wool in their first spring, so that the real ratio is more like one unit from every five ewes. Shortfall in the amount actually sent in is also carefully recorded, though we do not know what administrative action was taken if a flock failed to meet its target.

Another of the problems presented by these tablets has still not been completely solved. About two-thirds of the tablets record simply the name of the man responsible for the flock – it may perhaps be rash to term him 'shepherd' in our sense of the word – and the administrative area in which it was located. We must not suppose that all the flocks attributed to, let us say, Phaistos were actually on and around the hill where the town was built; the administrative area of Phaistos probably covered much of the western end of the Messará plain. But roughly one third of the tablets have a further entry in the top line, which is a man's name, usually but not always in the genitive case. There are also entries at this point which appear to be adjectives substituting for the genitive.

It would have been easy to conjecture that these men were the officials responsible for supervising the management of the flocks or collecting the wool; but this would leave the larger number of flocks without any manager, and, more worrying, the flocks attributed to the same man are not all grouped in the same area, but are widely distributed over the kingdom. Killen's researches have shown that the flocks without the additional name must be royal property; hence the remainder are in some sense not royal, though the mere fact of their inclusion in the palace archives shows that the king had an interest in their management. The best theory so far is that these men represented persons, presumably important members of the court, for whom the king needed to provide an income; and he did this by assigning to them the produce of certain flocks. As we shall see, this private concession applied not only to flocks, but equally to their wool and the textiles made from them. One at least of the beneficiaries of this concession seems to have been the goddess Potnia (see p. 93); but the exact status of the small number of human names in this category is still obscure.

The sheep records from Pylos differ in several ways. The most obvious is that the small tablets for each flock, if the information was collected in the same way, have been copied on to large tablets listing up to 25 flocks each. Then there are no details of breeding, nor is the flock broken down by age as it is sometimes at Knossos. But perhaps most significantly, there is no wool. This can mean only one thing: the spring sheep-shearing, which is usually in April, had not taken place. Such records as we have, are therefore likely to be an abstract of the state of the flocks in the previous year, and the information on this year's events has not yet been received. This agrees with the deduction (see p. 191) that Pylos was destroyed in the early spring.

Two facts are fairly well established. The great centres of sheep-raising are in the north of the Hither Province, especially the Kiparissía river valley, and on the west side of the Messenian valley in the Further Province. These areas are particularly suited for large numbers of flocks, and there is reason to think that sheep were probably bred in the Further Province and used as replacements for the flocks of the Hither Province. Secondly, the proportion of entries containing a second personal name in the genitive is much higher than at Knossos. The men who are named in this connexion are only four: *We-da-ne-u*, *A-ko-so-ta*, *A-ke-o* and *A-pi-me-de*. Of these the first two are undoubtedly high officials, the first perhaps the name of the *Lāwāgetās* (see p. 72); the other two are less well known, but the last is certainly an important land-holder. It would seem therefore that these are not just officials in charge of the management of flocks, but, as at Knossos, persons of high rank to whom is assigned the production of wool from some of the royal flocks.

Goats at Pylos are indexed on the same series of tablets as sheep. They were kept in much the same way in large flocks, and although we do not seem to have any records, we must assume that goats' hair was used, very much as wool; for comparison, in the 1950s Greece was producing over 2,000 tons annually of goats' hair.

At Knossos the goats are much less numerous than the sheep, though individual flocks are often large; one of 230 female goats is mentioned (C 911.4), there are also traces of breeding-flocks (e.g. C 7088). Goats too

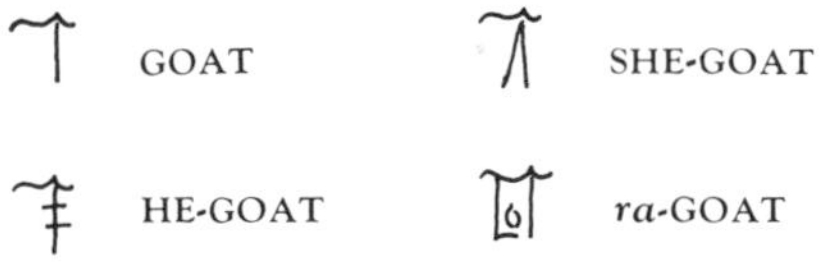

52 The ideograms for goats

are one of the species listed on the tablets dealing with the distant areas of Crete. But the most interesting possibility is that the native Cretan wild goat, the *agrími*, was hunted. A group of tablets (Mc) lists various places in Crete as contributing goats, horns and an unidentified commodity. The goats are distinguished into *ra*-goats and she-goats, the former being rather more numerous. Since *ra*-goats are contrasted with females, they are presumably male, but the abbreviation must be intended to distinguish some other feature, since male goats are indicated by a different variant of the sign (see fig. 52). A join between fragments (C 7064) has given us the word *agria* 'wild' applied to male and female goats; it is apparently not in the masculine gender as might be expected. But this is not followed by the special form of the goat sign with the abbreviation *ra*.

The problems of the Mc series remain unsolved. It would be possible to regard this as recording the product of the hunting of these creatures; but the goats themselves might be in fact only their skins; and the horns are clearly a product. The wild goat has extremely large curving horns, often measuring 70 cm in length. But the number of horns involves a problem: we should expect each carcase, whether male or female, to yield two horns, but the total number of horns is never more, and is usually about 10% less, than the number of '*ra*' carcases. We can perhaps account for some diminution by saying that some animals might be expected to have damaged horns; and perhaps the horns of the female were not suitable for whatever purpose was envisaged. But it is still true that each animal has two horns, so that however we look at it the figures are too low by a factor of two. Possibly the purpose for which they were required was such that only right or left horns, which would have opposite curvature, were acceptable.

Evans (1935, 832–6) speculated that the purpose of these goat products was the manufacture of the composite bow. There is some archaeological evidence for these weapons, which are made by gluing strips of horn between layers of wood to give much greater springiness to the bow. Actual specimens are known from contemporary Egypt. Hence the horns of the wild goat would have been much sought after for this purpose. Evans explained the unknown commodity in the same way; all we can say about it

53 Products of the Cretan wild goat

is that it is represented by a circular ideogram with a sort of ear projecting Fig. 53
from it and it was measured by weight. The weight in kilograms is always half the number of horns, except for a totalling tablet (Mc 4457) where the scribe appears to have made an error, repeating the figure 345 from the line above in place of the predictable 308; since it stands immediately below the figure 208, it is easy to see why the scribe thought that this was itself an error and so copied a wrong figure in this place. Evans suggested that this was gut, used for stringing the bows. Ingenious as this theory is, it does not

satisfactorily account for all the data; it fails to account for the indexing of the goats themselves, whether they are carcases or merely skins. An ingenious attempt (Melena, 1972) has been made to explain the products as needed for the manufacture of chariot bodies; these made use of leather-thongs to provide a floor which would lessen a little the jolting transmitted from the wheels. But there is still no easy way of accounting for the curious figures, and the attempt to see in these the operation of a fiscal process (Olivier, 1974) leaves even more questions unanswered.

Pigs appear as expected, widely distributed but never in very large numbers. There are traces at Knossos of a single pig, allocated to, less likely demanded from, each of a number of officials. At Pylos we have small herds of pigs indexed alongside the sheep and goats and an interesting list of *sialoi* 'fat porkers' which are apparently being fattened up in the various districts of the Hither Province. Here too the numbers are small, for the list totals only 25 in all. We know that pigs were used for sacrifice (see p. 96), so it is perhaps the purpose of these records to record the issue of small numbers of animals to local officials to enable them to conduct some religious rite.

Animal products

We can assume that meat was eaten, though as in later Greece probably only on special occasions, at least in the lower social classes, such as when a sacrifice took place. We can be sure of sacrifices from the presence of domestic animals in lists of religious offerings; and there are illustrations such as that on the famous Hághia Triádha sarcophagus, which show a sheep trussed ready for the knife.

Milk would be available from cows, goats and sheep; most of this would be made into cheese, and again we have mentions of cheeses in a list of offerings (PY Un 718). Goats' hair and wool have already been discussed.

But the chief animal product will have been their skins. The requisition of 234 ox-hides has already been mentioned, and we have references to what appear to be sheep-skins. But we have also some indication of the use to which skins were put in a long tablet from Pylos (Ub 1318). This uses two words for skins, one (*wrinos*) probably meaning 'raw-hide', the other (*diphthera*) meaning 'tanned leather'. The first is never qualified by the name of an animal and is probably used exclusively of ox-hide. The other is used either alone, much as leather unqualified in English usually means ox-leather, or with a series of epithets denoting goat, pig and deer. Some of the ox-leather is described as red; and it is interesting to note that a fragment of red leather has been recovered from a Mycenaean burial. It was used for bridles, halters and other harness-gear for chariots; for pack-saddles, straps and fastenings; and for foot-wear – the word in classical times meant sandals, but is probably more general. Rawhide is used for laces for foot-wear and 'covers for three pairs' – of shoes? At Knossos we also hear of horses' blinkers being made of raw-hide. Goat-leather too was used for foot-wear. Deer-leather would be too soft for that purpose, and we can only guess what it might have been used for. There are some records of deer at Pylos which are presumably wild animals hunted, and some slight confirmation in the term 'hunters', which in Greek means literally 'dog-leaders'. So by this roundabout route we can infer that they kept dogs. Cat-lovers will be disappointed to learn that so far we can find no trace of that indispensable animal.

54 The walls of Tiryns

8 CRAFT, INDUSTRY AND TRADE

Industry is a convenient heading under which to bring together all the productive processes which supplied the Mycenaean economy with man-made articles. It is perhaps rather too grand a word to describe the activities of carpenters or goldsmiths; but as we shall see, some of the productive services were organized on a scale which fully justifies the title industrial.

Building

Every visitor to Mycenae cannot fail to be impressed by the enormous walls, still standing in places after thirty-three centuries, though they have in part been reconstructed. The circuit of the walls measures over 1,100 m; and such is the size of the blocks of masonry that the later Greeks understandably concluded that the walls had been built by giants. The lintel block of the doorway of the great circular tomb known as the 'Treasury of Atreus' weighs about 100 tons; how with primitive equipment and power supplied only by human beings and oxen such massive blocks were manoeuvred into place is a matter of speculation, though it should be observed that the builders of Stonehenge in England performed a similar feat and at about the same period. But the technical skill revealed by the construction of the Mycenaean tombs is much greater. In the 'Treasury of Atreus' the diameter of the chamber is 14.50 m, and the vault above rises to a height of 13.20 m. True, the Mycenaeans had not discovered the principle of the arch; every opening had to be bridged either with a monolithic lintel or with overhanging courses of masonry until the gap could be closed. But this did not deter them from constructing monumental gateways such as the Lion Gate at Mycenae, or bridges carrying roads across ravines, like the one the remains of which are still to be seen a little way below the citadel at the same site.

Fig. 55

Fig. 56

The manpower needed to build such structures is hard to estimate. But a walled citadel like Mycenae must have taken a generation to construct, unless its builders had inexhaustible supplies of manpower. It is only in certain places that we have traces of Mycenaean fortifications; apart from the Argolid, there are Mycenaean walls on the Acropolis at Athens, though subsequent devastation and rebuilding prevent us from even guessing the extent of Mycenaean fortifications there. Perhaps the most striking use of manpower for building is the great circuit wall of Gla in Boeotia, three kilometres round, an area that would have contained not only the people but also their flocks from far and wide. There are traces of a Mycenaean wall across the isthmus of Corinth, though whether it was completed we do not know. On the other hand it is clear that the palace of Pylos was not fortified in its last phase, and doubtful whether it had earlier had any fortification walls, certainly not on the scale of Mycenae or Tiryns. Crete is strangely devoid of fortifications.

55 The walls of the citadel at Mycenae

56 The so-called 'Treasury of Atreus' at Mycenae

It is thus not surprising that we hear little in our documents of the crafts and materials of building. There is one Pylos tablet (An 35) which lists twelve masons – the word means literally 'wall-builders' – who are going to build at four different sites, Pylos itself being one of them. But we are not given any indication what they were going to build; in view of the small numbers this could hardly have been a last-minute attempt to provide for defence, even if the masons are merely the expert craftsmen who would direct the local unskilled labour. Indeed, if this were so, we should expect efforts to be concentrated on one site first, not started simultaneously at four. We may therefore presume that these are ordinary building operations.

A similar picture of normal house, or perhaps palace, building emerges from another Pylos tablet (Vn 46), which is quite clearly a list of building materials. In view of the regular numbers it is unlikely to be a random list; probably it enumerates all the timbers needed for a building operation, and this must be some sort of small hall, perhaps the characteristic Mycenaean type known as a *megaron*. Just as a modern list of building timbers might speak of purlins, rafters, newels, king-posts and so on, we must expect the Mycenaean lists to be equally full of technical terms, all doubtless clear enough to builders and carpenters of the period, but troublesome to us, since many of them either did not survive into classical usage, or, if they did, might have changed their meaning.

The list begins, after a broken heading, with a series of three entries, each containing the word *kapniās* 'of the chimney', and enumerating 12 beams, 4 roof-beams and 6 cross-beams. It was objected that a chimney could not be built of wood because of the risk of fire. But we must remember that a Mycenaean *megaron* had an open hearth at its centre, and the chimney was thus a wooden structure in the roof through which the smoke escaped by means of an earthenware pipe. We know this detail because Professor Blegen recovered from two such hearths at Englianós a number of fragments of coarse pottery. When he gave these to his pot-mender, the man was scornful and questioned whether it was worth while working on such crude stuff. Blegen told him to go ahead and see what came out. So he carefully assembled and joined the pieces, until he had, not as he expected crude cooking pots, but in each case two cylindrical pipes, about 65 cm in diameter and 50 cm long. These formed the smoke-duct, and must have been held in place by a complicated series of beams. Reconstructions of the palace show a kind of lantern standing up from the roof to support the chimney-stack; the woodwork of this must be what is here being listed. If we knew the precise meaning of the technical terms I have translated as various kinds of beams, we might even be able to hazard a guess at the structure of this lantern.

The next entries are both obscure words, but the numbers, 81 and 40, indicate that they are fairly small items. Then follow 23 (or more) 'wall-fittings', of what sort we can only guess, and 140 pegs or dowels. These were sometimes used in Cretan work to attach heavy layers of plaster to the wall. Then came 6 beams described as door-posts; since the term may include lintels, this probably means that there were two doors, for there is no item with the numeral 3 to be the lintels, if these were three doors. The next entry is 2 of something; could these be wooden thresholds? A further group of obscure entries has the numbers 10, 16 and 100. Finally we have 1 pillar with unclear definition, 2 roof-beams and 1 column. It is tempting to think that the last items belong to a small porch: the pillar standing between the two doors in the inner wall, the column supporting the two roof-beams at the outside. No doubt an architect will prove to me that I have got it wrong; but if this exercise of the imagination inspires someone to produce a better account of the woodwork of a Mycenaean *megaron*, I shall have achieved something.

Metals

The metals known to be in use were five: gold, silver, lead, copper and tin, the last two not normally employed in their pure forms, but alloyed in a mixture of up to ten per cent tin to make bronze. Iron was not unknown but was rare; the Mycenaeans' failure to exploit the iron ores of Greece was due to lack of technical skill. Thus bronze served all the main purposes for which metal was required, and provided the cutting edge for weapons and tools. Good bronze is superior for this purpose to poor iron; it is only with the advance in technology, which was introduced into Greece after the end of the Mycenaean age, that good iron tools and weapons could be made.

But although bronze plays such an important part in Mycenaean Greece, it must always have been a relatively scarce and expensive material, for, as far as we know, there is no adequate source of these metals in the country. Copper was easily obtained in Cyprus, and a Late Bronze Age wreck found off the south coast of Turkey eloquently demonstrates how cargoes of ingots were carried overseas. Indeed, it would seem that this ship carried a group of itinerant smiths, for pieces of metal that can hardly be anything but scrap were also recovered from the wreck. It is the source of tin which is a puzzle. One possible source is in what is now Czechoslovakia, another in Spain, or even Britain. But since only small quantities are needed, perhaps minor sources existed which have today been exhausted. The idea that Greece imported the two metals from east and west would explain its favourable position for establishing a metal industry.

Our knowledge of the bronze industry comes entirely from Pylos; there are objects of bronze recorded at Knossos, but only at Pylos do we have any information about smiths. Here there is a long series of documents listing the smiths at various places and the amounts of bronze issued to them. Clearly the palace was anxious to maintain a tight control over supplies of metals, and when it was issued to smiths to work into goods, a careful record of the quantity was kept at Pylos. Presumably the finished goods when received back were weighed to ensure that there was no deficiency.

Each tablet in this series (Jn) gives a place name, a list of the smiths and the amount of bronze issued to each, and a total; then often we have a list of smiths without an issue. We thus know the total number of smiths at each

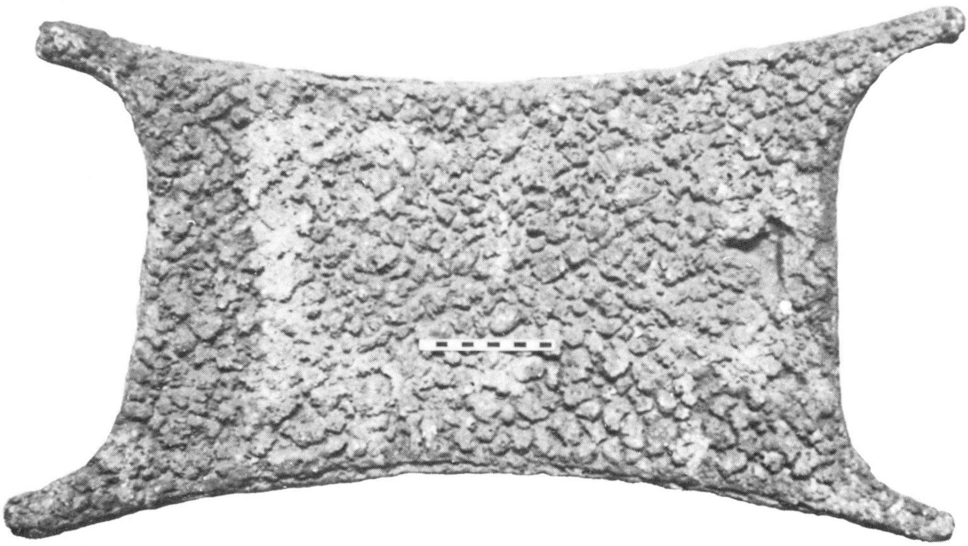

57 A copper ingot from Cyprus

site and how many of them were unemployed; the proportion in the latter class is about one third. However, the amount of bronze issued is small; one smith has as much as 12 kg, but 3 to 4 kg is normal, and some have as little as 1.5 kg.

We also have a document which gives a very large weight of bronze, which must be the sum of the quantities recorded as issued on each tablet. The difference between this sum, which amounts to 1,046 kg, and the sum of the bronze on all the surviving tablets gives us a measure of the number of tablets lost; it would seem that about one third of the tablets are missing. It is therefore necessary to increase the total of smiths on the extant tablets by a like amount, and this allows us to calculate that the total of smiths in the kingdom was nearly 400. This is an astonishing figure, for we must not imagine every village as having its forge; the smiths are in fact concentrated in groups of up to 26. Some of the groups are in the service of the goddess Potnia (see p. 93). The places where they work are sometimes in the main towns, though there are none at Pylos; more often they are at places of which we hear little or nothing elsewhere. An explanation of this may be the need to site metal foundries in areas with a good supply of fuel, and possibly on high sites where there is plenty of wind. It is easier to carry metal to the fuel than to bring the fuel into the towns.

A force of 400 workmen should have been able to produce many tons of goods annually, far more than we should expect the kingdom to need, for bronze was never a cheap metal, and substitutes would have been used wherever possible. Of course we may be wrong in thinking that craftsmen worked full time at their trade; it is possible that they also cultivated land and fed themselves. But even making such allowances, it seems unlikely that such a large force of craftsmen was required purely to meet domestic needs, and it is therefore probable that Pylos had a surplus of metal goods for export. If so, and it is an attractive theory to account for some of the wealth of the kingdom, then the economy was dependent upon sea-borne trade, since both the raw materials and the finished goods must have been carried by sea. Any interruption in trade routes would therefore have had drastic consequences for the kingdom.

Yet the evidence of these documents is clear. There was a shortage of metal, or this careful rationing would hardly have been necessary. This picture is confirmed by a unique document (Jn 829) which relates not to distribution, but to the collection of bronze. It begins with a long formula, stating that it is a list of contributions to be made by the local governors and their deputies; they are to contribute 'temple bronze as points for spears and javelins'. The purpose of the collection is thus to provide raw material for the armaments industry; a clear indication that Pylos was taking steps to improve its fighting strength. The word translated 'temple' might – such is the ambiguity of the dialect – equally mean 'ship'; but what is 'ship bronze' and how could the governors of inland districts have it at their disposal? If we accept the translation 'temple', we have to remember that the Mycenaeans did not, so far as we know, usually build free-standing temples, but carried out their religious rites in special parts of their palaces. We might legitimately substitute 'shrine' for 'temple'. The governor of each district and his deputy can be presumed to have had each a shrine in their houses. Now objects dedicated to a god were not thrown away; even when old and useless they were not treated as scrap, but were preserved for long periods. When a new temple was built the useless dedications from the earlier building were often buried in the foundations of the new, and such hoards have often provided archaeologists with rich treasures. The Mycenaean ivories from Delos are probably from a deposit of this kind. Thus shrines might be presumed to have quantities of bronze objects, often worn and useless; in an emergency the authorities might well demand that these, despite their dedication, be turned in for scrap. Again we catch a glimpse of an emergency looming over Pylos.

A group of much damaged tablets at Knossos (Oa 730, 733, 734) is apparently a record of bronze ingots, though only on one is the sign for bronze preserved. Sixty ingots are listed with a weight of *c.* 1,562 kg, that is to say, an average of 26.03 kg each. This agrees reasonably well with the weights of actual ingots recovered by the archaeologists (see p. 103).

The uses to which bronze was put are many. Obviously it is very useful for vessels of all types, cheaper than gold or silver, but much more durable than pottery. It is not always easy to judge what the vessels listed on the tablets were made of, since the word or the ideogram for bronze was only added when there was a risk of confusion; two similar cups on a Pylos inventory of vessels (Tn 996.4) are distinguished by the addition of the
Fig. 58 signs for bronze and gold. But this does not mean that all the other vessels

58 The ideograms for bronze and gold

in this list were pottery; even the great bath-tubs might have been of bronze, since a sealing at Knossos (Ws 8497) bears a rectangular pattern surmounted by the sign for bronze and on another face the word *asaminthos*, a very ancient Homeric word for 'bath'. The same problem recurs on the list of vessels which opens the so-called Pylos 'furniture' tablets; the descriptions, so far as intelligible, relate to their decoration, not to the basic material. It would be surprising if such trouble was taken to inventory even the finest painted pottery; but such a hoard of metal vessels is beyond the dreams of any excavator.

It would be easier to understand the epithets given to vessels if we knew whether the description applied to decoration or type. A jug (Ta 711.3) is described as 'queenly, womanly, ox-head, spirally'. Do we infer that the scene on the jug depicted women before a queen (seated on a throne?), between bands of ox-heads and spirals? Certainly the six large tripod-cauldrons were made of bronze; all but one were 'of Cretan work', though this need not mean more than made by Cretan craftsmen, and we need not suppose Cretan imports. One has an epithet which might fairly be translated 'goatish'; it has been suggested that this refers to the practice of ornamenting the rim of large vessels with small animal heads in the round attached on the outside; or did the goats' heads perhaps form the attachment of the handles? One cauldron is described as 'with one foot' and another as 'with the legs burnt off'. This shows that even when damaged these vessels were valuable enough to be carefully inventoried, and therefore they cannot have been mere earthenware. A series of vessels called *dipas* seem to be largish pitchers, not drinking cups as the classical *depas* suggests; here we have a word which has changed its meaning with time, but traces of its old sense still remain, if we take the trouble to look for them. These come in two sizes, and may have three or four handles, or none at all.

It is by no means clear whether all the other implements listed here (Ta 709) are of bronze. The list includes a rake, two fire-tongs, and two braziers. Bronze objects of this sort are rarely preserved, because they are inappropriate as the furnishings of tombs. There are also a number of words whose meaning is unknown or disputed.

We know of course that bronze was the material of weapons and any tools needing a cutting edge. Its use for armour is less expected, but since the discovery of the complete suit of bronze armour at Dhendrá, we cannot be surprised if the tablets refer to bronze in this connexion. The details of weapons and armour are discussed in Chapter 9, pp. 159–72. It was also used for bindings on chariot-wheels; presumably thin strips of bronze were applied to reinforce the joints between the spokes and the rim. One pair of wheels is described simply as 'of bronze'; since they are next to some pairs called 'bronze-bound', this must refer to something else, though it is difficult to imagine a wheel constructed entirely of bronze. One of the Knossos tablets (Sc 223) has the ideogram for bronze added underneath the sign for chariot; here too it is hard to guess exactly what is meant.

Silver is not infrequent in the archaeological finds, but is strangely absent from the documents, with one exception. This is a pair of chariot-wheels, which are said to be 'bound with silver'; I have already mentioned that some are bound with bronze, but this is a unique example of the use of silver for what clearly must have been a luxury vehicle. The absence of any other mention of silver on the tablets has led us to wonder if it lurks undetected behind another word or ideogram. But none of the unidentified ideograms appear to be a metal, and the only word which might conceivably mean 'silver' is *pa-ra-ku*, which cannot be matched with any appropriate Greek word. *Pa-ra-ku* is a material used for ornamental inlay; and although silver is possible for this purpose, other solutions can be contemplated, such as niello, a metallic compound used to give a black finish. One negative statement can be made: silver is not employed as a medium of exchange to give the value of the commodities. It must have been very scarce.

Lead on the other hand was known; it was used for small figurines and other objects which could be cast. A recent excavation at Thebes produced many small lumps of lead which represented some objects melted by the fire which destroyed the building. There is one reference in the tablets (KN Og 1527) to *mo-ri-wo-do*, and although far from certain this could be a Mycenaean form (*moliwdos*?) of the loan word meaning 'lead' which appears in later Greek in various guises such as *molybdos*, *molibos*, etc.

Gold is described either by an ideogram (see fig. 58) or by the normal Greek word *khrusos*. What is interesting about this word is that it is known to be a loan word from Semitic (Ugaritic *ḫrṣ*, Assyrian *ḫurāšu*). It is certain that a number of other words in Mycenaean Greek were borrowed from a Semitic language, such as *lewōn* 'lion', cf. Hebrew *lābī'*, Assyrian *labbu*, or the names of the spices cumin and sesame. It is thus clear that these borrowings cannot be ascribed to contact with the Phoenicians during the 'Orientalizing' period of Archaic Greece (eighth–seventh centuries). The traces of a sexagesimal system in weights and measures point in the same direction.

At Pylos we have a long, but unfortunately mutilated, list of contributions of gold (Jo 438). It seems clear that these are contributions because the individual entries are in the nominative case, where the dative is usually used for distributions; and nearly half the entries have added the 'check-mark' in the form of a small cross, probably indicating that in these cases payment has been received. The heading is totally lost apart from the last word, *koretēr* or 'governor' (see p. 73). Nine of the entries contain the same title; in two cases we have a *prokoretēr* or 'deputy governor'. Three people hold the rank of *mo-ro-qa* or 'share-holder'; one is a *guasileus* or 'chief'. But in a few cases we have a place name replacing a personal name or title; it would seem clear that the place is represented by its governor. Similarly some of the personal names appearing here can be identified from other documents. Nedwātās is the commander of one of the northern sectors and was probably the governor of a district; he is followed by Ekhemēdēs, who is the first of his subordinates in the coastguard list, and may well have been his deputy. We also meet here Augewās, the man appointed by the king to the office of *da-mo-ko-ro* (see p. 77). It is thus clear that the contributors in this list are high officials among the territorial nobility. Neither the king nor any officers of his household can be identified; the largest contributor who heads the list has only one sign of his entry preserved, but this cannot be restored either as the king, or *Lāwāgetās*, or their names, *E-ke-ra$_2$-wo* or Wedaneus.

The amounts of gold vary from 1 kg down to about 62 g; the most common figure is 250 g. The total of the amounts preserved is about 5 kg, and allowing for the missing figures is unlikely to have been more than 6 kg. But this is a very large quantity of what must always have been a scarce commodity; it does not seem to have been produced in more than tiny amounts within the kingdom, and was presumably imported. How did all the officials come to possess so much, and under what circumstances could the palace demand such a contribution? It would seem most unlikely that gold was so plentiful it could have been levied annually in such quantities. We are therefore forced to conclude that this was an extraordinary levy. The local officials might have possessed gold in the form of plate or jewellery; or on the analogy of the requisition of bronze discussed above, they could perhaps have found it in the shrines or temples under their control. But only in very exceptional circumstances could such a levy have been acceptable.

Thus it seems clear that we have in this document another indication of the emergency which confronted Pylos at the time of the tablets. Yet the purpose of the levy is obscure. Bronze might be collected for the fabrication of weapons; gold is useless for military purposes, except as a means of exchange. It could have been needed either to finance a trading mission sent to acquire armaments or fighting men from elsewhere; or directly as a kind of 'Danegeld', to buy off potential raiders.

Apart from this, gold appears either in descriptions of vessels or ornate furniture. At Knossos the word for gold occurs on an unhappily incomplete tablet which has pictograms of a very special kind of vessel; there are here two examples of what must be the so-called 'bull's head' rhyton, a vessel for libations shaped like a bull's head. Examples in silver are known from both Knossos and Mycenae, and both probably had the horns made of wood covered with gold foil. The mutilated description specifically mentions 'horns' (*ke-ra-a*). Gold, however, is only mentioned in the surviving text in connexion with a cup of the type famous from the gold examples found at Váphio in Lakonia; the previous word is incomplete but might mean something like 'cover'. Fig. 59 Fig. 60

At Pylos in a list of vessels of various kinds (Tn 996), the sign for gold is

59 Knossos tablet K 872 showing two bull's head rhyta

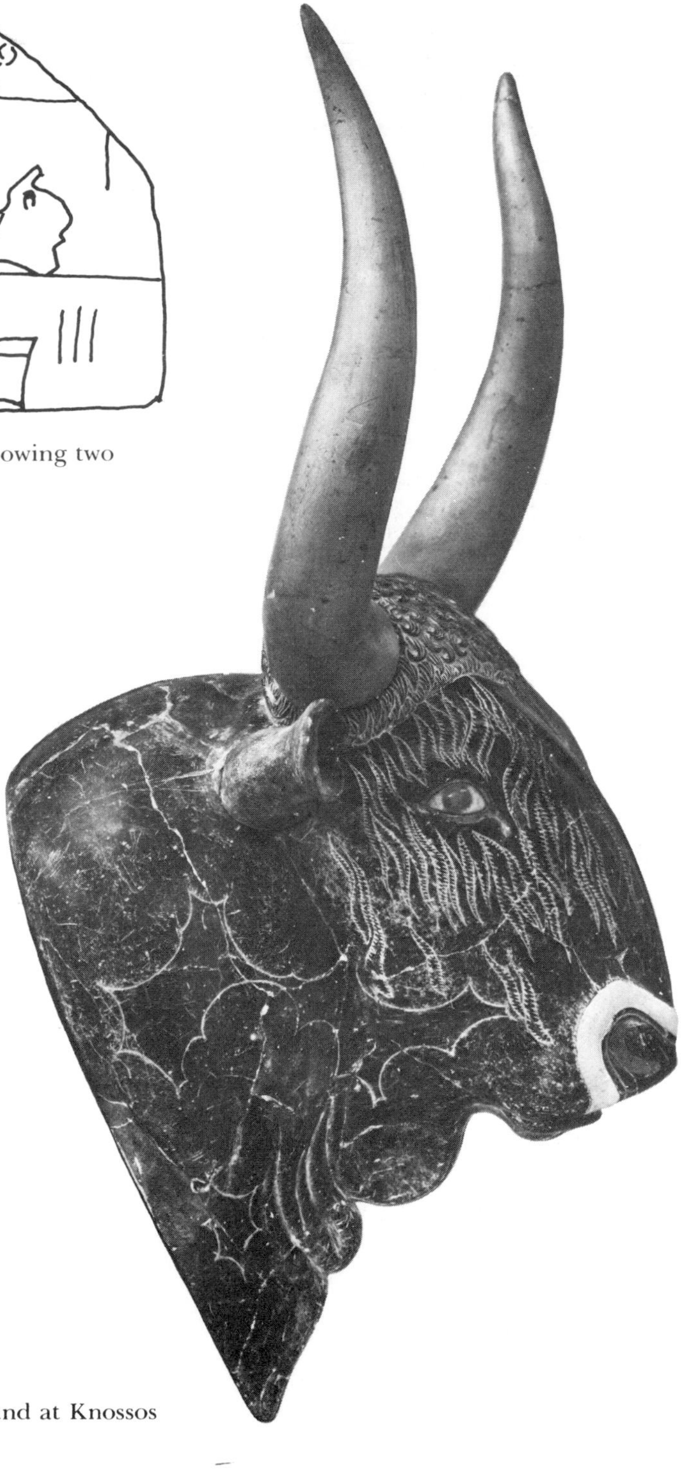

60 Bull's head rhyton found at Knossos

prefixed to a pictogram of some sort of dish, the name for which is obscure (*po-ka-ta-ma*); the numeral is only one, but it is followed by another similar pictogram with the prefix bronze, and there are three of these. The previous entry, perhaps another rhyton, may also have had the sign for gold as prefix. An entry in the previous line shows seven jugs of bronze, and was perhaps followed by an entry for similar jugs of gold.

But it is on the famous tablet of religious offerings (PY Tn 316, see p. 89) that gold vessels appear in quantity. Here we have no less than thirteen gold cups, some plain, others more elaborate and fitted with handles. No more than a tiny scrap of gold was found in the palace, for it had evidently been efficiently looted before being set on fire; but an unplundered *tholos* tomb at Peristeriá, just north of Kiparissía, produced several gold vessels, now to be seen in the Khóra Museum. The use of gold for inlay will be mentioned later (p. 148). Only once do we hear of goldsmiths; there is a group of four among a miscellaneous list of tradesmen at Pylos (An 207), which includes potters, bowyers and saddlers.

Furniture

Perhaps the most exciting list of valuable objects is the long series of tablets from Pylos known as the 'furniture tablets' (Ta). The purpose of the list is not clear, despite an admirably clear heading: '*Pu₂-ke-qi-ri* (a man's name) saw as follows, when the King appointed Augewās *da-mo-ko-ro* (a title).' This tells us that the list was the result of an inspection, but it does not tell us where all these goods were kept. They cannot have been the furnishings of a suite of rooms, for items such as beds are missing. L. R. Palmer translated the word rendered above 'appointed' as 'buried', which is difficult but theoretically possible, and identified the collection of goods as the contents of a *tholos* tomb reopened for another burial; but it was quickly pointed out that no known tomb in the Pylos area is large enough to hold them all, and again the list contains items unknown from any Mycenaean tomb so far found unplundered. The best explanation is that we have here the contents of a store-room, for which the official was responsible. This will explain the odd numbers of objects, and the damaged condition of some articles, which is expressly recorded.

The list begins with a collection of vessels of various kinds, which have already been discussed under the heading of bronze (p. 142), since this seems most likely to be the material of which they are made. Mixed up with them are various other objects also probably of bronze. It then passes on to the furniture proper, that is, tables, chairs and stools. The tables are called by what seems clearly to be an ancestral form of the classical word *trapeza*; but the new form does not resolve the argument about the etymology of this word. The second part clearly refers to 'feet'; and it has been thought that the first part is a reduced form of the numeral 'four', but the difficulty here is that in early times tables much more often had three than four legs, since a three-legged table will stand better on an uneven floor. The word for chair is the source from which English ultimately derived the word 'throne'; certainly these are no ordinary chairs, but regal seats of honour, as their elaborate decoration proves. The stools are in some cases paired with chairs, as if they were simply footstools; but since there are considerably more of them than chairs, they may have been used as seats.

The basic material of the furniture is apparently not mentioned; the officials no doubt thought it superfluous to record that it was made of wood, and perhaps they did not know what wood it was. One timber that is mentioned is called *kutisos*, which to the classical Greek was a name for a kind of laburnum, used for ornament and sometimes called in English 'bastard ebony'. We also hear of box-wood. Otherwise the epithets of material must refer to decoration rather than basic substance, for we have stone, rock-crystal and ivory. Blegen recorded fragments of marble table-tops in his dig, but all precious materials seem to have been removed before the destruction. Parts of the furniture are described as 'golden', but whether this means more than covered in gold foil one cannot tell. Feet and struts are 'of ivory'.

But in many cases the description of the ornamentation is specific, and was clearly intended to enable the reader to recognize a particular object. There is a word which must surely describe the process of inlay, though it cannot be explained by anything in later Greek. Inlay is mostly of ivory, but is also of gold, blue glass paste (*kuanos*) and an unidentified material (*pa-ra-ke-we*), which may conceivably have been silver (see p. 143). Another difficult word (*qe-qi-no-me-na*) seems to mean 'adorned with figures', but whether it refers to the pictorial effect or to a process of ornamentation it is impossible to say. The decorative motifs include human figures, helmets, bulls'-heads, calves, lions, a horse, an octopus, birds and other things which may be designs such as spirals. One stool (Ta 722.1) is described as inlaid in ivory with a man, a horse, an octopus and a *phoinix*; the choice for the last word seems to be between 'palm-tree' and 'griffin', the first being the more likely. This is probably not a single scene of a groom leading a horse while the octopus climbs a palm-tree, though we have it on the authority of the elder Pliny that octopuses do climb trees; the four motifs may be one on each side of the stool.

Recent finds in Cyprus (Karageorghis, 1969) have cast some light on

61 Ivory panel from Mycenae

Mycenaean furniture, for in this remote outpost of the Greek world Mycenaean traditions lingered on, long after they were forgotten in Greece. Several tombs at Salamis dating from the eighth to seventh centuries had the dead man's chariot, complete with its two horses slaughtered, buried in the entrance passage – a Mycenaean practice known from a tomb at Marathon in Attica. One of these tombs contained three richly decorated thrones or arm-chairs, which are strangely reminiscent of the description from Pylos. One, which has been reconstructed despite the fact that its woodwork had perished, was completely covered with thin plates of ivory. Another was covered with plates of silver and of ivory inlaid with blue glass paste; buttons of silver gilt were also used as decoration; a similarly decorated footstool lay near by. Some of the surviving Mycenaean ivories probably came from furniture of this sort.

There are still many unsolved problems in these descriptions, and I will quote one as an example. The tables in all but a few instances are described by terms which can easily be translated as 'nine-foot' and 'six-foot'. No other numerals occur. But a table with nine feet seems unlikely, unless it has three legs each ending in a triple foot; and this will of course destroy the point of having three legs. It is possible that the Mycenaeans, like the classical Greeks, used the foot as a measure of length – we have no recognizable measures of length in our documents. But it is surely surprising that so many tables should be nine feet long; one would have expected measurements other than six also to appear. Some of the other epithets undoubtedly refer to the type of table, but here again we cannot give them a certain meaning.

The decoration of chariots will be described in the next chapter, but it should be mentioned here that some of the same language occurs there, such as the words for ivory inlay.

Textiles

We turn now to a subject on which we have many documents, though they are not easy to interpret: the textile industry. Clearly the process of spinning wool into yarn and weaving this into cloth must have been commonly practised in Mycenaean Greece, as in all ancient societies. But we are not concerned with the ordinary everyday production of clothing. The royal archives disclose a special interest in this subject, and we must infer that these textiles are not the everyday goods, but special fabrics designed either for the royal family and household or very likely for export. The Mycenaean ambassadors shown on Egyptian monuments bringing what is boastfully described as 'tribute', but is presumably the customary gift, have among their offerings lengths of cloth. We cannot imagine that these were any ordinary textiles, they must have been elaborately ornamented fabrics of kinds not normally obtainable in Egypt.

The difficulties arise mainly from the technical terms employed. The technique for the production of luxuries like this will hardly have survived the Dark Ages which followed the Mycenaean collapse, so it is not surprising that these terms did not continue in use in the classical period. Little by little, however, they are beginning to become clearer, mainly thanks to more careful investigation by J. T. Killen. The other difficulty is the extremely fragmentary state of the Knossos texts, on which we rely for almost all details of textiles, since there are only a handful of short texts at Pylos dealing with this subject. The wool tablets at Mycenae at least prove that conditions there were similar, for some of the vocabulary reappears there.

A curious fact about the textile industry at Knossos is the degree of centralized control. When the wool from sheep in the area was received at Phaistos, the amount was carefully recorded on a clay tablet 50 km away at Knossos. There too we find the record stating that so much wool had been issued to 'women of Phaistos'; and in due course the records showed that the finished cloth had been received. Obviously the wool was not actually brought to Knossos, and then sent back to Phaistos; but all the details of the operation were meticulously recorded at Knossos. There must have been a good courier service to ensure that information could be collected centrally.

The details of the different kinds of textiles being produced are too technical for a book of this sort, and J. T. Killen proposes to discuss them at length in a future publication. We have the impression that certain towns specialized in certain kinds of fabric. Some wove the cloth, others provided the decorative elements which were attached to it. The women in these various establishments received their rations from the royal stores, and this indicates that they were not free workers, but regular employees, very likely slaves, though the legal implications of that term must be forgotten in dealing with Mycenaean society.

The labour force is best documented at Pylos, in two large series of tablets which have already been described (p. 79). We must now address ourselves to the identification of the occupational terms used to describe the groups of women. Here we have no clues to meaning other than the purely etymological search for appropriate Greek words; only the fact that all the trades appear to be humble and fall into two categories offers some sort of check. The two categories are domestic and industrial. Domestic trades are exemplified by corn-grinders, bath-attendants, servants and a term (*pa-wo-ke*) which I have interpreted as 'maids of all work' (Chadwick, 1967*a*). There is also an intriguing group called apparently 'wage-earners', but whether these are strictly free women must remain doubtful, for they appear to be treated like all the rest for rations.

The industrial sector is exclusively concerned with textiles; two terms used must mean wool-workers and linen-workers. The production of linen will be considered later, but where not specified we should probably conclude that the material was wool. We hear of spinners, carders and weavers; but more of the groups have names which we can associate with particular kinds of textile or article. For instance, some are called 'makers of headbands', a word we hear of again in connexion with horses, but which might also be made of cloth for human use; they would doubtless be embroidered or otherwise decorated. One of the kinds of textiles made is called *te-pa*, a word which cannot be equated with a later Greek word, though it bears a remarkable resemblance to *tapēs* 'carpet', remarkable because Killen has proved that the *te-pa* contained an enormous weight of wool and must therefore have been a heavy rug of some kind. Some specialized in the making of *o-nu-ke* (apparently the Greek word for 'finger-nails', but used in a technical sense of some decoration applied to cloth). Others are called *a-ke-ti-ri-ja*, a term with several possible interpretations, but Killen has demonstrated that it must be *askētriai* and mean 'finishers', that is, women who take the cloth as woven and work it up into the finished form. There are other words in this series which are clearly likewise occupational terms, but which we have not yet succeeded in solving.

Since many of the groups of women are defined merely by location or place of origin, it is impossible in these cases to know what were their duties; possibly the groups imported from the Asiatic coast (see p. 80) had special skills, and it would have been possible for an official to deduce their occupation from their name; these of course remain obscure to us. The analysis of the numbers involved in the series demonstrates two facts. About two-thirds of the total number of women, or around 500, are located in Pylos itself. The remainder are located at other places, in both Provinces; most of those in the Further Province are in Leuktron, which must be the administrative centre of that region. About a quarter of the women whose occupation can be classified are domestic, the remainder industrial. If the uncertain terms have the same distribution we arrive at the conclusion that between five and six hundred women were employed all over the kingdom on the production of textiles.

Flax

A large group of tablets at Pylos deals with a product which is denoted by the syllabic sign *SA*. As we know from other cases, these are not necessarily abbreviations of Greek words, but seem to have been taken over from Linear A. There was thus no reason to believe that *SA* indicated a Greek word for the commodity. Fortunately one document (Nn 228) has a heading to a list of *SA* entries which shows that the communities listed have an unfulfilled obligation to supply *linon*, the Greek word for both 'flax' and 'linen'. Since some of the slave-women are described as *lineiai* 'flax-workers', we clearly need some raw material for them to work on; and the main series (Na) could thus be explained as the production records of the areas where flax was grown. This equation of *SA* with flax, however, still seemed fragile, until I discovered that in modern times too large quantities of flax have been grown in the south-west Peloponnese. Indeed the area in Greece which produced most flax for fibre was almost exactly the kingdom controlled by the palace at Englianós. This cannot be an accident, but must be due to especially favourable conditions for the cultivation or preparation of flax. In fact, the west coast has the highest rainfall in Greece, and consequently has much more plentiful perennial water supplies; and the first stage in the process of preparing the fibres, known as retting, consists in immersing the bundles of stems in running water. It would thus be not surprising if flax-growing had been practised here from Mycenaean down to modern times; in recent years it has declined sharply owing to the competition of artificial fibres. The mention by Thucydides (4.26.8) of linseed in connexion with the rations smuggled in to the Spartans on Sphakteria island shows that flax was then grown in the neighbourhood; and medieval records too list flax among the products of the area. There is thus little doubt that the sign is correctly interpreted.

At Pylos the *SA* sign is always followed by numerals, so that we cannot see how it was measured. A figure of 100 units occurs once (Na 296), but the commonest figure is 30. J. T. Killen (1966), however, has shown that at Knossos flax is weighed; but here the quantities are much smaller, and rarely exceed 3 kg. We have a similar case of a commodity sign simultaneously denoting a unit of weight: the sign for 'wool' indicates a unit equivalent to 3 kg (see p. 128). But this is excluded in the case of *SA*, since 3 kg and even larger weights are recorded without the use of the major unit; moreover, the quantities produced would be very small, if the records refer to raw material. It is possible therefore that the unit indicated by *SA* is the major unit of weight, the talent, just as the signs for wheat or barley imply the major unit of dry measure. This would give the maximum production recorded for a single village as around three tons, with a little under a ton as the commonest amount. These are credible figures if they refer to bundles of retted fibre. In modern times the Peloponnese has produced over 300 tons annually, most of it from the Pylos area.

The Na series must indicate the production achieved or expected from the places named. There are about a hundred tablets or fragments in this group, so a total of at least eighty tablets seems certain. What is surprising here is that the assessment and collection has not been decentralized, so that only the sixteen administrative districts would be recorded, but that every productive area is treated separately. We should have expected the local governors to have been responsible for collection, as was certainly the case with the mixed agricultural produce recorded on the Ma tablets. In a few cases the place name on a flax tablet is that of an administrative district; in these cases it presumably refers to the lands occupied by the settlement itself, not the whole district, since most of the place names here are otherwise unknown. The tablets were originally filed in two baskets, since we have two totalling tablets for them (Ng), and these bear the names of the two Provinces into which the kingdom was divided. But there is no way of allocating the place names to the correct file, except for the few we can locate on other evidence. One of the totals has the numeral broken off, so that we cannot estimate what proportion of the individual records have been preserved. The total for the Hither Province, which is complete, is 1,239 units, or about 37 tons if the calculation suggested above is correct. That for the Further Province is smaller; it is a minimum of 200, but the damage would allow us to restore a figure up to 899.

The tablets are basically of two types, those with one and those with two or more flax entries. The simple type has usually a place name followed by *SA* and a number. This seems to represent the fulfilment by the village of its norm. Brief notes are sometimes added. The compound type is like the simple type, but has an additional entry stating that so many units of flax were 'free' or 'not given'. These therefore are rebates allowed against the original assessment; and it is significant that adding these rebates to the first entry usually produces a round number, from which we can infer that the first entry is the actual delivery, not a notional assessment. It is not clear why the rebates are expressed by two different formulas, for in the totalling tablets there is only a single additional entry headed 'not given'. The two formulas cannot refer merely to a distinction between failure to contribute and allowance of a rebate, as one might infer from cases where both appear with separate *SA* entries (Na 185), because there are entries which combine them: 'and so much the ship-builders do not contribute, *E-sa-re-u ke-po-da* (man's name and title?) made it free: *SA* 50' (Na 568). It would seem that the distinction was small enough to be ignored in adding up the amounts not received.

As this example indicates, the rebates are allowed not to the community as a whole, but to specified classes. We have also bronzesmiths, hunters and planters mentioned in this way. We might guess that bronzesmiths and ship-builders were given rebates as an incentive to the armaments industry, since we know that bronze scrap was being collected for the manufacture of weapons. In three cases confusion is caused by the absence of any Mycenaean notation for zero, for the whole assessment is cancelled by the rebate. One of these (Na 334) is particularly interesting, for it has also the note: 'the King holds it'. But royal ownership cannot be the only reason why a rebate has been allowed, since other places too have similar notes of ownership, but this does not invite any rebate.

In these cases the holders are in the plural, and the names used are those we find in the descriptions of the men employed as look-outs for the coastguard (see p. 175). Before the nature of the flax tablets was understood, this coincidence led to some curious theories, such as Palmer's suggestion (1963, 312) that the 'flax' was really linseed issued as an emergency ration. But the connexion depended upon the theory that the number of units of flax was equal to the number of men of the same designation in the coastguard detachments. It can now be seen that the agreement is either illusory or fortuitous, 30 being a common figure in both series of numbers (Chadwick, 1973, 470). I now prefer to regard these strange-sounding names as tribal groups, quite likely people of non-Greek origin, who occupied certain of the flax-producing villages, and were employed preferably on non-combatant duties in an emergency. It is interesting that one of these peoples is said to hold the important district capital of Kharadrō, perhaps modern Phinikoús; and they supply the coastguards for the adjacent area (Na 543; An 661.4–6). But this does not prove any direct connexion between the two sets of documents.

One minor problem about the flax is the presence of such records in an archive which appears (see p. 192) to be restricted to the early months of the year, since flax is harvested in autumn. The explanation is probably that after harvesting it was the duty of villages which cultivated it to ret the fibres. This might take as long as a month, and even in Messenia water is not so plentiful that it could all have been retted at once. Hence it might well have been early in the following year by the time the fibre was collected and taken to the production centres; once retted and dried the fibre will keep well. We know that groups of women called flax-workers were present at Pylos and another town in the Hither Province; but their greatest concentration seems to have been at Leuktron, the capital of the

Further Province; a minimum of 28 is recorded there, plus two groups of uncertain size. Since the production of the Hither Province was greater, it is probably an accident that we have fewer women there specifically said to belong to this class.

We do not appear to have any record of goods made of linen at Pylos. It would of course have been valuable for sails and cordage, as well as for clothing. There is good reason to think that some linen was used in the making of armour (see p. 160).

Trade

Production, whether agricultural or industrial, must either be balanced by consumption or the surplus must be exported. It is very hard to judge how large was domestic consumption in this sort of economy, with records as scanty as we possess; but it seems safe to assume that the productive capacity of the bronze industry at Pylos with its 400 workers was well beyond the needs of the community. The production of linen goods too may well have exceeded local demand; and if the Pylos area is the best in Greece for the cultivation of flax and the making of linen, there will certainly have been a demand for these products in other parts of Greece. At Knossos too agricultural surpluses may have existed; the quantities recorded of some spices are very large, and some of these may have been exported. In the subsequent period we appear to have evidence of stirrup-jars made in Crete found on the mainland, and these must have been containers for some export, probably olive oil. During the Mycenaean period containers made in Greece travelled as far as southern Italy, the Levant and Egypt. Thus without being able to quantify the data, we may reasonably infer that Mycenaean kingdoms produced a surplus for export.

We can also point to commodities in Mycenaean palaces that must have been imported. All the ivory which either has been found by digging or is mentioned in the documents obviously came from abroad, perhaps Syria. Very small amounts of gold may have been mined in Greece, but the small quantities found in digs must represent a very small fraction of the metal in use at the time, and again the documents confirm that it was not uncommon in palaces; a foreign origin is likely for at least some of this. We need hardly doubt that other luxuries too were imported. Some kind of foreign trade must therefore have been conducted.

The presence of a merchant class has been frequently supposed. Wace named the first of the houses he dug outside the walls of Mycenae 'the House of the Oil Merchant'. Certainly it was a building devoted to the preparation and storage of olive oil, and there was evidence of residential quarters on an upper storey. But there are two important reasons for questioning the existence of merchants. In all the Linear B documents so far known, there is not the slightest mention of merchants or their activity. Had they been an important class, it is incredible that we should not have had some indication of their existence. The palaces of the Near East speak of them frequently in their archives, for they are a valuable source of revenue. Secondly, the easy functioning of a commercial system depends upon the existence of some form of currency. It is possible in a non-monetary economy to carry on trade by barter; but this is a clumsy method, since exchanges can only take place between two parties both of whom need what the other has to dispose of. Hence it is common to find that some commodity, often gold or silver, is used as a standard, and the price of a commodity is expressed as a given weight of precious metal. Other commodities can serve as the medium of exchange; Homer puts a value on suits of armour by expressing their worth as equivalent to so many oxen. But despite our researches the Mycenaean documents have yet to yield unambiguous evidence of a standard of this kind.

There is a much mutilated fragment from Pylos (Un 1322) which may be a commercial text, for it contains a word *o-no* which seems to occur in these contexts. Its identification is difficult, because although there is a Greek word *ōnos* meaning 'price', on comparative evidence we should have expected the Mycenaean form to be *wōnos.* Nonetheless, it may be the association of similar words in cognate languages which is wrong. This text refers to an *o-no* consisting of wheat and figs, the standard elements of rations at Pylos, for a net-maker and a weaver. Then we have two entries which appear to refer to a fine type of cloth, followed by a sign which probably indicates some sort of textile and immediately afterwards a quantity of wheat. It is hard to see what this means unless the wheat is in some sense a measure of the value of the textiles. It is unfortunate that almost all the readings of the tablet are uncertain, for it appears to be unique.

There are, however, other texts containing the term *o-no*, and here too we get the impression that some sort of barter is being recorded. We have twice the expression *tu-ru-pte-ri-ja o-no* (PY An 35.5; Un 443.1), where the first word is likely to be *struptēriās* (classical *stypt-*, cf. English *styptic*) 'of alum'. Alum was a commodity imported into Greece, especially from Cyprus, and probably chiefly used as a mordant in dyeing. In each case the expression is followed by a list of goods: 6 kg of wool, 4 she-goats, 3 pieces of some textile, 288 litres of wine, and 384 litres of figs in one place, 30 kg of wool and 10 pieces of textile in the other. It would seem reasonable to infer that these goods constitute the 'price' paid for the alum. There are a number of similar uses of the word *o-no* at Knossos and Mycenae, where the commodities are either olive oil or wool. But a curious fact here is that in three Knossos tablets (Fh 347, Fh 361, Fh 372) the name of the person involved in the transaction is the same as one of the Pylos instances (Un 443.1). Obviously the same man cannot be meant, and it may be a simple coincidence; but the name in question is *Kuprios*, which means 'the man of Cyprus'. Is this perhaps not a personal name, but just describes him as 'the man from Cyprus'? If so, that would be documentary evidence of what we know well enough from archaeology, that the Mycenaeans traded with Cyprus; and as mentioned above, alum as well as copper was exported from that island.

Parallels with the Near Eastern kingdoms also suggest that in a non-monetary economy trading tends to be a state monopoly. It would have been simple for the king of Pylos or Knossos to equip a ship, fill it with valuable products such as metal-goods, jewellery, textiles or perfumed oil, and despatch it to trade these for gold, ivory and similar luxuries. Equally he will have needed officials to look after these aspects of the economy and their residences will be archaeologically indistinguishable from those of merchants trading on their own account. But it is difficult to imagine how in the rigidly controlled Mycenaean system a private individual could trade independently. It is not unlikely that some sort of a market existed in Mycenaean towns, at which surplus food could change hands; but the presence of a regular merchant class is highly questionable, so long as no documentary evidence can be found to support such a view.

9 WEAPONS AND WAR

The revelation of the Mycenaean archives fostered wild hopes that one day we might come across, let us say, the muster of ships at Aulis for the expedition against Troy, or an operation order for the attack of the Seven against Thebes. But it would be remarkable indeed if anything of this kind had survived on clay, for our tablets are only the everyday records of a short period before the fall of the palaces. Only at Pylos are there some indications which I believe can be related to the imminent disaster.

Minoan society in Crete seems to have been relatively peaceful; military scenes are not common in art, and the latest frescoes from Thera are unusual in showing lines of armed troops and a fleet of warships. No Minoan town seems to have been fortified. But with the coming of the Greeks to Crete in the second half of the fifteenth century, a change comes over the pacific face of society. Archaeologists were at first puzzled by the discovery of tombs of this period in the neighbourhood of Knossos, which they named 'warrior tombs' from the weapons and armour discovered in them. This impression is now supported by the Linear B tablets at Knossos which list military equipment, though not apparently armed forces. Greek rule in Crete is distinguished by this warlike aspect. Fig. 62

No document records the existence of an army, though there are lists of men assigned to military and naval duties. Efforts have been made to interpret some of the titles in use as military ranks; the *Lāwāgetās* has taken to be a generalissimo (see p. 71). But it is more likely that in such a society

62 Fresco of a fleet from Thera

soldiering was a duty required of every citizen, and there is little to indicate any special military skills. It is therefore from the records of equipment that we must begin our attempt to envisage Mycenaean society at war.

Armour

Fig. 64 A fine suit of bronze body-armour has recently been found in a Mycenaean tomb at Dhendrá in the Argolid. But much armour was probably made of leather or heavy linen, possibly reinforced with metal fittings. A large number of thicknesses of linen is a surprisingly effective protection against sword cuts; and wearing metallic armour in the Greek summer must have been extremely uncomfortable; small wonder that warriors are often represented half-naked. One of the shaft graves at Mycenae yielded a fragment of linen in many thicknesses. A document at Knossos (L 693) speaks of 'fine linen' apparently for a 'tunic' (*khitōn*), but the end of the entry reads '1 kg of bronze'; the second line also refers to 'tunic-fittings (*epikhitōnia*) 1 kg of bronze'. It is just possible that the bronze is a unit of exchange, but much more likely the 'tunic' mentioned is a linen garment reinforced with a fair weight of bronze; and a similar weight of metal goes into 'tunic-fittings' or perhaps the word means an overcoat which is worn over the tunic, possibly a reinforced cape to protect the shoulders and upper arms.

An interesting but very incomplete series (Sk) from Knossos deals in more detail with body-armour, but there is no indication of the materials used. There is a helmet (*korus*), four helmet accessories (metal reinforcing plates on a leather or felt base?), two cheek-pieces; two *qe-ro₂*, two shoulder-pieces, and an unknown number of further accessories of some kind. The order in which these items are enumerated suggests that the untranslated word *qe-ro₂* means 'arm-guards' of some kind, though others see it as the two large plates making up the 'lobster'-type corslet. I think

63 Knossos chariot tablet: Sc 217

rather the second set of 'accessories' may be the main body protection, but without knowing how many there were speculation is dangerous. The word here translated 'accessories' (*o-pa-wo-ta*) means literally 'things hung on'. The ordinary Greek word for 'corslet' is not found at Knossos, but there is little doubt that it is represented by an ideogram (see fig. 63).

65 Mycenaean helmet from Knossos

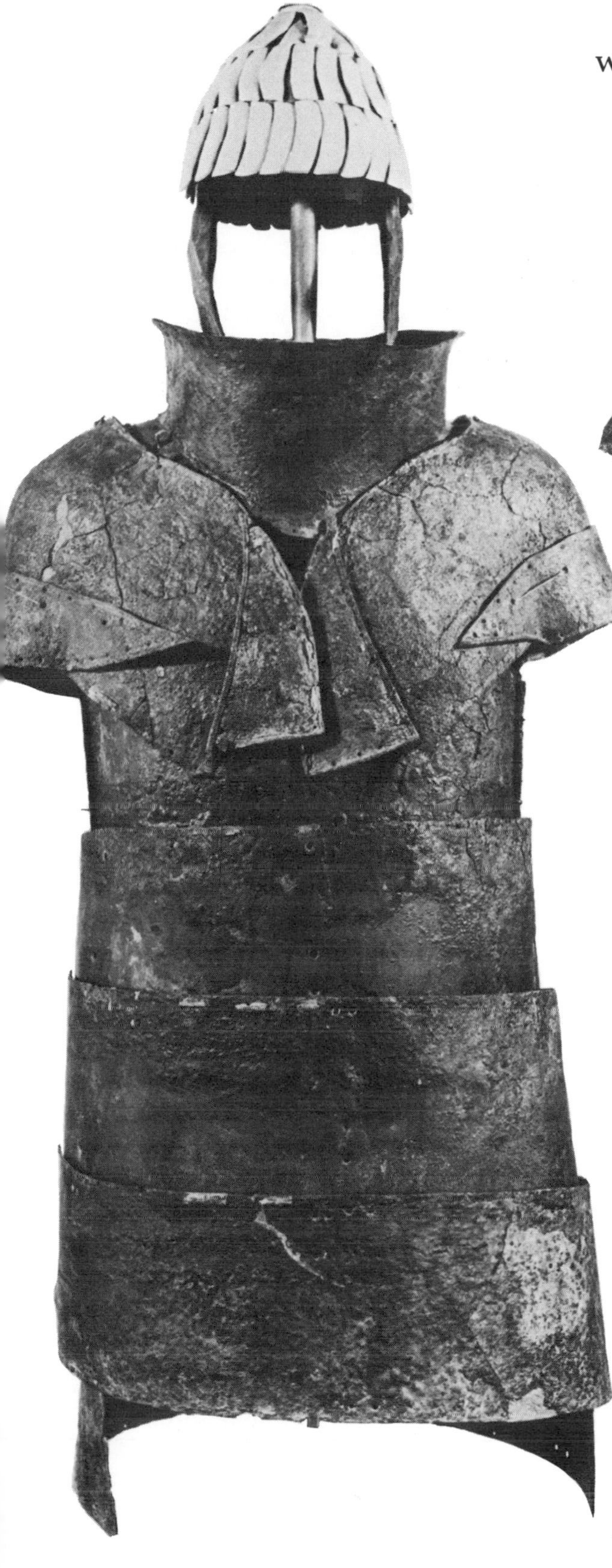

64 Bronze armour and helmet from Dhendrá

At Pylos we have the classical word for corslet (*thōrāx*) coupled with an
Fig. 66 ideogram which apparently depicts a short-sleeved tunic surmounted by a helmet. The closest parallel in shape is found in Egyptian paintings of
Fig. 67 slightly later date, which are of scale armour; some 250 to 500 metal plates were sewn onto a linen or leather tunic to reinforce it. At Pylos the formula is similar on each tablet, and although the words are usually abbreviated, each is spelt out at least once. Each corslet is listed as having twenty large and ten small 'accessories' (plates?); and, as at Knossos, four 'accessories' are added for the helmet together with two cheek-pieces. The helmet is not

66 Corslet and headdress from Pylos Sh tablets

67 Scale corslet from Egypt

difficult to imagine, if four petal-shaped plates are used to overcome the difficulties of fabricating a conical bronze object; and the cheek-pieces will be attached to its rim. But the corslet is much more difficult to envisage, since thirty plates is far too small a number for a 'scale' type corslet. Moreover, in four cases out of eleven the numbers are slightly higher: twenty-two large and twelve small plates.

Now it is evident that any suggestion for the distribution of these plates must account satisfactorily for these numbers. The absence so far of specimens from the archaeological record, either preserved *in corpore* or represented in art, must not hinder us in trying to reconstruct the appearance of this piece of armour. It is possible that the accessories or plates were sewn into the thickness of a linen tunic, so that the structure would not be apparent in drawings. All too often archaeological negatives in this field have been wrongly interpreted; no one had previously imagined the existence of such a suit of bronze body-armour as that found at Dhendrá.

In one case (Sh 740), where five 'old' corslets are listed, we have the abbreviation for 'pairs' in front of the numeral. It would be possible to have corslets made in matching pairs, for the warrior and his chariot-driver, as we might infer from the Knossos Sc series (see p. 167). But it is also possible that the pair refers to the two halves into which a corslet usually divides to enable the wearer to get into it. It is probably significant that all the figures referring to the plates are even: the 30 or 34 total will divide into two halves having respectively 15 and 17 plates. The problem therefore is to find an arrangement of 10 or 11 large plates and 5 or 6 small ones which will cover one side of the outline indicated by the ideogram (fig. 66). If the plates are irregularly distributed and vary greatly in size and shape almost any solution is conceivable; but if they are basically similar in size and shape, allowing only for the two sizes mentioned, the problem is more tractable. It is likely that 10 represents two rows of five, to match the five smaller ones. L. R. Palmer (1963, 333) proposed to interpret the 11 and 6 as allowing for shoulder-pieces; but the ideogram shows sleeves consistently in all cases, and again the argument of similarity of shape and size must be against it. Rather we should expect the large numbers to be disposed: 5+6+6. Palmer suggested that the 15 plates were arranged in five horizontal bands of three plates, two large at the side, one small in the middle. But as well as making it difficult to add the extra plates, this arrangement does not appear to have any particular reason. The fact quoted by Palmer, that the tunic ideogram of the Knossos Sc tablets is often divided into five horizontal bands, has to be balanced against the fact that the Pylos ideogram has often three horizontal bands, though the drawing is sometimes so careless that inferences must be doubtful. If we then imagine three horizontal rows, we can place five large, vertically elongated, plates to cover the chest, a row of five or six smaller plates to give the needed flexibility at the waist, and five or six larger ones again to protect the skirt. The increase in number will be accommodated on the lower Fig. 63

68 Suggested reconstruction of Pylos corslet

portion of the garment, since in several cases it has a pronounced flare. The plates will presumably overlap to give adequate protection; so that the final appearance might be something like fig. 68. This has two disadvantages; that the shoulders will not be well protected unless the plates are suitably curved at the top; and the sleeves carry no reinforcement. But no more satisfactory explanation has yet been given of these figures.

Mycenaean art has plenty of pictures of shields, apparently made of ox-hide and sometimes reinforced by metal bosses. The huge figure-of-eight shields of the earlier Mycenaean period were often used later as decoration, as in the famous shield fresco in the palace of Knossos. Yet there appears to be no record in our tablets of shields. We have ox-hides, but they are used, as far as we can tell, for other purposes. There is no ideogram which looks like a shield, nor any word which can be equated with classical or Homeric words for various kinds of shield. Set alongside the information we do have on weapons and body-armour, the absence of shields from the documents is puzzling. It is just possible that the shields lie hidden beneath a conventional ideogram which we have failed to recognize; but as more and more of the series of tablets can be assigned a function in the archives, this seems progressively less likely. We can only suppose that the palace did not reckon to supply such equipment to its troops; indeed it is not improbable that the weapons of the ordinary infantry-man were his own responsibility, and such supplies as the palace arsenal contained were for the officer class only.

Chariots

The Mycenaean warrior, however well armed, is incomplete without means of locomotion. Hence the need for a means of transport for the heavily armed warrior, though we must suppose the larger mass of regular troops moved on foot. The use of massed chariots in battle, which we know was the practice of contemporary neighbours of the Mycenaeans such as the Hittites, will hardly have been practicable in most parts of Greece, since the deployment of such forces demands open level plains unencumbered by trees or watercourses. On suitable terrain such tactics might have been employed; but in areas such as Messenia or Crete chariots can hardly have served other than as means of transport and perhaps as a prestige symbol.

The Mycenaean chariot is depicted on many Knossos tablets and is frequently to be seen in art, both frescoes such as the Pylos picture of two warriors riding in a chariot (fig. 69), and numerous scenes on vases. The chariot consists of a light body, possibly with wickerwork sides and front, with a fixed axle on which are mounted the two four-spoked wheels. It is ordinarily pulled by two horses, and actual skeletons of horses prove that the breed of horses then known in Greece was very small, hardly bigger than Shetland ponies. On the mid-Aegean island of Skyros a similar breed of half-wild horses survives to this day, and it is perhaps not too fanciful to see in them the descendants of this ancient breed. The absence of cavalry, despite evidence that horses could be ridden, is no doubt due to the lack of strength and stamina in this breed. Two horses, however, pulling a light car could offer a fast, if rather uncomfortable, ride on suitable roads.

We could therefore infer from the presence of chariots the existence of roads to permit their use. Suitable roads for unshod horses will have had a loose surface and will have been planned on inclines to avoid too steep a gradient. The difficulty for us lies in dating an ancient road, since roads of some sort have existed in Greece at every period since the Mycenaean; but until modern times many have been pack-horse trails, which can follow much steeper gradients than the carriage roads. Such for instance are the Turkish *kalderim*, traces of which are still often to be seen. But some stretches of Mycenaean road have been fairly certainly identified, especially by the structure of culverts and even small bridges still surviving, like that close to the modern road between Návplion and Epídhavros. On the route between modern Kalamáta and Pílos an ancient road has been

69 Mycenaean chariot on a Pylos fresco

detected with the S-curves on a gradient typical of a carriage road (McDonald and Rapp, 1972, 27, 245). South of the great palace of Knossos there was a viaduct crossing the ravine, and traces of a bridge over the ravine near Mycenae are still visible. We are still a long way from drawing a map of Mycenaean land routes; but it now seems certain that a proper road network existed within each kingdom. How far it was feasible to travel long distances by road is uncertain, and in Crete the more remote areas probably did not have satisfactory land communications. Fig. 70

Some details of the chariot and its fittings emerge from the inventories at Knossos; at Pylos the records of chariots are missing, but their existence can be inferred from the inventories of wheels. The chariot frames or

70 The viaduct just south of the palace at Knossos

bodies are indexed separately from the wheels. Some are fully equipped with yokes, bridles and other necessary fittings; but others are apparently stripped down, and in one case we have an entry which may mean 'reduced to constituent members', 'knocked down' (*me-ta-ke-ku-me-na*). Some of the technical terms remain obscure or at least opaque, but the main items listed in addition to the framework are: ivory inlay; bridles or harness; eye-pieces or blinkers (of leather or ivory); a mysterious set of fittings (*o-pi-i-ja-pi*) made of horn or bronze; a pair of 'heels', probably steps at the rear for mounting; a 'horse-follower' which may be a harness saddle of some kind; and a tube (*aulos*), again of obscure function. Some are said to be painted red (*phoinikiai*) or vermilion (*miltowessai*).

Most of the fully equipped vehicles are single or in pairs; but the numbers of plain chariot frames are much larger, for we have twice the entry 80, once 56 and smaller numbers. The wheels are also listed in considerable numbers. The reconstruction of a large tablet (Sg 1811), still unfortunately far from complete, gives on a single document a total of at least 246 chariot-frames and 208 pairs of wheels. It would seem likely that as well as a number of luxury vehicles, Knossos could put in the field around 200 chariots.

But in addition to these inventories of chariots, which come mainly from the arsenal building outside the palace proper, we have the remains of a curious series of small tablets (Sc) showing fully-equipped chariots with the wheels in position (see fig. 63, p. 160). Relatively few of these tablets are complete, but the formula can be worked out as follows. The first word is apparently always a man's name: but whether he is the owner (i.e. warrior) or the driver remains unclear. Then follows a sign for a tunic, probably a piece of armour rather than an ordinary garment, with the numeral 2, a complete chariot with the numeral 1, and a pair of horses. This at least is the maximum offered by the formula; but large numbers of tablets apparently fall short of this maximum. Any one of the three items may be omitted: e.g. Sc 236 has the tunic sign written but then deleted, no horse entry, so only the chariot; Sc 222 has two tunics and the pair of horses, but no chariot. Moreover, the number of tunics can also be one (e.g. Sc 243); at least eighteen times this sign was written and deleted. Even more remarkable, the number of horses can also be one; in this case instead of the sign for pair (*ZE* = *dzeugos*), we have *MO* (= *monwos*) 'single'. The ideogram for chariot can be seen on ninety-one of these tablets, but the whole series must have been rather larger; owing to their fragmentary condition a straight count of tablets is impossible, since some will appear twice in the lists.

Now it would be easy enough to explain a series of 100 tablets with the maximum formula as an inventory of the Knossian chariot force. The two tunics, or corslets, would be for the warrior and his charioteer; surely not the two pieces of a jointed 'lobster' corslet. But if this is an inventory of the present readiness of this force, it is woefully ill equipped; hardly any units are ready to take the field, some have only one horse or none, some have horses but no chariot, and a lot are devoid of corslets. Either the force has just met with a disaster, or it has not been used for so long that half its equipment is missing. Neither of these alternatives sounds probable; can we imagine another solution?

We must consider first the curious deletions on this series. A sign incised on clay can easily be deleted at the time of writing, but usually leaves traces which remain visible even when written over. Hence we can say without hesitation that on this series about twenty tablets originally had the tunic sign written, but subsequently deleted. Deletions and corrections are not uncommon on the tablets, but it is curious here how the deleted sign is almost always the one for tunic. Moreover, the deleted sign has in at least two cases been replaced by another, quite different, sign. What this sign means is not entirely certain. It bears a close resemblance to a sign identified as an ingot, apparently used in inventories of stores of copper or bronze; and although this is a probable value for it here too, some doubt must attach to it, since there is no sign to indicate the metal of which it is made, nor is any weight given. There is also one case where this same sign replaces not the tunic but the horse entry.

The suggestion was therefore made that in some cases the charioteer was able to draw an ingot of bronze instead of a bronze-plated corslet; instead of the finished article you get the raw materials, or rather a part of the raw materials, needed to make it. The absence of the linen, leather or whatever was used as a foundation, is a problem; it is not a complete do-it-yourself kit for the home-made corslet, though of course the quantity of bronze would be the item hardest to come by. Yet supposing this were true, can we seriously imagine a situation in which the individual warrior was supplied with raw materials instead of the finished object? How long would it have taken to turn the ingot into a serviceable piece of armour? This suggestion does little more than compound our perplexity in the face of these documents.

But we must explore further the idea that the chariot-force is being mustered, perhaps as a part of regular spring manoeuvres, and the stores have been instructed to issue any equipment that is found to be missing or unserviceable. One man possesses a chariot, but has to draw two tunics and a pair of horses; another has one horse, but no other equipment; and so on. Now the consequence of this theory is that if a man had all his equipment complete, a tablet would be made out recording his name, but nothing else. There are such small tablets, belonging to the same archive as the Sc tablets, often ending after the name with the figure 1 (Vc). Are these really part of the same list? There is at least one name that figures on both lists, but this could perhaps be explained away as another man of the same name; most of the names certainly do not repeat in the other list. The situation would then be somewhat improved, since the number showing deficiencies would be less than two-thirds of the total. But we are still faced with the difficulty that the chariot-force would have been desperately short of equipment, and the issue of raw bronze will hardly have contributed to its battle-readiness.

This was one reason why I put forward the suggestion (Chadwick, 1968, 17–21) that all the tablets from what Evans called the Room of the Chariot Tablets, including the Sc and Vc series, were not genuine documents, but were in some sense scribal exercises. The other main reason was that all the tablets from this area are written in a very distinctive style of writing; not apparently by a single hand, but by a number of writers all copying a single style. The very least that is necessary is to suppose that the man in charge of this office was a strict master who made all his clerks imitate his own handwriting. And is this likely, unless the master was in fact a teacher? It is also very noticeable that all the tablets in the group are singularly uninformative: they rarely give as much information as the cryptic Sc series discussed above. Nor are there any certain links between these tablets and the main archive; some places of course are mentioned in both, but although some of the men's names reappear elsewhere, there is no proof that the same persons are meant. Since some of them are elsewhere in charge of flocks of sheep, it would seem unlikely. Nor are the repeated names more frequent than those which repeat at other sites, where identity is of course excluded. Whatever the true solution of this mystery, it is impossible to ignore the problem. Merely to protest, as one writer did, that this is to discard much valuable evidence is no help; if the evidence is valuable, it must be capable of rational explanation. If it is valueless, we must beware of building theories upon it.

At Pylos no tablets listing chariots have been found; possibly they were kept in an outlying building which has not been excavated. One must continually bear in mind that the excavated area is only the central palace-complex, and the surroundings undoubtedly contain the remains of other less important buildings, which, on the analogy of other Mycenaean palaces, would certainly have had minor archives of tablets. Unfortunately the cost of extending the excavation was too high, and the results would perhaps not have justified the expense.

There is, however, a large series of tablets (Sa) which records wheels. It is impossible to be sure that they are not wheels for something else, but the fact that they are commonly listed as one pair per tablet certainly suggests a two-wheeled vehicle, which can hardly be anything but a chariot. The usual formula runs: 'The vehicle of X, (doubtful word), one pair of wheels with borders.' X is a man's name; very few of the names in this series are found elsewhere. One is, understandably, found on an armour tablet (Sh 736); two are among the names of shepherds at other places in the kingdom and are probably therefore duplicated names. We can conclude from this that the series is not a list of chariots belonging to high officials, unless of course the name is that of the driver. The doubtful word is thought to mean 'in good condition', 'serviceable', since it apparently contrasts with a word definitely meaning 'unfit for use', 'unserviceable'. But there are problems in equating it with the classical word for this, and other interpretations have been proposed; one 'turning upon an axle' is very unlikely for the factual reason that the Mycenaean chariot has a fixed axle secured to the chariot, and the wheels are mounted on this and secured by a lynch-pin. Wheels with borders (*termidwenta*) are mentioned frequently at Knossos, but we do not know to what the 'border' or 'edge' refers. One is tempted to think of some kind of tyre, but it is not the word used for this in Homeric and later Greek; since it is once said to be of ivory, it is presumably some decorative element. A few men have two pairs of wheels, none more.

There are, however, other tablets in this series which list wheels not allocated to a particular vehicle. These are presumably spares in stock, e.g.: 'bound with silver, one pair of wheels' (Sa 287); 'of cypress-wood, one pair of wheels with borders and one single wheel' (Sa 488); 'wrought, unfit for use, six pairs of wheels' (Sa 682); 'Zakynthian, unfit for use, 32 pairs of wheels with borders' (Sa 751); 'Followers'-type wheels, unfit for use, 6 pairs of wheels with borders' (Sa 790): 'with ivory borders, old, thin (?), 11 pairs of wheels with borders' (Sa 793); 'bound with bronze, unfit for use, 1 pair of wheels' (Sa 794). There are also two totalling documents: 'so many serviceable, new, 20 pairs of wheels with borders' (Sa 843); 'so many old, serviceable, 31 pairs and one single wheel'; 'old, Followers'-type, 12 pairs of wheels; Zakynthian, 32 pairs of wheels' (Sa 787). The last entry on this tablet matches Sa 751 so closely that it must surely refer to the same lot; but it is not clear how the other figures square with these tablets. There are 22 pairs of wheels assigned to particular vehicles.

From all this we can safely conclude that Pylos had a chariot force of some sort, but this evidence suggests that it was on a smaller scale than at Knossos. One can only speculate about the reason; possibly the smaller size of the kingdom has something to do with it, but the absence of the chariot records must leave the true size of the force at Pylos in doubt.

Weapons

Evans had called attention to a cache of tablets (Ra) showing pictures of what appear to be short swords. It is difficult from the sketch to be sure whether these are swords, somewhat foreshortened by the need to draw them in vertical position on a horizontally arranged tablet, or whether they are really daggers. The problem is not resolved by the word used on the

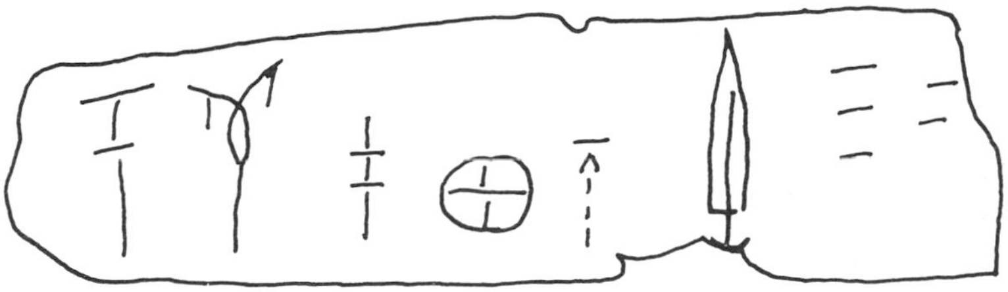

71 Knossos tablet showing swords or daggers: Ra 1540

tablets to describe them; *pa-ka-na* is certainly the Homeric *phasgana*, and in Homer this is one of the three words in use for 'swords'. But the analogy of other words suggests that the Homeric use may have been a later confusion of terms which in Mycenaean had distinct meanings, so that 'daggers' remains an equally plausible translation.

Whatever the truth of this argument, it may not be too fanciful to see in this group of tablets an inventory kept in the armoury of the king's bodyguard. The tablets were found in a corridor on the east of the central court, not far from the royal apartments, and it would have been necessary for the body-guard to have a store of weapons available for immediate use; they may even have been intended for issue to members of the court in case of emergency. If we may use the *Odyssey* as evidence, however anachronistic, this shows that weapons were ordinarily kept in royal residences; for one of the major problems confronting Odysseus in his attack on the suitors was how to get the weapons out of the hall without attracting attention, so that when the shooting began they would be unable to arm themselves. A tablet serving as total to this series (Ra 1540; fig. 71) has a number not smaller than 50 for these swords or daggers. Some of them have descriptions which are not easy to interpret; 'fitted with band' may refer to baldrics on which the weapon could be slung and worn. Some are described as 'bound with ivory' (Ra 984, 1028); but other terms so far resist satisfactory interpretation.

At Pylos this word for 'sword' or 'dagger' does not recur; but a strange tablet which belongs with the inventory of vessels and furniture (Ta 716) records two swords; the word is here the classical *xiphos*, though the spelling is surprising. There are also two double-axes, if we may trust the drawing, but the word describing them cannot be equated with an appropriate classical form. The tablet ordering contributions of bronze (Jn 829; see p. 141) states that these are needed to make tips for spears and *pa-ta-ja*. This word recurs at Knossos on some sealings (Ws 1704, Ws 1705, Ws 8495), which show a short pointed stick (see fig. 72). Evans found in association with these sealings what he described as arrowheads, and we

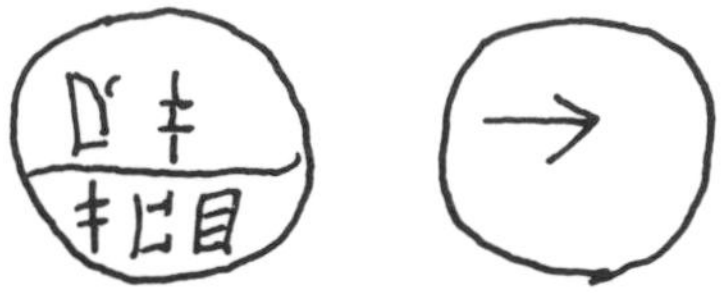

72 Javelins on a Knossos sealing: Ws 1704

jumped to the conclusion *pa-ta-ja* meant arrows. But there is another ideogram with flights on the tail (see fig. 73) which is quite certainly an arrow, and that leads us to consider the pointed stick as more likely a light throwing-spear or javelin; some of the many objects catalogued in museums as arrowheads may belong to this type of weapon. There seems no doubt that this kind of spear was used for hunting by the Mycenaeans,

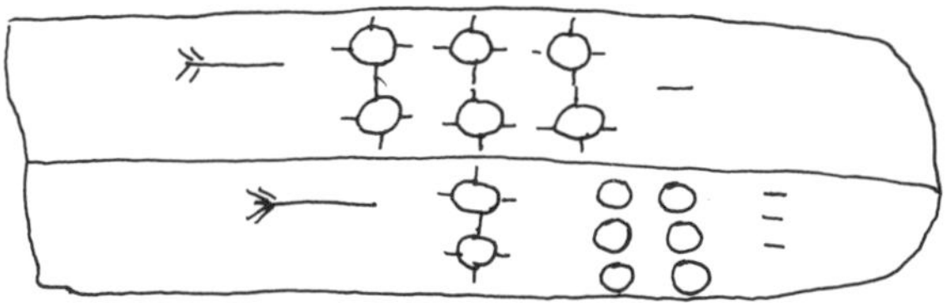

73 Arrows on a Knossos tablet: R 4482

and if Homer were to be trusted we could extend it to use in war. But the scenes in art which are certainly military show the use of the single heavy thrusting spear, and this is clearly what is called *enkhos* (the classical word too) on the tablets.

Military organization

The dearth of weapons on the tablets is not to be read as proof that the Mycenaeans were a peaceful people. We must remember that the tablets record the areas of life which the palace interested itself in; obviously therefore the kings of Pylos and Knossos did not keep a well-stocked arsenal from which the army on mobilization could draw its weapons. It is more likely that, as in classical Greece, every man was expected to possess personal weapons, and to use them when required for military service.

The absence of any lists of troops at Knossos is disappointing; for the king must have had powerful forces to maintain his hold over such a wide territory, and the 'warrior tombs' around Knossos fit this picture. They must have belonged to some of the Followers who are mentioned, rather infrequently and in small numbers, on the Knossos tablets.

At Pylos the situation is a little better. There are at least large numbers of men referred to as 'rowers', and from this we can perhaps infer something of the naval organization. It must, however, be admitted that the word translated 'rower' appears at Knossos in contexts which do not appear to be appropriate; e.g. in C 902 where a 'rower' intrudes into a list which consists mainly of local governors. But at Pylos we have a list (An 1) of 30 men who are drawn from five places and are 'going as rowers to Pleuron'. Where this Pleuron was we have no means of knowing; it might, but need not, be the town of this name on the north of the Corinthian gulf. A much larger list (An 610) has its heading badly damaged, but the word 'rowers' is visible on it. A total of 569 men can be counted on the preserved part, but the figures are missing for five entries and some of the others may be incomplete, so the true total was probably between 600 and 700. It has been suggested that 30 rowers might be the complement of one ship, so that this force would be enough to man more than 20 ships. But the newly discovered ship fresco from Thera seems to show that Minoan warships had a complement of 42 oarsmen; whether this can be extended to Mycenaean ships is uncertain, for the other representations of ships in art are usually too crude to allow us to place any confidence in the count of oars. Homer appears to reckon on a complement of 52 men per ship, but two of these are the officers. If the season of the year permitted an enemy to attack by sea, then the Pylian fleet too could have put to sea.

The strategic problem confronting the king of Pylos was clear. In the disturbed times which ended the thirteenth century a few Mycenaean monarchs had been able to construct massive fortifications behind which their people and at least some of their animals could shelter. The enormous circuit of walls at Gla in Boeotia could have contained tens of thousands of sheep; the problem would have been to feed them. But virtually no trace of fortifications came to light at Pylos; the only traces of heavy walls seem to date from an earlier period and to have been dismantled by the thirteenth century. Thus the king must have relied for defence on keeping the enemy away from his palace. The kingdom, if the reconstruction given in Chapter 3 is accepted, is difficult to invade by land. The eastern frontier is a high mountain range; a lower but difficult tract of mountain forms the northern boundary. In the north-east corner there is a route, followed by the modern road and railway, which by a stiff climb allows access to the central plateau of Arcadia. This valley would not be difficult to hold against an enemy; but to have reached this area an enemy would presumably have first subdued the whole of the northern Peloponnese. There was little to fear from this direction so long as Mycenae held out. Only along the west coast is there an easy line of approach from the north; and here too there is a convenient little pass which could easily be held. The king of Pylos cannot have been much worried about invasion by land; but the sea is another story.

The total coastline of the kingdom is about 150 km. The figure is approximate because no one can tell me how to measure coastlines; it depends whether you follow exactly every inlet and promontory, or take a more general line. If the enemy came by sea, he would have the choice of a number of areas for a landing, but on a largely rocky coastline some areas would be obviously unsuitable, and others would be difficult, so the real points of danger are actually fairly few. Starting in the north there is a region to the north of the modern Kiparissía, with good beaches and easy access to the important sites stretching up the river valley which ultimately leads to the upper Messenian valley. South of Kiparissía the coast is less favourable for landing, and the country inland is broken and rather difficult. Just north of the Bay of Navaríno is the little harbour of Voïdhokiliá, which may have been the main port. The bay itself is an ideal landing site with some 5 km of sandy beach protected by the island of Sphakteria. This is the obvious route to the palace about 6 km away and constitutes the point of maximum danger. To the south of modern Pílos there are cliffs, and landing would be impracticable before reaching Methóni, the south-western tip of the peninsula. Either here or at Phinikoús, 12 km to the east, landing would have been possible, but the area is remote from the palace and the main centres of population. The southern tip of the peninsula, Cape Akrítas, is again inhospitable and rocky. Inside the Messenian gulf landing would be impossible almost anywhere as far as the frontier at modern Kalamáta, except for a stretch along the north shore which is now marshy, and although the coastline may have been different in antiquity was probably a marsh then too. But however easy to land here, it is again remote from the palace; and the gulf is a dangerous place to enter if there is any risk of finding your exit blocked by a hostile fleet. It was precisely this consideration that in 1941 forced a British squadron, which had been sent to take off the troops withdrawing in the face of the German invasion, to withdraw without completing its mission. If an Italian fleet had appeared on the scene, it might have led to a major naval disaster. Thus the Messenian gulf, although attractive in some ways, would not be a very likely point to choose to attack.

But from the point of view of the defence, the paramount need was for an organization to keep watch over the long coastline and give warning of an enemy fleet or landing. It so happens that one of our most important documents is just that. It is headed: 'Thus the watchers are guarding the coastal regions', a clear indication of its purpose. But it needs to be described in detail.

This single document is contained on a set of five tablets (An 657, An 654, An 519, An 656, An 661); the pages are not numbered and the reconstructed order just given depends upon a series of complicated arguments. But when so arranged a pattern emerges clearly. The whole coast is divided into ten sectors. In each sector the name of the official responsible is given, followed by a few other names who are presumably his subordinates. We know one or two of these officials from other documents, and it seems they belong to the local governing class. Thereafter follow groups of men, who are described in various ways: their number is always a multiple of 10 and may be as high as 110. A few figures may be missing or incomplete, but the surviving total comes to 800. This is a large force, if concentrated, but if spread out along 150 km of coastline amounts to little more than one man every two hundred metres. Such a force could never offer effective resistance; but it would be quite adequate to maintain look-outs. Indications of place are given, but these cannot all be located; it is, however, established that the sectors begin on the Nédha river in the north, follow the west coast down to Cape Akrítas and then turn north into the Messenian gulf.

Some of the groups of men are described by reference to their native town. Thus the sector at *Owithnos* (or some such name; it has no known classical form) is manned by the men of that town. But there are a number of other terms used to describe these groups of men, none of which can be identified as words known to the later Greek vocabulary; some of them look like derivatives of place names, but again no such places are mentioned elsewhere on the tablets. A possible, but I must emphasize only a possible, solution is that these names are tribal designations of groups of people resident in the kingdom, but not full citizens. They might for instance be the remains of the pre-Greek population which had not been absorbed by the Greek newcomers. Such tribes would hardly have been trusted to serve in the army; but they could well have provided the manpower needed for non-combatant duties such as look-outs, if properly officered by Greeks.

Now there is a further piece of information contained in this document. At intervals we come across the entry: 'and with them [is] the Follower So-and-so'. There are in all eleven such entries, though in one case the name is not given; elsewhere the name is usually given in its full form, that is with patronymic. There are ten sectors and eleven Followers; but the arrangement is not regular. A table will show this best:

	Sector
Ke-ki-jo	I, II north
A₃-ko-ta	II south
A-re-ku-tu-ru-wo	III
Ro-u-ko	IV, V, VI
Pe-ro-qo-ni-jo	VII north
Di-wi-je-u	VII south
Di-ko-na-ro	VIII north
Pe-re-u-ro-ni-jo	VIII central
Ka-e-sa-me-no	VIII south
Wo-ro-tu-mi-ni-jo	IX
(unnamed)	X

The first suggestion for the function of the Follower was that he was some sort of liaison officer. It is no use having a look-out organization, if it cannot communicate rapidly with headquarters. As we have seen (p. 170), Pylos knew 'wheels of Follower type'; therefore Followers must have had chariots. These Followers would thus have been able to receive reports from the look-out units, and send off their charioteers as despatch-riders to take messages back to the king at Pylos. But although this is probably part of the truth, it does not explain the irregular distribution of the Followers; why should one sector need three liaison officers, while another officer had to cover three sectors?

I have therefore suggested another explanation. The most marked concentration of Followers, five in all, is in Sectors VII and VIII, which must be towards the southern end of the west coast, in fact, the area of the Bay of Navaríno and the coast immediately north of it. This, as we have already seen, is exactly the point of maximum danger upon a strategic appraisal of the situation. There is also a minor concentration of two Followers in Sector II, up in the north; this clearly represents the coastal end of the Kiparissía river valley, another important strategic location. We know that the Followers are senior officials of the royal household; all we have to suppose is that each of the eleven listed on this document is in command of a regiment of the Pylian army, and it is at once clear that we have a convincing picture of the king's military dispositions to meet the threatened invasion.

Two regiments are stationed in the Kiparissía area and just to the north of it (Sector II); they will serve to protect the important route inland and the settlements in it, and incidentally they can cover the coastal road from further north. The area south of Kiparissía is less suitable for landing; one regiment covers Sector III but Sectors IV, V and VI are weakly defended. They will represent the rather unfavourable coastline in this area. The real danger is that the enemy will land on the beaches just north of Navaríno (including the likely port at Voïdhokiliá), or in the Bay itself. Thus Sector VII has two regiments, Sector VIII (the Bay?) no less than three; nearly half the available forces are concentrated in this area, a perfectly correct disposition to meet this threat. One regiment is in the south of the peninsula, though not so far south as Phinikoús or Koróni; it could therefore quickly come to support the main force; or if the attack developed in the Gulf of Messenia, it could act jointly with the regiment stationed at the north of the Gulf. This is perhaps a weak point in the system; a major landing at the head of the Gulf would encounter only a weak force, and if successful the way would be open to the important settlements in the Messenian valley. But its approach to the palace would still be blocked by the main force in the Navaríno area; for all or part of this could rapidly be moved to occupy the high ground over which an attacking force would have to pass. The king's decision to leave this area weakly defended was probably right. Everything must have depended upon the resistance of the five regiments of the main army group; for if they were defeated, the palace could not be defended.

What actually happened remains a tantalizing mystery. All we know is that the palace was looted and burnt. The absence of human remains suggests that no resistance took place there; probably as soon as news was received of the army's defeat, or even earlier, the non-combatant inhabitants had withdrawn to the shelter of the mountains, carrying with them perhaps a few treasures. Any women and children captured by the raiders would of course have been carried off as slaves; the men would have been butchered. Something drastic must have happened to account for the paucity of sites which appear to have continued in occupation in the subsequent phase (LH III C); the archaeological picture suggests that the population was reduced to something like a tenth of its earlier numbers. No doubt many of the survivors abandoned sites too easily reached by sea-borne raiders, and moved further inland. The dispersal of place names found on the tablets may have been caused by this movement (see p. 40). There is also archaeological evidence suggesting that some found refuge in the north-west of the Peloponnese, and even the Ionian islands, where there seem to have been flourishing settlements in the LH III C period.

But who were the raiders? The indications that they came by sea are very strong; and if one reaction to the attack was a withdrawal northwards, the raiders must have come from the south, and presumably therefore the east. No positive evidence will take us further. But if we can allow ourselves a speculation, it is hard to dismiss from our minds the attacks on Egypt which were launched about this time by what the Egyptians called 'the Peoples of the Sea'. There is little doubt that these 'Sea-peoples' came from the Aegean area; the Egyptians even list their names, but as usual they are hard to identify. Even if we think we recognize the Philistines and the Lycians, we cannot tell whether they had at this date already occupied their positions of historical times. The Philistines at least are likely to have settled in Palestine only after being repulsed from Egypt, and there is reason to think that they had earlier Aegean connexions. The evidence such as it is suggests that these people had their base in Anatolia.

Now among these Sea-peoples was a tribe called by the Egyptians by a name which suggests vaguely 'Achaeans'; but the phonetic resemblance is not close, and in any case we doubt whether the Mycenaeans called themselves by that name. But the date of their two attacks on Egypt, 1225 and 1183 B.C. on the usual chronology, fits so closely with the date for the destruction of Pylos that it is very tempting to bring them into connexion. The Sea-peoples' attack on Egypt appears to have been no mere raid, but a serious attempt at invasion for the purpose of settlement, since the force comprised wagons laden with women and children as well as ships. But since they possessed a powerful fleet, even a small division of it would have been enough to mount a raid on a small kingdom, if the main force was only repelled with difficulty by one of the major powers of the time. They may well have been like the Vikings; a collection of pirates who combined from time to time to tackle major targets, but often operated in smaller groups against weaker enemies. If their bases were in the eastern Aegean, they would have made the trade routes to Cyprus and the Levant insecure, and this would square with the evidence (see p. 141) that there was a shortage of raw material for the metal industry. But whatever the truth, and we shall perhaps never know for sure, these are the prime suspects in the case.

The time of year at which the attack came must have been the spring, for reasons shown in Chapter 11. The extraordinary document listing offerings is headed with what is probably a month name signifying 'sailing time' (p. 90). This too fits well with the theory of a sea-borne raid; it will have been one of the first operations attempted at the start of a new campaigning season.

The fall of Knossos is much less well documented, for despite our searches it has yet to be shown that any of the tablets there relate to military preparations. Only the issue of armour, chariots and horses might be read in this context as an attempt to bring a fighting force up to strength; and as we have seen (p. 170), this theory is not without its difficulties. Rather it would seem that the king of Knossos had little warning of the impending blow; it may have been an internal *coup d'état*, rather than a military operation. But what is surprising is that in these circumstances the palace was set on fire. There are still many problems about the destruction of Knossos which have no solutions, and it is unwise to speculate when evidence is so scanty.

10 HOMER THE PSEUDO-HISTORIAN

Somewhere around the year 700 B.C. a poet whose name was known to later ages as *Homēros*, a word meaning 'hostage', put together two large epic poems. The *Iliad*, named after Ilium, the alternative name of Troy, describes a short but vital period in the tenth year of the siege of that city by a Greek expeditionary force. The *Odyssey* is the story of the homecoming of Odysseus from the Trojan War. Thus both poems are set in the same period, and at a great remove from the date of their composition. Yet they are the sole prime source for the history of the Trojan War. When did it happen? Did it even happen at all?

Greece in the eighth century B.C. was a disorganized collection of petty states, still living at a comparatively low level of civilization; houses were mainly of wood and mud-brick; precious materials were very scarce; the arts of painting and sculpture were primitive. Yet the Greece Homer describes is a network of well-organized kingdoms capable of joint military action; its kings live in luxurious stone-built palaces, adorned with gold, ivory and other precious materials. The scenes attributed to the shield made for Akhilleus by the god Hēphaistos argue a high degree of artistic competence. Nor does this situation square with what little we know of conditions in the ninth, tenth or eleventh centuries, the so-called Dark Age. In order to find a plausible setting for the Greece Homer describes we need to go back to the Mycenaean age, to the twelfth or more likely the thirteenth century at the latest.

Is it possible that a poet of the eighth century could accurately describe events which happened five hundred years earlier? The answer to this question is perhaps yes. We have for example the parallel of the medieval *Song of Roland* which, apparently composed in the twelfth century, relates an event that occurred in the year 778. But the comparison with other epics is both encouraging and disappointing. They show that oral tradition could perfectly well preserve historical facts for many centuries, but they also show that it has a habit of distorting the truth and introducing serious errors into the account. The *Song of Roland* has even the wrong enemy; and other epics introduce into the story characters who were not contemporaries. We cannot therefore accept the Homeric story as historical as it stands; much of it is unverifiable, but we must estimate Homer's credibility by testing his account where we do have evidence.

It is to the eternal credit of the American scholar Milman Parry (1902–35) that he demonstrated the way in which oral poetry works. It is of course possible to preserve a work of literature by transmitting it word for word from one reciter to another; some of the Vedic hymns were so transmitted in India for many centuries before they were committed to writing. Once composed, the epics of Homer might have been so preserved before they were written down; but the date at which writing came into the tradition is hard to determine, because the text we possess is based upon an edition in modernized spelling published in the third century B.C. If Homer is rightly dated to the eighth century, this is just the period at which alphabetic writing was spreading throughout Greek lands.

But in an illiterate or semi-literate community the process of oral composition leaves characteristic traces on the poem. The creative singer is no mere record-player; he creates new poems as he recites. He is able to perform this feat because he has stored in his memory groups of lines, single lines, half-lines and even smaller units suitable for all the normal situations. He does not have to waste time wondering how to describe nightfall, he has ready to hand the line: 'And so the sun went down and all the streets became darkened.' If a warrior is struck down in battle: 'Down he fell with a thud and his armour clattered around him.' There are numerous formulas for speech, such as: 'Thus indeed he spoke and addressed him with words that went flying.' Every hero has his stock epithet: Akhilleus is 'fleet of foot', Odysseus 'much-devising', Agamemnon 'king of men'. Since Greek is an inflected language, these names have different patterns of scansion in different cases so that the epithet has to change too; 'Akhilleus fleet of foot' will not scan in the genitive, and he may therefore become 'Akhilleus the son of Peleus' in that case. Every common object has its series of stock epithets: a ship is 'swift' or 'rounded at both ends'; a hand is 'stout', even when it belongs to a queen; a porch is 'echoing', even when assigned to a stranger as his room for the night. This quaint system has two advantages: it makes the task of the composer practicable, for the formula gives him time to arrange in his head the next line: and it gives the hearer the comfortable feeling of recognizing part of a poem he has never heard before – a totally original composition is rarely fully appreciated at first hearing. The disadvantage is that such poetry quickly becomes jejune and repetitious. The Yugoslav singers recorded by Parry and his successors may have sounded well enough around a camp-fire; studied in cold print they are largely devoid of poetic merit.

Homer shows a great deal of evidence of formulaic composition, but his work is generally at a far higher level. He was not merely a clever story-teller, but one of the world's great poets. He took the oral tradition and transformed it into superb poetry. This is not to say that there are not tedious sections, but the plot, the characterization and the descriptions are

74 Fresco from Pylos showing a lyre-player

all so well handled that the devices of oral composition become a specific merit. But it is evident that Homer inherited much of his technique from his unknown predecessors; he may equally have inherited much of the story.

In this tradition, handed down from one singer to the next, lies the explanation of the link which binds Homer to the Mycenaean age. No written records survived from the Mycenaean palaces, or if they did, no one remained who knew how to read them. The secrets of Linear B were lost. When Homer describes a letter entrusted to a traveller – it was, ironically, a request for the bearer to be quietly liquidated – Homer describes it as something exotic and almost magical; writing was no more than a dim memory. But some idea of the Mycenaean world could well have been passed down through the Dark Ages to Homer, and the tradition of verse-making may go back to the Mycenaean palaces. The so-called theatral areas of the Cretan palaces are much better adapted to vocal performances than bull-sports. There is a fresco from Pylos showing a lyre-player sitting on a rock; was he perhaps a distant fore-runner of Homer? Fig. 74

There are more than a few indications that elements in the Homeric poems go back not to the end of the Mycenaean period but an earlier phase. One character in the *Iliad* has the great body-shield described as 'like a tower', yet these seem to have gone out of use a couple of centuries earlier; the parallel of epics which combine historical but not contemporary characters suggests that this may have happened here. There is an exact description in Homer of a helmet covered in plates cut from boars' tusks; such an object was known in the early Mycenaean period, but seems to have gone out of fashion by the thirteenth century. One of the striking formulas used to name a hero is to call him 'the holy might of Alkinoos' (or whatever his name might be); but he does not have to be particularly pious to deserve this appellation, and the word which to the later Greeks meant 'holy' may have started by meaning little more than 'powerful'. What is interesting about it is that this same phrase (without the proper name) occurs also in the Vedic hymns; the Greek *hieron menos* is exactly paralleled by Vedic *ishiram manas*, not just in sense, 'mighty power', but these are in origin the very same two words. It would seem probable that both languages have here preserved a very ancient expression. At the same time it must not be supposed that Homer's language is simply inherited from the Mycenaean period; some phrases might well be, but such a passage as the description of the boars' tusk helmet contains language of later origin. Not all of Homer, if transcribed back into Mycenaean, would still scan.

Tradition tells us very little about Homer himself. It says he was blind, which may be a guess based upon the blind singer Demodokos who appears in the *Odyssey*, but since the blind often have an abnormally good memory, and this a singer must have, there might have been some truth in it. We do not know the name of Homer's father; yet this is the essential patent of respectability which any free Greek citizen must possess. This, combined with his unusual name, has led to speculation that he was not perhaps a Greek speaker, but introduced poetry to the Greeks by translating from his native language, just as the first Roman poet was a Greek who translated Homer into Latin. Such a theory is incompatible with the evidence of a long Greek oral tradition; Homer's predecessors undoubtedly spoke Greek. Perhaps worst of all we do not know where he came from, for the fact that seven cities could claim to be his birthplace proves that the Greeks had no reliable information. On the evidence of the dialect of the poems he must have lived in Ionia, the central part of the west coast of Anatolia, and this accords with the location of most of the claimants.

So far I have spoken of Homer as the author of both the *Iliad* and the *Odyssey*. But was he one man or two? Although there is in each poem a monumental structure, which implies a single architect, no matter how many builders, it is uncertain whether the same architect designed both structures. Superficially they are very much alike; but if you probe deep enough, you can detect differences, some of which would be hard to explain if they were the product of the same brain. Given sufficient time and ingenuity, it could doubtless be proved that *Paradise Lost* and *Paradise Regained*, or the *Inferno* and the *Paradiso* of the *Divina Commedia*, were by different hands, for no man's style remains unchanged throughout his life. Yet there are differences between the *Iliad* and the *Odyssey* which seem to require more explanation than the process of ageing. There is a striking difference of attitude between the gory warfare of the *Iliad* and the light-hearted adventures of the *Odyssey*. Perhaps the explanation is not that the same small area produced almost contemporaneously two geniuses, but that the one Homer inherited two different traditions which account for these differences underneath the superficial uniformity.

It has for the past century been fashionable to use archaeology to 'prove the truth' of legends. Mind you, not all legends yield to this treatment; we have yet to dig up the bones of the Sphinx or discover the Linear B tablet on which Phaidra accused Hippolytos. But if a fact recorded by Homer can be shown to agree with archaeological remains, this is thought to increase the probability that he is telling the truth where we cannot verify his statements. There is a close analogy here with what is known as biblical archaeology; since digging has disclosed the existence of towns mentioned in the Old Testament, its moral authority is thought to be vindicated – as if the excavation of the walls of Jericho proved that they were brought down by the vibration of passing traffic. It is not enough to demonstrate that a few facts in Homer's account are correct; we need to examine all the points where his picture can be checked by archaeology and then see what sort of a balance sheet we can draw up. The disclosures of Linear B have significantly changed that balance.

Whatever Heinrich Schliemann failed to do, he must at least have the credit for correctly locating at Hisarlık the city later ages knew as Troy, and by his unauthorized digging he pioneered the archaeological exploration of the Aegean world in the Bronze Age. Troy was inhabited with only short breaks from the fourth millennium B.C., for the remains of nine or more cities lie one on top of another in layers, now dissected and exposed as some monstrous kind of anatomical specimen by the labours of generations of devoted archaeologists. One of these layered cities, known as Troy VIIA, seems to have been destroyed by enemy action around 1250 B.C., a date which will fit well enough with Homer's Trojan War. The date is in fact so suspiciously close to the general collapse of Mycenaean Greece that it may yet prove to have been an incident in that saga of destruction. But those who want to save Homer's reputation can claim it as confirmation of the Trojan War.

There is, however, a vast difference between the detail which fits the legend and the truth which confirms it. Archaeology has no means of telling us the names of the generals, nor even who the attackers were. While we need not press our scepticism to the point of rejecting the story of the Trojan War altogether, we must, I believe, express considerable reservations about the details of that war: its date, its cause, the participants and so on. Nor does there seem much hope that we shall ever know more; but in history a bad source is sometimes worse than none. We shall do well to keep an open mind.

What we need to do is to test the accuracy of Homer where we have independent evidence. Some facts have been long known and recognized. For instance, Homer while successfully giving his heroes weapons of bronze occasionally drops in an anachronistic mention of iron. Iron was of course not unknown in the Bronze Age; it was the technique of fabrication which was lacking. The most striking example is the method of disposal of the dead: Mycenaean rulers were buried in great family vaults, Homer's heroes are cremated. Here it has been suggested that an expeditionary force encamped upon enemy soil might have been compelled to abandon its usual custom; yet there is never a hint in Homer of the huge circular tombs which must have been a prominent feature of the Mycenaean world.

The evidence of the Linear B tablets now presents us with many more points of comparison. The official titles of the tablets, *hequetās*, *telestās*, *lāwāgetās*, are all absent from Homer, the last it is true perforce, because its metrical shape excludes it from Homer's verse. Where Homer confuses two words for 'king', the tablets have a sharp distinction; *wanax* is there the King, and the other word means only 'chief', and now we know the facts we can point to relics of the old distinction still surviving in Homer.

Even better as a test is the geography. Homer gives us, in several passages, accounts of the south-west Peloponnese. There is, first of all, the so-called Catalogue of Ships in Book 2 of the *Iliad*. It lists nine towns, beginning with Pylos, which are subject to Nestor. The tablets also show nine areas of the Hither Province (see pp. 41–6); but Pylos is not one of these nine, for it stands aloof from the tribute lists. Not one of the other names matches, though one Homeric name, *Kyparissēeis*, does appear to be a variant of a place name found on the tablets. Moreover, Homer appears to ignore the Further Province, which in the *Odyssey* he makes into a separate kingdom. One of the Homeric names, *Helos*, is found on the Pylos tablets, but in the Further Province; since it is the ordinary Greek word for 'marsh', it is probably no more than a coincidence. As shown in Chapter 3, the northern frontier of the kingdom was along the line of the River Nédha; Homer in the *Iliad* speaks of the Alpheios, 35 km further north, as the frontier, and this account cannot be reconciled with the location of Pylos at Englianós.

Our suspicion that Homer does not know in detail the geography of western Greece can be confirmed elsewhere. When he describes the location of Odysseus' home, Ithaca, his geography is so palpably faulty that scholars have tried to argue that it was not modern Itháki at all. The truth is simpler: Homer was an Ionian Greek who had probably never even sailed across the Aegean, let alone round the west coast of Greece. He knew that Mycenae was the chief town of Greece at this time, and its archaeological riches confirm this; but it would seem that Homer did not know where it was, for he gives Agamemnon a kingdom along the southern shore of the Corinthian Gulf, as if Mycenae lay much further to the west, while he assigns the port of Mycenae, Tiryns, now a kilometre from the sea, to another kingdom. Instead of trying to make sense of Homer's geography, we should be well advised to regard it as the sort of information about distant parts which a stay-at-home may glean from sailors' yarns.

The important thing to remember about Homer is that he was a poet not an historian. Poetic truth and historical truth are two quite different commodities. Poetry is concerned with unchanging, eternal values; history with facts and events. Poetry may take, like history, the form of narrative; but we are not really concerned with the fate of a few warrior-princes of a long distant past. What does concern us is the human values, the emotions and attitudes of the poet's characters; for these are constants of human nature, as important today as at any time in the past. The death of a warrior or the sack of a city in the remote past may mean nothing to us. But the tragedy of Hector and of Troy is still capable of moving our emotions and thus inspiring our actions. To look for historical fact in Homer is as vain as to scan the Mycenaean tablets in search of poetry; they belong to different universes.

75 The walls of Tiryns from the air

11 THE END OF THE MYCENAEAN WORLD

Knossos

It is self-evident that the documents which were stored in the Mycenaean palaces at the time of their destruction can tell us nothing about what happened afterwards. The disaster at Knossos early in the fourteenth century remains the earliest known case of a Mycenaean palace destroyed by fire and never rebuilt on the same scale, whatever use was made of the site by later occupants. The other palaces seem to have fallen towards the end of the thirteenth century; but neither the exact date nor the sequence in which they fell can be determined. The evidence from Mycenae suggests a first destruction of the buildings outside the massive walls as early as the middle of the century; and the constant attempts by archaeologists to depress the date of the destructions on the mainland may have been, consciously or not, motivated by the conviction that the Trojan War is to be dated to the middle of the same century.

But coming events often cast their shadows before; a prosperous, well-ordered society does not usually collapse overnight. It is therefore tempting to read our documents in the light of subsequent events, in the hope of detecting the causes. Despite all our efforts, the Knossos documents remain inscrutable on this subject. The evidence strongly suggests that Knossos was half way through a perfectly normal year when the blow suddenly fell. The sheep had been shorn, their wool issued to groups of women to work into cloth; the grain harvest, in some areas at least, seems to have been gathered in.

But although this is the date suggested by the agricultural calendar, it does not agree with Evans's deduction that the palace was destroyed in spring. A strong southerly wind was blowing at the time, as is proved by the blackening by smoke of masonry immediately on the north side of the position of wooden beams; and such winds are most frequent in Crete in the spring. In order to try to resolve this conflict of evidence I obtained from the Greek Meteorological Service a table showing the percentage of south, south-east and south-west winds recorded at Iráklion with force 6 or higher on the Beaufort scale. The figures are as follows: January 2.4, February 4.4, March 3.5, April 3.5, May 1.0, June 0.5, July 0.0, August 0.1, September 0.1, October 0.6, November 1.5, December 3.6. Thus the chances of a southerly gale between July and September are negligible; they are possible in May, June, October and November; most likely between December and April.

Now a date for the destruction between December and April seems impossible. The spring shearing was not merely completed, but large quantities of wool had been issued to the textile workers. The grain harvest was beginning to be recorded, but, unless our records here have suffered especially badly, was incomplete. The earliest date in the year which will fit this picture is late May to early June; and a southerly gale is not excluded at this time.

The presence of records of the collection of spices such as coriander might suggest the autumn; but if so, why have we no records of the vintage? It seems more likely that seed-crops which would not suffer from keeping might be kept back during the busiest season of the year, and only transmitted to Knossos during the winter.

Attempts have been made to confirm the date by reference to the Mycenaean calendar. Now we have only a few tablets with month names, and these are exclusively concerned with religious offerings (see p. 97). The reason may be that almost all the operations recorded in the archives are basically annual ones, and since they happen at a fixed time of year there is no need to specify the date. Six month names were known until very recently, when two fragments which do not physically join (Oa 745+7374) were identified as belonging to the same tablet, and this discloses a partially preserved month name, which cannot be restored as any of the other six. It would seem therefore that Knossos was in at least the seventh month when the end came; for there may have been other names on tablets that have not survived. This raises the awkward question of the point from which the Mycenaeans reckoned the beginning of the calendar year. It is likely to have been one of the four astronomically determined points: the solstices and the equinoxes. Classical practice is not much help here, since different cities had calendars starting at different dates. If Knossos had a calendar beginning at the autumn equinox, then we have to explain the absence of records for the vintage and other agricultural events of the autumn; we could still obtain a date of May/June by supposing that one or two month names had not survived. But the evidence of Pylos suggests the winter solstice as a more likely point. If so, there is still a way to escape from the dilemma. One of the tablets in this series (Fp 1), which bears an otherwise unknown month name, is of quite different shape and format from the remainder; is it perhaps a summary of the records of the last month in the calendar year, made and filed for reference at the grand winter clearance, when other sets were generally destroyed? This would allow us to date the destruction to the sixth month, corresponding to our June, when southerly winds are still possible.

Evans was attracted by the earthquake theory to account for the early fourteenth-century destruction. In a seismic area such as Crete, which lies near the southern edge of the 'plate' carrying the Aegean, earthquakes are frequent and there is no way of verifying their occurrence from the archaeological record, unless there is evidence of major displacements of heavy masonry, such as could not have occurred in the course of a fire. No such unequivocal evidence has yet been produced for Knossos at this date, though it remains a possibility.

But wherever a flourishing community suffers a major earthquake, the immediate reaction is to rebuild. This had happened before at Knossos, and the same sequence of events is known from sites such as Thera or Troy. But there is still no proof that any rebuilding took place after this destruction. That people continued to live in parts of the building is certain; but there is still, if we can accept that the tablets are all associated with fourteenth-century destruction, no sign that the palace was ever afterwards a royal residence or administrative centre. Whatever the cause of the destruction, something induced the survivors to abandon the site. If Knossos remained in the following period the centre of a kingdom, the palace must have been moved to another site, still undiscovered.

There is but one clue in the Knossos tablets which may be significant. We have seen the evidence that the royal administration there sought to control the activities of thousands of people, not merely in the immediate neighbourhood, but at distances of 70 km or more; the most distant place which can be identified on the tablets is *Kudōnia* about 150 km away. It is clear that the local governor of Phaistos more than 50 km away had little autonomy; he had to report to Knossos in detail the agricultural produce and the industrial activity of his region. It is easy to believe that the administration was over-centralized, and that this led to discontent among the towns which were thus administered by remote control. Crete splits naturally into separate areas, and the existence of five major palaces with administrative records in Minoan times demonstrates that, whatever hegemony Knossos exercised before the coming of the Greeks, the local rulers enjoyed a large measure of autonomy. I heard a modern parallel to this when the Bishop of Míres in the area of Phaistos was talking about a remarkable social enterprise the Orthodox Church had carried out in his diocese; someone asked him if he had been helped in raising funds by the

Archbishop and by other parts of the island, and he indignantly denied this, assuring us that it was entirely the work of his own diocese. Not only are the Cretans still very jealous of the control exercised over the island by the national government in Athens; their local patriotism extends to fierce rivalry between the different parts of the island.

But amusing as it is to speculate on the continuity of attitudes between ancient and modern times, we must admit that we have still no clear indication of the cause of the breakdown or of the subsequent course of events in Crete. This is an area of darkness which archaeological work can probably illuminate; we need to know exactly what sites were occupied in the latter half of the fourteenth and thirteenth centuries, and what sort of activity continued then. There is so far very little evidence of writing, though apparently Linear B inscriptions were occasionally painted on jars. But so far not a single scrap of clay tablet written in Linear B has been found at any site but Knossos. Did Crete dissolve into such tiny states that the need for written accounts disappeared? Or is their absence due merely to chance? Since a good fire is needed to give them the durability to survive, it may well be that conditions at other places were inimical to the preservation of records. It seems hard to believe that the Messará, for instance, which had needed written records in Minoan times, was now so broken up and poor that no accounts were kept.

I should prefer to think that following the destruction of the palace of Knossos the Greek-speaking population of Crete established much smaller administrative units, which after many centuries emerged as the petty city-states of classical times, when we find Tylisos, which had been subject to Mycenaean Knossos, concluding a treaty with its fifth-century successor. We must hope that future work will cast more light on this question.

Pylos

At Pylos, the situation is quite different. Here we think we can detect clear evidence of the parlous situation the king was facing. There are still far too few documents from Mycenae and Thebes for us to draw any conclusions of this kind.

The time of year when Pylos fell is easier to guess than at Knossos. There are records of sheep, but no shearing of wool, and only a few scraps of records of textiles. There is no trace of a grain harvest or vintage. Everything points to a date very early in the year. The calendar seems to confirm this, but unfortunately only one name is accompanied by the word for month and must be a month-name. This is *Sphagiānios*, evidently the month in which the major festival at Sphagiānes took place; classical months are similarly named after places. But there are two other words which, from their use, look as if they must be names of months. I am not impressed by one which superficially suggests the meaning 'new wine'; if correctly so interpreted, and there are serious difficulties in this, it would have to belong to the late autumn. But the heading of the list of human sacrifices (Tn 316; see p. 90) is *po-ro-wi-to-jo*, and L. R. Palmer (1963, 447) very attractively suggested that this was *Plowistoio* '(in the month) of sailing'. Since for the ancients the sailing season opened about the end of March, this would be the name of a spring month; and since, as has been demonstrated, this document very likely belongs to the last days of the palace, it follows that Pylos was destroyed in early spring. Even the shearing of the sheep had not been completed.

The evidence that Pylos expected an attack from the sea has been fully discussed in Chapter 9 (pp. 173–9). The so-called Sea-peoples are the prime suspects, but there is no positive evidence to incriminate them. But the state of affairs disclosed by the documentation of the bronze industry (pp. 140–2) certainly confirms the idea that at this time the seas had become unsafe, for it is clear that Pylos depended upon imports of metal to maintain the manufacture and very likely export of finished goods. An industry so dependent upon shipping would be the first victim of a period of naval anarchy. The collection of gold too may have had defence as its motive (see p. 145).

Conclusion

Whatever the causes, one after another the main Mycenaean sites were overthrown and burnt. All over Greece the settled order which had lasted for more than three centuries was coming to an end. Depopulation followed, whether as the result of war, pestilence or famine hardly matters; there is no positive evidence that any of these factors were to blame. The theory of Rhys Carpenter (1966) that the collapse of Mycenaean Greece was due to climatic change is a mere speculation which seems to be contradicted by the evidence of palaeobotany; we must demand scientific proof before accepting such an explanation. For the least satisfactory part of the theory is the bland assumption that areas such as Attica, which appears to have flourished in the twelfth century, suddenly enjoyed a wetter climate, when modern figures show that it had only half the rainfall of Messenia, where depopulation is so well attested.

It used to be fashionable to cast the Dorians for the rôle of villains in the Mycenaean tragedy. The Dorians were in later times the dominant people of the southern and western mainland of Greece, and they retained a traditional hostility to the Ionians, the dominant people of the central Aegean, which culminated in the twenty-seven years of war in the fifth century. Since they undoubtedly profited by the Mycenaean collapse, it was natural to blame them for it. But the major difficulty has always been the absence of any archaeological evidence of the series of Dorian invasions necessary to account for the change of dialect. One by one the material innovations ascribed to the Dorians have been shown to be unconnected; there is no common element which distinguishes the linguistically Dorian areas and only these.

It is traditionally believed that the Dorians moved south to occupy their classical homes, and there is no doubt that there were major shifts in population at this period. But where were all the Dorians during the Mycenaean period? And why were they content to wait in the wings until the time was ripe for their intervention? The period from the eleventh to the eighth century is deservedly called the Dark Age of Greece, for we have still very little information about it except from the miserable contents of simple tombs.

I want to end therefore with a question mark. I do not think the Dark Age will remain totally obscure, and I am beginning to see some outlines emerge from the darkness. But this lies outside the scope of this book. Some sort of continuity made possible the transmission, in however mangled a form, of some stories of the great days of Mycenaean Greece down to the time when a master poet could use them as the background to two great narrative poems. But by then the real knowledge of the Bronze Age was dead, and the documents upon which this book is based were lying buried awaiting their resurrection in the twentieth century A.D.

BIBLIOGRAPHY

Baumbach, L. (1968): *Studies in Mycenaean Inscriptions and Dialects 1953–1964*, Rome (continuing annual volumes edited by L. J. D. Richardson, published by London Institute of Classical Studies).

Bennett, E. L., Jr (1957): Review of *Documents in Mycenaean Greek. Language*, **33**, 553–68.

(1958): Tentative identifications of the hands of the scribes of the Pylos tablets. *Athenaeum*, **46** (n.s. 36), 328–31.

Bennett, E. L., Jr and Olivier, J.-P. (1973): *The Pylos Tablets in Transcription*, Rome.

Carpenter, R. (1966): *Discontinuity in Greek Civilization*, Cambridge.

Caskey, J. L. (1970): Lead weights from Ayia Irini in Keos. *Arkheologikón Dheltíon*, **24**, 95–106.

Catling, H. W. and Millett, A. (1965): A study of the inscribed stirrup-jars from Thebes. *Archaeometry*, **8**, 3–85.

Chadwick, J. (1958): *The Decipherment of Linear B*, first edition, Cambridge.

(1963): The Two Provinces of Pylos. *Minos*, **7**, 125–41.

(1967*a*): Mycenaean *pa-wo-ke*. *Minos*, **8**, 115–17.

(1967*b*): *The Decipherment of Linear B*, second edition, Cambridge.

(1968): The organization of the Mycenaean archives. *Studia Mycenaea* (Brno), 11–27.

(1970): Linear B tablets from Thebes. *Minos*, **10**, 115–37.

(1973): *Documents in Mycenaean Greek*, second edition, Cambridge. (See Ventris and Chadwick.)

(1975): Thebes Tablets II. Supplement to *Minos* No. 4.

Chadwick, J., Killen, J. T. and Olivier, J.-P. (1971): *The Knossos Tablets*, fourth edition, Cambridge.

Evans, A. J. (1975): *The Palace of Minos at Knossos*, Vol. **4**: 2, Oxford.

Graves, R. (1958): *The Greek Myths*, London.

Karageorghis, V. (1969): *Salamis in Cyprus*, London.

Killen, J. T. (1964): The wool industry of Crete in the Late Bronze Age. *Annual of the British School at Athens*, **59**, 1–15.

(1966): The Knossos Nc tablets. *Proceedings of Cambridge Colloquium on Mycenaean Studies*, 33–8.

Lang, M. (1964): The Palace of Nestor excavations of 1963, Part II. *Amer. J. of Archaeol.*, **68**, 99–105.

Lejeune, M. (1966): Le récapitulatif du cadastre Ep de Pylos. *Proceedings of Cambridge Colloquium on Mycenaean Studies*, 260–4.

Lindgren, M. (1973): *The People of Pylos*. Parts I and II, Uppsala.

McDonald, W. A. and Rapp, G. (1972): *The Minnesota Messenia Expedition:* Reconstructing a Bronze Age Regional Environment, Minneapolis.

Melena, J. L. (1972): On the Knossos Mc tablets. *Minos*, **13**, 29–54.

(1974): *ki-ta-no* en las tabillas de Cnoso. *Durius*, **2**, 45–55.

NILSSON, M. P. (1927): *The Minoan-Mycenaean Religion and its Survival in Greek Religion,* first edition (second edition 1950). Lund.
NINKOVICH, D. and HEEZEN, B. C. (1965): Submarine geology and geophysics. *Colston Papers* (Bristol), **15**, 413–52.
OLIVIER, J.-P. (1967): *Les Scribes de Cnossos,* Rome.
(1969): *The Mycenae Tablets IV,* Leiden.
(1974): Une loi fiscale mycénienne. *Bulletin de Correspondance Hellénique,* **98**, 23–35.
OTA, H. (1959): Pyurosu monjo ni okeru DA oyobi TA. *Shigaku Zasshi,* **68**, 60–72.
PALMER, L. R. (1955): A Mycenaean calendar of offerings, *Eranos,* **53**, 1–13.
(1959): Methodology in 'Linear B' interpretations. *Die Sprache,* **3**, 128–42.
(1961): *Mycenaeans and Minoans,* London.
(1963): *The Interpretation of Mycenaean Greek Texts,* Oxford.
SHELMERDINE, C. W. (1973): The Pylos Ma tablets reconsidered. *Amer. J. Archaeol.,* **77**, 261–75.
TAYLOUR, Lord William (1964): *The Mycenaeans,* London.
TRITSCH, F. J. (1958): *Minoica:* J. Sundwall Festschrift, 406–45.
VENTRIS, M. and CHADWICK, J. (1956): *Documents in Mycenaean Greek,* Cambridge, first edition (second edition see CHADWICK, 1973).
VERMEULE, E. (1964): *Greece in the Bronze Age,* Chicago.
WYATT, W. F., Jr (1962): The Ma tablets from Pylos. *Amer. J. Archaeol.,* **66**, 21–41.

INDEX

Note: only leading references are given under Crete, Knossos and Pylos